每天读一点英文

Everyday English Snack

那些激励我前行的身影

Those great addresses that encouraged me to go on

章华◎编译

与美国人同步阅读的英语丛书
——美国英语教师协会推荐——

陕西师范大学出版社

图书在版编目(CIP)数据

那些激励我前行的身影:英汉对照/章华编译. —西安:
陕西师范大学出版社,2009.9
(每天读一点英文)
ISBN 978-7-5613-4788-1

Ⅰ.那… Ⅱ.章… Ⅲ.①英语—汉语—对照读物
②名人—演讲—世界—选集 Ⅳ.H319.4:I

中国版本图书馆 CIP 数据核字(2009)第 146811 号

图书代号：SK9N0801

上架建议：英语学习

那些激励我前行的身影(成功卷)

作　　者：章　华	
责任编辑：周　宏	
特约编辑：辛　艳　刘宇圣	
封面设计：张丽娜	
版式设计：风　筝	
出版发行：**陕西师范大学出版社**	

（西安市陕西师大 120 信箱　邮编：710062）

印　　刷：北京嘉业印刷厂	
开　　本：880×1230　1/32	
字　　数：290 千字	
印　　张：10	
版　　次：2009 年 10 月第一版	
印　　次：2009 年 10 月第一次印刷	

ISBN 978-7-5613-4788-1

定　　价：23.80 元

目录

Contents

·········· Those elegant spirits ··········

优雅的灵魂

········· Glorious mind ·········
光辉的信念

那些激励我前行的身影

Those great addresses that encouraged me to go on

我有一个梦

I have a dream

Gettysburg Address

林肯葛底斯堡演说

Abrabam Lincoln/亚伯拉罕·林肯

Four score and seven years ago，our fathers brought forth upon this continent a new Nation，conceived in Liberty，and dedicated to the proposition that all men are created equal. Now，we are engaged in a great Civil War，testing whether that Nation，or any nation so **conceived** and so dedicated，can long **endure**. We are met on a great battlefield of that war. We have come to dedicate a portion of that field as a final resting-place for those who here gave their lives that Nation might live. It is altogether fitting and proper that we should do this.

But，in a larger sense，we cannot dedicate，we cannot consecrate，we cannot **hallow** this ground. *The brave men，living and dead，who struggled here，have consecrated it far above our poor power to add or detract.* The world will little note nor long remember what we say here，but it can never forget what they did here. *It is for us，the living，rather to be dedicated here to the unfinished work which they who fought here have thus far* *so nobly advanced*. It is rather for us to be here **dedicated** to the great task remaining before us；that from these honored dead，we take increased devotion to that cause for which they gave the last full measure of devotion；that we here highly resolve that these dead shall not have died in vain；that this Nation，under God，shall have a new birth of freedom；and that government of the People，by the People，and for the People，shall not perish from the earth.

87年前，我们的先辈们在这块大陆上创建了一个新的国家，她孕育于自由之中，奉行一切人生来平等的原则。现在我们正从事一场伟大的内战，以考验这个国家，或者任何一个孕育于自由和奉行上述原则的国家是否能够长久存在下去。我们在这场战争中的一个伟大战场上集会。烈士们为使这个国家能够生存下去而献出了自己的生命，我们聚集在这里，是要把这个战场的一部分奉献给他们作为最后的安息之所。我们这样做是完全应该而且是非常恰当的。

但是，从广义上来说，我们不能奉献，不能圣化，更不能神化这块土地。那些曾在这里战斗过的勇士们，活着的和去世的，已经将这块土地圣化了，这远不是我们微薄的力量所能增减的。今天，我们在这里所说的话，全世界不大会注意，也不会长久地记住，但那些勇士们在这里的所作所为，全世界却永远不会忘记。换言之，我们这些依然活着的人，应该把自己奉献于那些勇士们已经向前推进但尚未完成的崇高事业。我们应该在这里把自己奉献于仍然摆在我们面前的伟大任务——我们要从那些光荣牺牲的勇士们身上汲取更多的奉献精神，来完成他们投入毕生精力并为之献身的事业；我们要在这里下定决心，不能让那些勇士们白白牺牲；我们要使我们的祖国在上帝的保佑下得到自由的新生，要使这个民有、民治、民享的政府永世长存。

导读

1863年7月初，北军为夺取位于宾夕法尼亚州的葛底斯堡与南军激战，伤亡2万余人，为纪念阵亡将士，同年11月在葛底斯堡建起了国家公墓。时任总统的林肯在公墓落成典礼上的致辞简短却令人难忘。

单词注解

conceive [kən'si:v] *v.*构想出，想象

endure [in'djuə] *v.* 忍耐，忍受

hallow ['hæləu] *v.*使神圣，把……视为神圣

dedicated ['dedikeitid] *adj.*专注的；献身的

诵读名句

Four score and seven years ago, our fathers brought forth upon this continent a new Nation, conceived in Liberty and dedicated to the proposition that all men are created equal.

The brave men, living and dead, who struggled here, have consecrated it far above our poor power to add or detract.

It is for us, the living, rather to be dedicated here to the unfinished work they who fought here have thus far so nobly advanced.

Inaugural Address

奥巴马就职演说：
选择希望，未来就在我们手中

Barack Obama/巴拉克·奥巴马

My fellow citizens：

I stand here today **humbled** by the task before us，**grateful** for the trust you have bestowed，mindful of the sacrifices borne by our ancestors. I thank President Bush for his service to our nation，as well as the generosity and cooperation he has shown throughout this transition.

Forty-four Americans have now taken the presidential oath. The words have been spoken during rising tides of prosperity and the still waters of peace. Yet，every so often the oath is taken amidst gathering clouds and raging storms. At these moments，America has carried on not simply because of the skill or vision of those in high office，but because We the People have remained faithful to the ideals of our forbearers，and true to our founding documents.

So it has been. So it must be with this generation of

Americans.

That we are in the midst of crisis is now well understood. Our nation is at war, against a far-reaching network of violence and hatred. Our economy is badly weakened, a consequence of greed and irresponsibility on the part of some, but also our collective failure to make hard choices and prepare the nation for a new age. Homes have been lost ; jobs shed ; businesses shuttered. Our health care is too costly ; our schools fail too many ; and each day brings further evidence that the ways we use energy strengthen our adversaries and threaten our planet.

These are the indicators of crisis, subject to data and statistics. Less measurable but no less profound is a sapping of confidence across our land—a nagging fear that America's decline is inevitable, and that the next generation must lower its sights.

Today I say to you that the challenges we face are real. They are serious and they are many. They will not be met easily or in a short span of time. But know this, America—they will be met.

On this day, we gather because we have chosen hope over fear, unity of purpose over conflict and discord.

On this day, we come to proclaim an end to the petty grievances and false promises, the recriminations and worn out dogmas, that for far too long have strangled our politics.

We remain a young nation, but in the words of Scripture, the time has come to set aside childish things. The time has come to reaffirm our enduring spirit ; to choose our better history ; to carry forward that precious gift, that noble idea, passed on from generation to generation : the God-given promise that all are equal, all are free, and all deserve a chance to pursue their full measure of happiness.

In reaffirming the greatness of our nation, we understand that greatness is never a given. It must be earned. Our journey has never been one of short-cuts or settling for less. It has not been the path for the faint-hearted—for those who prefer leisure over work, or seek only the pleasures of riches and fame. Rather, it has been the risk-takers, the doers, the makers of things—some celebrated but more often men and women obscure in their labor, who have carried us up the long, rugged path towards prosperity and freedom.

For us, they packed up their few worldly possessions and traveled across oceans in search of a new life. For us, they toiled in sweatshops and settled the West ; endured the lash of the whip and plowed the hard earth. For us, they fought and died, in places like Concord and Gettysburg ; Normandy and Khe Sanh.

Time and again these men and women struggled and sacrificed and worked till their hands were raw so that we might live a better life. They saw America as bigger than the sum of our individual ambitions ; greater than all the differences of birth or wealth or faction.

This is the journey we continue today. We remain the most prosperous, powerful nation on Earth. Our workers are no less productive than when this crisis began. Our minds are no less inventive, our goods and services no less needed than they were last week or last month or last year. Our capacity remains undiminished. But our time of standing pat, of protecting narrow interests and putting off unpleasant decisions—that time has surely passed. Starting today, we must pick ourselves up, dust ourselves off, and begin again the work of remaking America.

For everywhere we look, there is work to be done. The state of the economy calls for action, bold and swift, and we will act—not only to create new jobs, but to lay a new foundation for growth. We will build the roads and bridges, the electric grids and digital lines that feed our commerce and bind us together. We will restore science to its rightful place, and wield technology's wonders to raise health care's quality and lower its cost. We will harness the sun and the winds and the soil to fuel our cars and run our factories. And we will transform our schools and colleges and universities to meet the demands of a new age. All this we can do. And all this we will do.

Now, there are some who question the scale of our ambitions—who suggest that our system cannot tolerate too many big plans. Their memories are short. For they have forgotten what this country has already done ; what free men and women can achieve when imagination is joined to common purpose, and necessity to courage.

What the cynics fail to understand is that the ground has shifted beneath them—that the stale political arguments that have consumed us for so long no longer apply. The question we ask today is not whether our government is too big or too small, but whether it works—whether it helps families find jobs at a decent wage, care they can afford, a retirement that is dignified. Where the answer is yes, we intend to move forward. Where the answer is no, programs will end. And those of us who manage the public's dollars will be held to account—to spend wisely, reform bad habits, and do our business in the light of day—because only then can we restore the vital trust between a people and their government.

Nor is the question before us whether the market is a force for good or ill. Its power to generate wealth and expand freedom is unmatched, but this crisis has reminded us that without a watchful eye, the market can spin out of control—and that a nation cannot prosper long when it favors only the prosperous. The success of our economy has always depended not just on the size of our Gross Domestic Product, but on the reach of our prosperity ; on our ability to extend opportunity to every willing heart—not out of charity, but because it is the surest route to our common good.

As for our common defense, we reject as false the choice between our safety and our ideals. Our Founding Fathers, faced with perils we can scarcely imagine, drafted a charter to assure the rule of law and the rights of man, a charter expanded by the blood of generations. Those ideals still light the world, and we will not give them up for expedience's sake. And so to all other people and governments who are watching today, from the grandest capitals to the small village where my father was born : know that America is a friend of each nation and every man, woman, and child who seeks a future of peace and dignity, and that we are ready to lead once more.

Recall that earlier generations faced down fascism not just with missiles and tanks, but with sturdy alliances and enduring convictions. They understood that our power alone cannot protect us, nor does it entitle us to do as we please. Instead, they knew that our power grows through its prudent use ; our security emanates from the justness of our cause, the force of our example, the tempering qualities of humility and restraint.

We are the keepers of this legacy. Guided by these principles once more, we can meet those new threats that demand even greater effort—even greater cooperation and understanding between nations. We will begin to responsibly leave Iraq to its people, and forge a hard-earned peace in Afghanistan. With old friends and former foes, we will work tirelessly to lessen the nuclear threat, and roll back the specter of a warming planet. We will not apologize for our way of life, nor will we waver in its defense, and for those who seek to advance their aims by inducing terror and slaughtering innocents, we say to you now that our spirit is stronger and cannot be broken ; you cannot outlast us, and we will defeat you.

For we know that our patchwork heritage is a strength, not a weakness. We are a nation of Christians and Muslims, Jews and Hindus—and non-believers. We are shaped by every language and culture, drawn from every end of this Earth ; and because we have tasted the bitter swill of civil war and **segregation**, and emerged from that dark chapter stronger and more united, we cannot help but believe that the old hatreds shall someday pass ; that the lines of tribe shall soon dissolve ; that as the world grows smaller, our common humanity shall reveal itself ; and that America must play its role in ushering in a new era of peace...

As we consider the road that unfolds before us, we remember with humble gratitude those brave Americans who, at this very hour, patrol far-off deserts and distant mountains. They have something to tell us today, just as the fallen heroes who lie in Arlington whisper through the ages. We honor them not only because they are guardians of our liberty, but because they **embody** the spirit of service ; a willingness to find meaning in something greater than themselves. And yet, at this moment— a moment that will define a generation—it is precisely this spirit that must inhabit us all.

For as much as government can do and must do, it is ultimately the faith and determination of the American people upon which this nation relies. It is the kindness to take in a stranger when the levees break, the selflessness of workers who would rather cut their hours than see a friend lose their job which sees us through our darkest hours. It is the firefighter's courage to storm a stairway filled with smoke, but also a parent's willingness to nurture a child, that finally decides our fate.

Our challenges may be new. The instruments with which we meet them may be new. But those values upon which our success depends—hard work and honesty, courage and fair play, tolerance and curiosity, loyalty and patriotism—these things are old. These things are true. They have been the quiet force of progress throughout our history. What is demanded then is a return to these truths. What is required of us now is a new era of responsibility—a recognition, on the part of every American, that we have duties to ourselves, our nation, and the world, duties that we do not grudgingly accept but rather seize gladly, firm in the knowledge that there is nothing so satisfying to the spirit, so defining of our character, than giving our all to a difficult task.

This is the price and the promise of citizenship.

This is the source of our confidence—the knowledge that God calls on us to shape an uncertain destiny.

This is the meaning of our liberty and our creed—why men and women and children of every race and every faith can join in celebration across this magnificent mall, and why a man whose father less than sixty years ago might not have been served at a local restaurant can now stand before you to take a most sacred oath.

So let us mark this day with remembrance, of who we are and how far we have traveled. In the year of America's birth, in the coldest of months, a small band of patriots huddled by dying campfires on the shores of an icy river. The capital was abandoned. The enemy was advancing. The snow was stained with blood. At a moment when the outcome of our revolution was most in doubt, the father of our nation ordered these words be read to the people :

"Let it be told to the future world...that in the depth of winter, when nothing but hope and virtue could survive...that the city and the country, alarmed at one common danger, came forth to meet [it]."

America. In the face of our common dangers, in this winter of our hardship, let us remember these timeless words. With hope and virtue, let us brave once more the icy currents, and endure what storms may come. Let it be said by our children's children that when we were tested we refused to let this journey end，that we did not turn back nor did we falter；and with eyes fixed on the horizon and God's grace upon us，we carried forth that great gift of freedom and delivered it safely to future generations.

同胞们：

今天我站在这里，面对眼前的诸多困难，深感重任在肩。我感谢你们对我的信任，并铭记先辈们为了这个国家所做的献身。我感谢布什总统为国家做出的贡献，感谢他在两届政府过渡期间给予的慷慨与合作。

迄今为止，已经有44个美国总统宣誓就职。总统宣誓有时面对的是国家的和平繁荣，但通常面临的是乌云密布的紧张形势。在紧张的形势中，支持美国前进的不仅仅是领导人的能力和远见卓识，更是因为美国人民始终坚信国家先驱者的理想，并对我们的建国理念忠贞不渝。

前辈们如此，我们这一代美国人也必须如此。

现在我们都深知，我们身处危机之中。我们的国家在战斗，我们面对的敌人是分布广泛的暴力和仇恨势力；我们的经济也受到严重的削弱，原因虽有一些人的贪婪和不负责任，但更为重要的是我们作为一个集体在一些重大问题上决策失误，同时也未能做好应对新时代的准备。一些人失去了家园，一些人失去了工作，很多企业纷纷倒闭。社会的医疗保险费用过度昂贵、学校教育让许多人失望，而且每天的情况都在不断显示，我们使用能源的方式助长了敌人的威风，同时也威胁着我们星球的安全。

　　统计数据证实，我们已身陷危机。危机难以测量，但更难以测量的是其对美国人信心的动摇——现在一种认为美国衰落不可避免，我们的下一代不得不降低对美国的期望的说法正在吞噬着人们的自信。

　　听我说，这些威胁并非子虚乌有，它们不仅迫在眉睫而且多乱如麻。要想一挥而就解决这些问题绝非易事。我们要相信，我们一定会渡过难关。

　　今天，我们在这里齐聚一堂，因为我们选择希望而不是恐惧，选择齐心协力而不是冲突对立。

　　今天，我们宣布要为无谓的摩擦、不实的承诺和指责画上句号，我们要打破牵制美国政治发展的若干陈旧教条。

　　美国仍是一个年轻的国家，借用《圣经》的话说，"放弃幼稚的时代已经到来了。"重拾坚韧精神的时代已经到来，我们要为历史做出更好的选择，我们要秉承历史赋予的宝贵权利，秉承那种代代相传的高贵理念：上帝赋予我们每个人以平等和自由，以及每个人尽全力去追求幸福的机会。

　　在重申我们国家伟大精神的同时，我们深知伟大从来不是上天赐予的，伟大需要靠努力赢取。我们的历程从来不是走捷径或退而求其次的历程。它不是弱者的道路——它不属于好逸恶劳或只图名利享受的人；这条路属于冒险者、实干家，创造者——有些人享有盛名，但大多数是默默无闻耕耘劳作的男女志士，是他们带我们走向通往繁荣和自由的漫长崎岖之路。

为了我们，先辈们打点起贫寒的行装上路，远涉重洋，寻找新生活；为了我们，先辈们忍辱负重，用血汗浇铸工厂；为了我们，先辈们在荒芜的西部原野辛勤耕作，定居他乡；为了我们，先辈们奔赴疆场，英勇捐躯，长眠于康科德城、葛底斯堡、（第二次世界大战中的）诺曼底和（越战中的）溪山。

一次又一次，我们的先辈们战斗着、牺牲着、操劳着，只为了我们可以生活得更好。他们看到的美国超越了我们每一个人的雄心壮志，也超越了所有种族、财富或派系的差异。

今天我们继续先辈们未尽的旅程。美国依然是地球上最繁荣、最强大的国家。同危机初露端倪之时相比，美国人民的生产力依然旺盛；与上周、上个月或者去年相比，我们的头脑依然富于创造力，我们的商品和服务依然很有市场，我们的实力不曾削弱。但是，可以肯定的是，维持现状的时代、保护狭隘利益的时代以及对艰难抉择犹豫不决的时代已经过去了。从今天开始，我们必须振作起来，拍拍身上的泥土，重新开启再造美国的事业。

无论我们把目光投向何处，都有工作在等待着我们。经济状况要求我们采取大胆且快速的行动，我们即将行动起来，不仅是要创造就业，更要为（下一轮经济）增长打下新的基础。我们将造桥铺路，为企业铺设电网和数字线路，将我们联系在一起。我们将回归科学，运用科技的奇迹提高医疗保险的质量，降低医疗成本。我们将利用风能、太阳能和地能驱动车辆，为工厂提供能源。我们将改革中小学以及大专院校，以适应新时代的要求。这一切，我们都能够做到，而且我们都将会做到。

现在，有人怀疑我们的雄心壮志，他们认为我们的体制承载不了太多的宏伟计划。他们太健忘了。他们已经忘了这个国家过去所取得的成就；他们已经忘了当创造力与共同目标以及必要的勇气结合起来时，自由的人民就会爆发出无穷的创造力。

这些怀疑论者的错误在于，他们没有意识到政治现实已经发生了变化，长期以来耗掉我们太多精力的陈腐政治观点已经过时。今天，我们的问题不在于政府的大小，而在于政府能否有效运转，政府能否帮助家庭成员找到薪水合适的工作、提供给他们可以负担得起的医疗保障并让他们体面地退休。哪个方案能给予肯定的答案，我们就推进哪个方案。哪个方案的答案是否定的，我们就选择终止。而掌管纳税人税金的人应当承担起责任，合理支出，摒弃陋习，磊落做事，这样才能重塑人民与政府的信任纽带。

我们面临的问题也不是市场好坏的问题。市场创造财富、拓展自由的能力无可匹敌，但是这场危机提醒我们，没有严格的监管，市场很可能就会失控——如果一个国家仅仅施惠于富裕者，其富裕便不能持久。国家经济的成败不仅仅取决于国内生产总值的大小，而且取决于繁荣的覆盖面，取决于我们是否有能力让每一位愿意致富的人都有机会走向富裕。我们这样做不是慈善，而是因为这是确保实现共同利益的途径。

就共同防御而言，我们绝不接受安全与理念不可两全的荒谬论点。当年，我们的先辈们面对我们几乎无法想象的危险，起草了确保法治和人权的宪章。一代代人民的鲜血夯实了这一宪章。今天，这些理念依然照耀着世界，我们不会为一时之利而弃之。因此我想对正在观看这一仪式的其他国家的人民和政府说，不论他们现在各国伟大的首府还是在如同我父亲出生地一般的小村落，我想让他们知道：对于每个追求和平与尊严的国家和个人而言，美国是你们的朋友，我们愿意再次领导大家踏上追寻之旅。

回想起先辈们从容地面对法西斯主义的时候，他们不仅依靠手中的导弹和坦克，他们还依靠稳固的联盟和坚定的信仰。他们深知单凭自己的力量我们无法保护自己，他们也深知我们强大并不足以使我们有权利为所欲为。他们明白，正是因为谨慎使用实力，我们才日益强大；我们的安全通过我们正义的事业、榜样的力量以及谦卑和克制的品质得以保障。

我们继承了这些遗产。在这些原则的再次指引下，我们有能力应对新的威胁，我们需要付出更多的努力、进行国家间更广泛的合作以及增进国家间的理解。首先，我们将以负责任的态度，将伊拉克交还给伊拉克人民，同时巩固阿富汗来之不易的和平。对于老朋友和老对手，我们将继续努力，不遗余力，削弱核威胁，遏制全球变暖的幽灵。我们不会在价值观念上退缩，也不会动摇捍卫它的决心。对于那些企图通过恐怖主义或屠杀无辜平民达成目标的人，我们要对他们说：我们的信仰更加坚定，不可动摇，你们不可能拖垮我们，我们定将战胜你们。

因为我们知道，我们的多元化遗产是一个优势，而不是劣势。我们是一个由基督教徒和穆斯林、犹太教徒和印度教徒，以及无宗教信仰者组成的国家。我们民族的成长受到许多语言和文化的影响，我们吸取了这个星球上任何一个角落的有益成分。正是因为我们民族曾亲尝过内战和种族隔离的苦酒，并且在经历了这些黑色的篇章之后变得更加强大更加团结，因此我们才确信一切仇恨终有一天都会成为过去，种族的划分不久就会消失，而且随着世界变得越来越小，我们共同的人性将得到彰显。在迎接新的和平时代到来的过程中，美国需要发挥自己的作用。

思索前方的路，我们无时无刻不在铭记那些远征沙漠和偏远山区的英勇美国战士，并对他们充满感激之情，他们和那些安息在阿灵顿国家公墓之下的战争英雄们一样，给予我们启示。

我们向他们致敬，不仅因为他们是自由的守护者，更因为他们体现了为国服务的精神，他们愿意在比自身更伟大的事业中发现人生的意义。此时此刻，在这个要塑造一代人的时刻，我们需要的正是这样一种精神。

虽然政府能有许多作为也必须有许多作为，但最终离不开美国人民的信仰和决心，这才是我们的立国之本。于防洪堤坝决堤之时收留陌生受难者的善意，于经济不景气的时候宁愿减少自己工时也不肯看着朋友失业的无私，正是这些，支撑着我们走过黑暗的时刻。消防队员冲入满是浓烟的楼梯抢救生命的勇气，父母养育孩子的坚持，正是这些决定了我们的命运。

我们面临的挑战可能前所未闻，我们应对挑战的措施也可能前所未有，但那些长期以来指导我们成功的价值观——勤奋、诚实、勇气、公平竞争、包容以及对世界保持好奇心，还有对国家的忠诚和爱国主义——却是历久弥新。这些价值观都是千真万确的。他们是创造美国历史的无声力量。我们现在需要的就是回归这些古老的价值观。我们需要一个新的负责任的时代，一个觉醒的时代，每个国人都应意识到：我们对自己、对国家和世界负有责任。对于这些责任，我们并非勉强接受，而是心

我有一个梦

甘情愿主动承担。我们应该坚定这一认识，即没有什么比全身心投入一项艰巨的工作更能锻炼我们的性格，更能获得精神上的满足。

这是公民应尽的义务，应做出的承诺。

这就是我们自信的来源，上帝号召我们要掌握自己的命运。

这就是我们自由和信仰的意义，这也是为何不同种族、不同信仰、不同性别和年龄的人可以同聚一堂在此欢庆的原因，也是我今天能站在这里庄严宣誓的原因，而在 50 多年前我的父亲甚至都不能成为地方餐馆的服务生。

所以，让我们铭记自己的身份，镌刻自己的足迹。在美国诞生的时代，那最寒冷的岁月里，一群勇敢的爱国人士围着篝火在冰封的河边取暖。首都被占领，敌人在挺进，冬天的雪被鲜血染成了红色。在美国大革命最受质疑的时刻，我们的国父们这样说："我们要让未来的世界知道……在深冬的严寒里，唯有希望和勇气才能让我们存活……面对共同的危险时，我们的城市和国家要勇敢地上前去面对。"

今天的美国也在严峻的寒冬中面对共同的挑战，让我们记住国父们不朽的话语。带着希望和勇气，让我们再一次勇敢地面对寒流，迎接可能会发生的风暴。我们要让我们的子孙后代记住，在面临挑战的时候，我们没有屈服，我们没有逃避也没有丝毫动摇，我们脚踏实地、心怀信仰，我们将自由一代一代，薪火相传！

🍃导读🍃

2009 年 1 月 20 日第 56 届(第 44 任)美国总统奥巴马发表了就职演说。奥巴马说，美国仍然是个年轻的国家，且这个时代受到了挑战，我们必须凝聚力量，重新塑造美国。但他并没有涉及有关经济刺激计划的更多细节。

🍃单词注解🍃

humble ['hʌmbl] *adj.* 谦逊的；卑微的

grateful ['greitful] *adj.* 感激的，感谢的

segregation [ˌsegri'geiʃən] *n.* 隔离

embody [im'bɔdi] *v.* 象征，具体表现

🍃诵读名句🍃

Forty-four Americans have now taken the presidential oath. The words have been spoken during rising tides of prosperity and the still waters of peace.

Now，there are some who question the scale of our ambitions – who suggest that our system cannot tolerate too many big plans.

America. In the face of our common dangers，in this winter of our hardship，let us remember these timeless words.

I Have a Dream
我有一个梦

Martin Luther King/马丁·路德·金

Five score years ago, a great American, in whose symbolic shadow we stand today, signed the Emancipation Proclamation. This momentous decree came as a great beacon light of hope to millions of Negro slaves who had been seared in the flames of withering injustice. It came as a joyous daybreak to end the long night of their captivity.

But one hundred years later, the Negro still is not free. One hundred years later, the life of the Negro is still sadly crippled by the manacles of segregation and the **chains** of discrimination. One hundred years later, the Negro lives on a lonely island of poverty in the midst of a vast ocean of material prosperity. One hundred years later, the Negro is still languished in the corners of American society and finds himself an exile in his own land. And so we've come here today to dramatize a shameful condition.

...

And so even though we face the difficulties of today and tomorrow, I still have a dream. It is a dream deeply rooted in the American dream.

I have a dream that one day this nation will rise up and live out the true meaning of its creed : "We hold these truths to be self-evident, that all men are created equal."

I have a dream that one day on the red hills of Georgia, the sons of former slaves and the sons of former slave owners will be able to sit down together at the table of brotherhood.

I have a dream that one day even the state of Mississippi, a state sweltering with the heat of injustice, sweltering with the heat of oppression, will be **transformed** into an oasis of freedom and justice.

I have a dream that my four little children will one day live in a nation where they will not be judged by the color of their skin but by the content of their character.

I have a dream today !

I have a dream that one day, down in Alabama, with its vicious racists, with its governor having his lips **dripping** with the words of "interposition" and "nullification" —one day right there in Alabama little black boys and black girls will be able to join hands with little white boys and white girls as sisters and brothers.

I have a dream today !

I have a dream that one day every valley shall be exalted, and every hill and mountain shall be made low, the rough places

will be made plain, and the crooked places will be made straight,
" and the glory of the Lord shall be revealed and all flesh shall see
it together?"

This is our hope, and this is the faith that I go back to the
South with. With this faith, we will be able to hew out of the
mountain of despair a stone of hope. With this faith, we will
be able to transform the jangling discords of our nation into a
beautiful symphony of brotherhood. With this faith, we will be
able to work together, to pray together, to struggle together,
to go to jail together, to stand up for freedom together, knowing
that we will be free one day. And this will be the day—this will be
the day when all of God's children will be able to sing with new
meaning : My country'tis of thee, sweet land of liberty, of thee
I sing. Land where my fathers died, land of the Pilgrim's pride.

From every mountainside, let freedom ring ! And if America
is to be a great nation, this must become true.

And so let freedom ring from the **prodigious** hilltops of New
Hampshire.

Let freedom ring from the **mighty** mountains of New York.

Let freedom ring from the heightening Alleghenies of
Pennsylvania.

Let freedom ring from the snow-capped Rockies of
Colorado.

Let freedom ring from the curvaceous slopes of California.

But not only that ; let freedom ring from Stone Mountain of
Georgia.

Let freedom ring from Lookout Mountain of Tennessee.

Let freedom ring from every hill and molehill of Mississippi.

From every mountainside, let freedom ring.

And when this happens, when we allow freedom ring, when we let it ring from every village and every hamlet, from every state and every city, we will be able to speed up that day when all of God's children, black men and white men, Jews and Gentiles, Protestants and Catholics, will be able to join hands and sing in the words of the old Negro spiritual : Free at last! free at last! Thank God Almighty, we are free at last!

　　一百年前，一位伟大的美国人——今天我们就站在他的雕像下——正式签署了《解放宣言》。这项重要法令的颁布，如一座伟大的灯塔，照亮了当时挣扎于不义之火焚烧下的数百万黑奴的希望；它像欢快的破晓曙光，结束了黑人陷于囹圄的漫漫长夜。

　　然而，整整一百年过去了，我们却仍然得面对这个悲惨的现实：黑人依然得不到自由；整整一百年过去了，黑人依然被种族隔离的镣铐和种族歧视的锁链羁绊着，举步维艰；整整一百年过去了，在物质繁荣的汪洋大海中，黑人却依然独自生存在贫穷的孤岛之上；整整一百年过去了，黑人依然在美国社会的阴暗角落里向隅而泣，在自己的土地上却依然流离失所。

因此，我们今天来到这里，把这种骇人听闻的情况公布于众。

……

朋友们，今天我要告诉你们，尽管此刻困难挫折重重，但我仍然有一个梦想。这个梦深深扎根于伟大的美国梦之中。

我有一个梦想：总有一天这个国家会奋然而起，实现其信条的真谛："我们认为这些真理是不言而喻的。每个人生来就是平等的。"

我有一个梦想：总有一天在佐治亚州的红色山冈上，昔日奴隶的儿子与昔日主人的儿子能够如兄弟手足般同桌而坐。

我有一个梦想：总有一天就算是密西西比这样一个被不公正与种族压迫的热潮所统治着的荒漠之州，也能转变成一方自由和正义的绿洲。

我有一个梦想：总有一天我的四个孩子将生活在一个不以他们的肤色，而是以他们内在品质来评价他们的国度中。

今天，我有一个梦想。

我有一个梦想：总有一天阿拉巴马州——该州州长今天仍在喋喋不休地说着不同意也不执行联邦法令的话语——能有所不同，黑人的小男孩与小女孩能够和白人的小男孩与小女孩如兄弟姐妹般携手同行。

今天，我有一个梦想。

我有一个梦想：总有一天幽谷会上升，高山会下降，崎岖之地将变为坦荡的平原，曲折之路将变为笔直的大道；主的荣光将会显现，芸芸众生同声赞叹。

这是我们的渴望，也是将随我返回南方去的信念。靠着这个信念，我们就能从绝望之山开凿出希望之石。靠着这个信念，我们就能把我们国家里种族争斗的不和谐之音，转谱成一曲兄弟般友爱的动人交响曲。靠着这个信念，我们就能共同工作、共同祈盼、共同战斗、共同昂首入狱、共同维护自由。我们知道，总有一天，我们会获得自由。当这一天到来时，上帝所有的子民都能以全新的意义高唱：我的祖国，亲爱的自由之邦，我为你歌唱。这是祖先安息的故园，这是朝圣者为之自豪的土地。让自由之声在每一座山峰回响！

当美国成为真正伟大的国家时，这一切必将成真。

因此，让自由之声在新罕布什尔州的巍峨高峰回响！

让自由之声在纽约州的雄伟山脉中回响！

让自由之声在宾夕法尼亚州高耸的阿勒格尼山峰回响！

让自由之声在科罗拉多州白雪皑皑的洛基山回响！

让自由之声在加利福尼亚州的柔美群峰回响！

不，不仅如此，让自由之声在佐治亚州的石山回响！

让自由之声在田纳西州的远眺山峰回响！

让自由之声在密西西比州的每一座山巅，每一座丘陵回响！

让自由之声在每一处山坡回响！

当我们让自由之声回响时，当我们让自由之声在每一个山村、每一处村寨、每一个州、每一座城回响时，我们就能让这一天早日降临。到那时，上帝所有的孩子——白人与黑人，犹太人与非犹太人，基督教徒与天主教徒——携手同唱那首古老的黑人圣歌："终于自由了！终于自由了！感谢全能的上帝，我们终于自由了！"

实战提升
Practising & Exercise

🍃 导读 🍃

1963 年 8 月 23 日，马丁·路德·金组织了美国历史上影响深远的"自由进军"运动。他率领一支庞大的游行队伍向首都华盛顿进军，为全美国的黑人争取人权。他在林肯纪念堂前向 25 万人发表了著名的演说《我有一个梦想》，号召大家为反对种族歧视、争取平等而努力。

🍃 单词注释 🍃

chain [tʃein] *n.* 链，链条；项圈

transform [trænsˈfɔːm] *v.* 改造；改革；改善

drip [drip] *v.* 滴下

prodigious [prəˈdidʒəs] *adj.* 巨大的；庞大的

mighty [ˈmaiti] *adj.* 强大的；强有力的

🍃 诵读名句 🍃

Five score years ago, a great American, in whose symbolic shadow we stand today, signed the Emancipation Proclamation.

I have a dream that one day this nation will rise up and live out the true meaning of its creed : "We hold these truths to be self-evident, that all men are created equal."

This is our hope, and this is the faith that I go back to the South with With this faith, we will be able to hew out of the mountain of despair a stone of hope.

Farewell Address
布什告别演说

George Walker Bush/乔治 · 沃克 · 布什

Fellow citizens：

For eight years，it has been my honor to serve as your President. The first decade of this new century has been a period of consequence—a time set apart. Tonight，with a thankful heart，I have asked for a final opportunity to share some thoughts on the journey we have traveled together and the future of our Nation.

Five days from now，the world will witness the vitality of American democracy. In a tradition dating back to our founding，the presidency will pass to a successor chosen by you，the American people. Standing on the steps of the Capitol will be a man whose story reflects the enduring promise of our land. This is a moment of hope and pride for our whole Nation. And I join all Americans in offering best wishes to President-elect Obama，his wife Michelle，and their two beautiful girls.

Tonight I am filled with gratitude—to Vice President Cheney and members of the Administration ; to Laura, who brought joy to this house and love to my life ; to our wonderful daughters, Barbara and Jenna ; to my parents, whose examples have provided strength for a lifetime. And above all, I thank the American people for the trust you have given me. I thank you for the prayers that have lifted my spirits. And I thank you for the countless acts of courage, generosity, and grace that I have witnessed these past eight years.

This evening, my thoughts return to the first night I addressed you from this house—September 11, 2001. That morning, terrorists took nearly 3, 000 lives in the worst attack on America since Pearl Harbor. I remember standing in the rubble of the World Trade Center three days later, surrounded by rescuers who had been working around the clock. I remember talking to brave souls who charged through smoke-filled corridors at the Pentagon and to husbands and wives whose loved ones became heroes aboard Flight 93. I remember Arlene Howard, who gave me her fallen son's police shield as a reminder of all that was lost. And I still carry his badge.

As the years passed, most Americans were able to return to life much as it had been before Nine-Eleven. But I never did. Every morning, I received a briefing on the threats to our Nation. And I vowed to do everything in my power to keep us safe.

Over the past seven years, a new Department of Homeland Security has been created. The military, the intelligence community, and the FBI have been transformed. Our Nation is equipped with new tools to monitor the terrorists'movements, freeze their finances, and break up their plots. And with strong allies at our side, we have taken the fight to the terrorists and those who support them. Afghanistan has gone from a nation where the Taliban harbored al Qaeda and stoned women in the streets to a young democracy that is fighting terror and encouraging girls to go to school. Iraq has gone from a brutal dictatorship and a sworn enemy of America to an Arab democracy at the heart of the Middle East and a friend of the United States.

There is legitimate debate about many of these decisions. But there can be little debate about the results. America has gone more than seven years without another terrorist attack on our soil. This is a tribute to those who toil day and night to keep us safe— law enforcement officers, intelligence analysts, homeland security and diplomatic personnel, and the men and women of the United States Armed Forces.

Our Nation is blessed to have citizens who volunteer to defend us in this time of danger. *I have cherished meeting these selfless patriots and their families.* America owes you a debt of gratitude. And to all our men and women in uniform listening tonight : There has been no higher honor than serving as your Commander in Chief.

The battles waged by our troops are part of a broader struggle between two dramatically different systems. Under one, a small band of fanatics demands total obedience to an oppressive ideology, condemns women to subservience, and marks unbelievers for murder. The other system is based on the conviction that freedom is the universal gift of Almighty God and that liberty and justice light the path to peace.

This is the belief that gave birth to our Nation. And in the long run, advancing this belief is the only practical way to protect our citizens. When people live in freedom, they do not willingly choose leaders who pursue campaigns of terror. When people have hope in the future, they will not cede their lives to violence and **extremism**. So around the world, America is promoting human liberty, human rights, and human dignity. We are standing with dissidents and young democracies, providing AIDS medicine to bring dying patients back to life, and sparing mothers and babies from malaria. And this great republic born alone in liberty is leading the world toward a new age when freedom belongs to all nations.

For eight years, we have also strived to expand opportunity and hope here at home. Across our country, students are rising to meet higher standards in public schools. A new Medicare prescription drug benefit is bringing peace of mind to seniors and the disabled. Every taxpayer pays lower income taxes. The addicted and suffering are finding new hope through faith-based programs. Vulnerable human life is better **protected**. Funding for our veterans has nearly doubled. America's air, water, and lands are measurably cleaner.

When challenges to our prosperity emerged, we rose to meet them. Facing the prospect of a financial collapse, we took decisive measures to safeguard our economy. These are very tough times for hardworking families, but the toll would be far worse if we had not acted. All Americans are in this together. And together, with determination and hard work, we will restore our economy to the path of growth. We will show the world once again the resilience of America's free enterprise system.

Like all who have held this office before me, I have experienced setbacks. There are things I would do differently if given the chance. Yet I have always acted with the best interests of our country in mind. I have followed my conscience and done what I thought was right. You may not agree with some tough decisions I have made. But I hope you can agree that I was willing to make the tough decisions.

The decades ahead will bring more hard choices for our country, and there are some guiding principles that should shape our course.

While our Nation is safer than it was seven years ago, the gravest threat to our people remains another terrorist attack. Our enemies are patient and determined to strike again. America did nothing to seek or deserve this conflict. But we have been given solemn responsibilities, and we must meet them. We must resist complacency. We must keep our resolve. And we must never let down our guard.

At the same time, we must continue to engage the world with confidence and clear purpose. *In the face of threats from abroad, it can be tempting to seek comfort by turning inward.* But we must reject isolationism and its companion, protectionism. Retreating behind our borders would only invite danger. In the 21st century, security and prosperity at home depend on the expansion of liberty abroad. If America does not lead the cause of freedom, that cause will not be led.

As we address these challenges—and others we cannot

foresee tonight—America must maintain our moral clarity. I have often spoken to you about good and evil. This has made some uncomfortable. But good and evil are present in this world, and between the two there can be no compromise. Murdering the innocent to advance an ideology is wrong every time, everywhere. Freeing people from oppression and despair is eternally right. This Nation must continue to speak out for justice and truth. We must always be willing to act in their defense and to advance the cause of peace.

President Thomas Jefferson once wrote, "I like the dreams of the future better than the history of the past." As I leave the house he occupied two centuries ago, I share that optimism. America is a young country, full of vitality, constantly growing and renewing itself. And even in the toughest times, we lift our eyes to the broad horizon ahead.

I have confidence in the promise of America because I know the character of our people. This is a Nation that **inspires** immigrants to risk everything for the dream of freedom. This is a Nation where citizens show calm in times of danger and compassion in the face of suffering. We see examples of America's character all around us. And Laura and I have invited some of them to join us in the White House this evening.

We see America's character in Dr. Tony Recasner, a principal who opened a new charter school from the ruins of Hurricane Katrina. We see it in Julio Medina, a former inmate who leads a faith-based program to help prisoners returning to society. We see it in Staff Sergeant Aubrey McDade, who charged into an ambush in Iraq and rescued three of his fellow

Marines.

We see America's character in Bill Krissoff, a surgeon from California. His son Nathan, a Marine, gave his life in Iraq. When I met Dr. Krissoff and his family, he delivered some surprising news : He told me he wanted to join the Navy Medical Corps in honor of his son. This good man was 60 years old—18 years above the age limit. But his petition for a waiver was granted, and for the past year he has trained in battlefield medicine. Lieutenant Commander Krissoff could not be here tonight, because he will soon deploy to Iraq, where he will help save America's wounded warriors and uphold the legacy of his fallen son.

In citizens like these, we see the best of our country—resilient and hopeful, caring and strong. These virtues give me an unshakable faith in America. We have faced danger and trial, and there is more ahead. But with the courage of our people and confidence in our ideals, this great Nation will never tire ... never falter ... and never fail.

It has been the privilege of a lifetime to serve as your President. There have been good days and **tough** days. But every day I have been inspired by the greatness of our country and uplifted by the goodness of our people. I have been blessed to represent this Nation we love. And I will always be honored to carry a title that means more to me than any other : citizen of the United States of America.

And so, my fellow Americans, for the final time : Good night. May God bless this house and our next President. And may God bless you and our wonderful country.

各位同胞：

过去的8年，我很荣幸地成为你们的总统。这个世纪的头10年是一个非常重要的时期。今晚，带着一颗感恩的心，我将利用这最后的机会和你们一起分享我的一些看法，回顾过去一起走过的时光以及我对国家未来的展望。

再过5天，世界将见证充满活力的美国民主政治。根据我们建国时创立的传统，总统职位将交给你们——美国人民选举出来的继任者。届时站在国会台阶上的那个人，他的经历将折射出我们这个国家长久以来的承诺。对于我们整个国家来说，这是一个充满希望和自豪的时刻。我将和其他所有美国人民一起，向当选总统奥巴马、他的妻子米歇尔以及他们两个漂亮的女儿送去最美好的祝愿。

今晚，我满怀感激之情，感谢我的副总统切尼以及白宫的每一位工作人员；我还要感谢我的妻子劳拉和我的女儿芭芭拉和詹娜，是她们给我的生活带来了无尽的快乐和爱意；我要感谢我的父母，他们给了我前进的动力。最重要的是，我要感谢所有美国人民给予我的信任。谢谢你们的祈祷让我斗志昂扬。

在过去的 8 年里，你们给了我无穷的勇气和极大的宽容，我对此表示深深的感谢。

今晚，我的思绪回到了 2001 年 9 月 11 日，那是我第一次在这里发表晚间演说。那天上午，恐怖分子对美国发动了自珍珠港事件以来最为严重的恐怖袭击，造成约 3，000 人死亡。我记得自己 3 天后站在世贸大楼的废墟前的情景。我周围是那些夜以继日抢救伤者的救援人员。我记得我同那些穿过五角大楼浓烟密布的走廊进行救援的勇士们交谈，同 93 号航班的英雄们的爱人们对话。我记得阿勒内·霍华德，她当时把她死去儿子的警徽交给了我，以表达对逝者的思念之情。直到现在，我仍然珍藏着他的徽章。

随着时光流逝，绝大多数美国人都已从悲痛中走了出来，恢复了 9·11 之前的生活。然而，我还没有解脱。每天早上，我都会收到一份关于国家安全威胁的简报，那时我发誓要尽最大的努力来保证我们的安全。

在过去的 7 年中，我们成立了新的国土安全部。我们的军队，军事情报部门，以及 FBI 都进行了改革。为了监视恐怖分子的行动，我们已经做了充分的准备，我们冻结了恐怖分子的账户，并屡屡粉碎了他们的阴谋。我们与强大的同盟国一道共同打击恐怖分子以及那些支持恐怖分子的人。在我们的帮助下，阿富汗已经由恐怖主义的天堂转变成了一个逐步成熟的民主国家，那里的人们正和恐怖主义作斗争。此外，女孩子上学也得到了应有的尊重。伊拉克也已经摆脱了萨达姆的残酷统治，不再与美国为敌，成为了中东心脏地带的民主国家，美国的朋友。

针对这些决策，存在着一些合理的争论，但对于这些结果却没有任何争议。在过去的 7 年多时间里，美国本土再也没有遭受过恐怖袭击，这要归功于那些日夜辛劳保卫我们安全的人们：执法人员、情报分析人员、国土安全人员和外交官员，以及美军的士兵们。

承蒙上帝恩典，美国拥有这些愿意在国家危难之际挺身而出的人们。我非常珍视与这些无私的爱国者以及他们家人进行的会面，美国人民感谢你们。对于那些今晚正在聆听这次演讲的美军士兵们，我想说的是：这个世界上再也没有比成为你们的总司令更让人感到荣幸的事了。

美军正在进行的战争，广义上来看其实是两种不同体系之间的战争。一种是一小撮狂热分子要求人们完全臣服于受压迫的意识形态，他们迫害妇女并且杀害那些和他信仰不一样的人们。另外一种体系则建立在普世的民主基础上，自由和正义是通往和平的道路。

美国，正是基于这样的信念诞生的。从长远来看，倡导这种信念是保卫我们国民的唯一切实有效的方法。当人们生活在民主政治中时，他们就不愿再去选择那些追随恐怖势力的领导者。当人们对未来充满希望时，他们就不会选择放弃生命来发动暴力袭击。因此，美国一直在全世界倡导自由、人权和尊严。我们向那些新兴的民主政体提供支持，向艾滋病人提供药物，让垂死的病人起死回生，让母亲和婴儿们免受疟疾的困扰。自由是美国成立的唯一基石，并领导世界向一个自由普照全球的时代发展。

过去8年里，我们也努力增加美国人民所拥有的机会和希望。在美国，学生们现在可以在公立学校接受条件更好的教育；新的医疗福利政策让老人和残疾人更加安心；每一位纳税人的个人所得税降低了；通过信心重建计划，那些吸毒者也找到了新的希望；人们脆弱的生命得到了更好的保护；对于退伍老兵的补助几乎增加了一倍；美国的空气、水源以及土地比以前更加清洁了。

当繁荣遇到挑战时，我们勇敢地面对。当金融危机发生时，我们采取了果断的措施来保护我们的经济。对于那些辛勤工作的家庭来说，这是一个非常艰难的时期，但是如果我们不采取行动的话，后果会更严重。所有的美国人都受到了影响。团结一心的美国人将通过坚定的信心和辛勤的工作将我们的经济重新拉回到增长的车道上。我们将向世界再次展示美国自由企业制度的复兴。

和所有前任一样，我也经历过挫折，如果可能的话，我会采取不一样的方式来应对这些挫折。不过，我总是以国家利益最大化为出发点。我对得起自己的良心，采取了我认为是正确的措施。你们可能不同意我所作出的一些艰难决定。但是我希望，你们能认为，我是一位愿意作出艰难决定的总统。

我们的国家在未来将面临更多的艰难选择，必须用一些指导性原则来指引我们的路线。

虽然我们的国家现在比 7 年前更为安全，但目前美国最严峻的威胁仍然是恐怖袭击。我们的敌人很有耐心，并且决意要再次发动袭击。美国没有试图挑起冲突或者做过任何导致冲突的错事。但我们肩负着庄严的责任，必须同恐怖主义作斗争。我们不能骄傲自满，要坚定决心，绝不能放松警惕。

与此同时，我们必须抱有信心和明确的目的参与世界事务。面对来自海外的威胁，在国内寻求安慰是一种诱人的举措。但是我们必须抵制孤立主义和保护主义，退缩只会招来危险。在21 世纪，国内的安全和繁荣需要依靠国外自由的扩展。如果美国不领导自由事业，那么自由事业将无所适从。

在我们应对这些挑战时，我们今晚还无法预测其他的挑战，美国必须保持道德上的纯洁。我们经常谈及善恶问题，这可能令一些人颇感不适，但是目前这个世界确实存在着正义和邪恶，两者之间无法达成妥协。无论何时何地，杀害无辜者来推动一种意识形态都是错误的，把人们从压迫和绝望中解放出来永远是正确的。美国必须坚持为正义和真理而呼喊。我们必须保护正义和真理，并且推进和平事业的发展。

托马斯·杰斐逊总统曾写道，"相对于过去的历史，我更喜欢未来的梦想。"在我即将离开他两个世纪前所居住过的白宫时，我也持这种乐观的态度。美国是一个年轻的国家，充满了活力，在不断地发展与更新。即便是在最艰难的时候，美国仍然没有放弃对未来的梦想。

我对美国的未来充满信心，因为我了解我们民族的特质，这是一个鼓励移民们为自由的梦想而去尝试一切事情的国家，这是一个面对危险仍能保持镇定的国家，这是一个面对苦难仍抱有同情心的国家。在身边的每一个人身上，我们都能看到美国的特征。

我们可以在托尼·里卡斯尼尔的身上看到美国的特质，这位校长在卡特里娜飓风的废墟上重建了他的学校。我们可以在胡利奥·梅迪纳身上看到这种特质，这位曾经的犯人领导着一个基于信仰的项目，帮助囚犯们重返社会。我们也可以在奥布里·麦克达德参谋军士身上看到这种特质，他在伊拉克时，冲入包围圈并成功营救出了三名海军陆战队队员。

我们在加州医生比尔·克里索夫身上看到了美国的这种特质，他的儿子纳塔恩，作为一名海军陆战队队员，在伊拉克献出了自己的生命。当我遇到克里索夫和他的家人时，他告诉我一个令我意想不到的消息：为了缅怀儿子，他想加入海军医疗团。这位好人已60岁，超过规定年龄的上限18年，但他的申请得到了批准。在过去的一年中，克里索夫得到了很好的锻炼，可惜已荣升中校的他今晚不能来到这里，因为他很快就会前往伊拉克，在那里他可以救助我们受伤的勇士，并继续他儿子未完成的事业。

我们在这些公民身上看到了我们国家最优良的品质：坚韧且充满希望、有爱心且坚强。这些品质使我对美国有不可动摇的信心。我们曾面临危险和考验，未来还会有更多的危险和考验。然而，依靠你们的勇气和信心，伟大的美国永远会坚如磐石，永远不会走向没落。

对我来说，能够担任你们的总统是我一生的荣耀。任期内，我有过欢乐也有过困苦。但我每天都被我们国家的伟大所鼓舞，为我们人民的善良所振奋。我对自己有机会代表我们所热爱的国家感到幸福，并且我也一直在为我们的国家祈祷。在以后的时光里，我会永远珍视这样的身份：美利坚合众国的公民。

所以，我亲爱的美国同胞，让我最后一次对你们说：晚安。愿上帝保佑白宫和我们的下一任总统。愿上帝保佑你们和我们这个美好的国家。

实战提升
Practising & Exercise

✎导读✎

2009 年 1 月 15 日晚 8 时 (北京时间 16 日上午 9 时),美国总统布什发表电视告别演说,正式向美国国民道别。这位在任期内倍受争议及批评的美国总统在告别演说中,表示在国内外政策上取得了一系列成功,同时也向国民承认了一些错误。布什称自己的总统任期为"在危机中取得重大成就"的时期。

✎单词注释✎

debate [di'beit] *n.* 辩论,讨论

extremism [iks'tri:mizəm] *n.* 极端性;极端主义

protected [prə'tekid] *adj.* 受 (法律) 保护的

inspire [in'spaiə] *v.* 鼓舞,激励

tough [tʌf] *adj.* 坚韧的,牢固的,折不断的

✎诵读名句✎

As the years passed, most Americans were able to return to life much as it had been before Nine-Eleven. But I never did.

I have cherished meeting these selfless patriots and their families.

In the face of threats from abroad, it can be tempting to seek comfort by turning inward.

See China in the Light of Her Development

温家宝在剑桥大学的演讲：
用发展的眼光看中国

Wen Jiabao/温家宝

Vice Chancellor Alison Richard，Ladies and Gentlemen，

It gives me great pleasure to come to Cambridge，a world-renowned university that I have long wanted to visit. Cambridge has produced many great scientists and thinkers Isaac Newton, Charles Darwin and Francis Bacon，to name but a few，and made important contribution to the progress of human civilization. This year marks the 800th anniversary of the university. Please accept my warm congratulations.

This is my fourth visit to your country. Despite the great distance between China and Britain，the friendly exchanges between our peoples have been on the rise. The successful resolution of the question of Hong Kong and **fruitful** cooperation between our two countries in areas such as economy，trade，culture，education，science and technology have cemented the foundation of our comprehensive strategic partnership.

Here, I wish to pay high tribute to all those who have been working tirelessly to promote friendly ties between our two countries.

The title of my speech today is "See China in the Light of Her Development".

My beloved motherland is a country both old and young.

She is old, because she is a big Oriental country with a civilization stretching back several thousand years. *With **diligence** and wisdom, the Chinese nation created a splendid civilization and made significant contributions to the progress of humanity.*

She is young, because the People's Republic is just 60 years old, and the country began reform and opening-up only 30 years ago. The Chinese people established the New China after unremitting struggles and ultimately found a development path suited to China's national conditions through painstaking efforts. This is the path of socialism with Chinese characteristics. Following this path, our ancient civilization has been rejuvenated.

The key element of China's reform and opening-up is to free people's minds and the most fundamental and significant component is institutional innovation. Through economic reform, we have built a socialist market economy, where the market plays a primary role in allocating resources under government macro-regulation. We have carried out political reform, promoted democracy and improved the legal system. People are the masters of the country. We run the country according to law and endeavor to build a socialist country under the rule of law.

The essence of China's reform and opening-up is to put people first and meet their ever growing material and cultural needs through releasing and developing productive forces. It aims to give everyone equal opportunities for all-round development. It aims to protect the democratic rights of the people and promote stability, harmony and prosperity across the land. And it aims to safeguard the dignity and freedom of everyone so that he or she may pursue happiness with ingenuity and hard work.

Over the past three decades, more than 200 million Chinese have been lifted out of poverty, the average life expectancy has increased by 5 years, and the 83 million people with disabilities in China have received special care from the government and society. All this points to the tremendous efforts China has made to protect human rights. We have introduced free nine-year compulsory education throughout the country, established the cooperative medical system in the rural areas and improved the social safety net. The age-old dream of the Chinese nation is being turned into reality a dream to see the young educated, the sick treated and the old cared for.

I want to **quote** from a Tang Dynasty poem to describe what is happening in China, "From shore to shore it is wide at high tide, and before fair wind a sail is lifting." The Chinese people are working hard to modernize their country. This is a great practice in a large developing country both ancient and new. The Chinese people, with destiny in their own hands, are full of confidence in their future.

My beloved motherland is a country that stood numerous

vicissitudes but never gave up.

Earlier in my career, I worked in northwest China for many years. There, in the boundless desert, grows a rare variety of tree called euphratespoplar. Rooted over 50 meters down into the ground, they thrive in hostile environments, defying droughts, sandstorms and salinization. They are known as the "hero tree", because a euphrates poplar can live for a thousand years. Even after it dies, it stands upright for a thousand years, and even after it falls, it stays intact for another thousand years. I like the euphrates poplar because they symbolize the resilience of the Chinese nation.

Over the millennia, the Chinese nation has weathered numerous disasters, both natural and man-made, surmounted all kinds of difficulties and challenges, and made her way to where she proudly stands today. The longsufferings have only made her a nation of fortitude and perseverance. The experience of the Chinese nation attests to a truth : what a nation loses in times of disaster will be made up for by her progress.

I am reminded of the experience that I had in Wenchuan, Sichuan Province after the devastating earthquake there last May. That earthquake shocked the whole world. It flattened Beichuan Middle School and **claimed** many young lives. But only 10 days after the earthquake, when I went there for the second time, I had before my eyes new classrooms built on debris by local villagers with planks. Once again, the campus echoed with the sound of students reading aloud. I wrote down 4 Chinese characters on the blackboard, meaning "A country will emerge stronger from adversities." I have been to Wenchuan seven times since the earthquake and witnessed countless touching scenes like this. I am deeply moved by the unyielding spirit of my people. This great national spirit is the source of strength which has enabled the Chinese nation to emerge from all the hardships stronger than before.

With hard work over the past half century and more, China has achieved great progress. Its total economic output is now one of the largest in the world. However, we remain a developing country and we are keenly aware of the big gap that we have with the developed countries. There has been no fundamental change in our basic national condition : a big population, weak economic foundation and uneven development. China's per capita GDP ranks behind 100 countries in the world and is only about 1/18 that of Britain.Those of you who have been to China as tourists must have seen the modern cities, but our rural areas are still quite backward.

To basically achieve modernization by the middle of this century, we must accomplish three major tasks : first, achieve industrialization, which Europe has long completed, while keeping abreast of the latest trends of the scientific and technological revolution ; second, promote economic growth while ensuring social equity and justice ; and third, pursue sustainable development at home while accepting our share of international responsibilities. The journey ahead will be long and arduous, but no amount of difficulty will stop the Chinese people from marching forward.Through persistent efforts, we will reach our goal.

My beloved motherland is a country that values her traditions while opening her arms to the outside world.

The traditional Chinese culture is rich, extensive and profound.Harmony, the supreme value cherished in ancient China, lies at the heart of the Chinese culture. *The Book of History*, an ancient classic in China for example, advocates amity among people and friendly exchanges among nations.

The Chinese cultural tradition values peace as the most precious. This has **nurture**d the broad mind of the Chinese nation. The Chinese nation is generous and tolerant, just as Mother Earth cares for all living things.She is in constant pursuit of justice, just as the eternal movement of the Universe.

In the 15th century, the famous Chinese navigator Zheng He led seven maritime expeditions to the Western Seas and reached over 30 countries. He took with him Chinese tea, silk and porcelain and helped local people fight pirates as he sailed along. He was truly a messenger of love and friendship.

The argument that a big power is bound to seek hegemony does not apply to China. Seeking hegemony goes against China's cultural tradition as well as the will of the Chinese people. China's development harms no one and threatens no one. We shall be a peace-loving country, a country that is eager to learn from and cooperate with others. We are committed to building a harmonious world.

Different countries and nations need to respect, tolerate and learn from each other's culture. Today, 300 million Chinese are learning English and over one million of our young people are studying abroad. The cultures and arts of various parts of the world are featured daily on China's television, radio and print media. Had we not learned from others through exchanges and enriched ourselves by drawing on others'experience, we would not have enjoyed today's prosperity and progress.

In the 21st century, economic globalization and the information network have linked us all together. Different cultures live together and influence each other. No culture can flourish in isolation. How much a country or a nation contributes to the culture of humanity is increasingly determined by her ability to **absorb** foreign cultures and renew herself.That is why China will remain open and receptive, value her own traditions while drawing on others'successful experience, and achieve economic prosperity and social progress in a civilized and harmonious way.

...

Ladies and Gentlemen,

Britain is the last leg of my European trip. I have gained a deeper understanding of Europe through this visit. China–EU cooperation is now standing at a new historical starting point and I am all the more confident about the China–EU comprehensive strategic partnership. There are no outstanding issues left over from history or conflict of fundamental interests between the two sides. What we have is a solid foundation and a bright future for cooperation. As the first industrialized country, Britain has accumulated rich experience in economic development and environmental protection. We hope to learn from your experience and strengthen exchanges and cooperation with you.

The future belongs to the younger generation. It is incumbent upon you to build an even more splendid future of China—Britain relations. Here and now, I cannot but mention Dr. Joseph Needham, a Cambridge alumnus who made important contributions to cultural exchanges between China and Britain.With his monumental masterpiece, Science and Civilization in China, he built a bridge between the two great civilizations of East and West. To honor tradition and innovation is the outstanding character of Cambridge.I hope more of you will turn your eyes to China, see my country in the light of her development, and act as ambassadors of China—Britain friendship. I believe that as long as you, the young people of China and Britain learn from each other and strive for progress hand in hand, you will add a brilliant new chapter to the annals of our relations.

Thank you!

尊敬的理查德校长，女士们，先生们：

来到向往已久的剑桥大学，非常高兴。剑桥举世闻名，培养出牛顿、达尔文、培根等许多杰出的科学家、思想家，为人类文明进步作出了重要贡献。今年是剑桥建校 800 周年，我谨致以热烈祝贺！

这是我第四次访问英国。中英相距遥远，但两国人民的友好交往不断增多。香港问题的圆满解决，经贸、文教、科技等领域的有效合作，为发展中英全面战略伙伴关系奠定了坚实基础。在此，我向长期致力于中英友好的朋友们表示崇高的敬意！

今天，我演讲的题目是：用发展的眼光看中国。

我深深爱着的祖国——古老而又年轻。

说她古老，她是一个有着数千年文明史的东方大国。中华民族以自己的勤劳和智慧，创造了灿烂的古代文明，对人类发展作出过重大贡献。

说她年轻，新中国成立才 60 年，改革开放才 30 年。中国人民经过长期不懈的斗争建立了新中国，又经过艰苦的探索，终于找到了适合国情的发展道路——中国特色社会主义道路，文明古国焕发了青春活力。

中国改革开放，最重要的是解放思想，最根本、最具有长远意义的是体制创新。我们推行经济体制改革，建立了社会主义市场经济体制。在政府的宏观调控下，充分发挥市场对资源配置的基础性作用。我们深化政治体制改革，把发展民主和完善法制结合起来，实行人民当家作主，依法治国，建设社会主义法治国家。

改革开放的实质，就是坚持以人为本，通过解放和发展生

我有一个梦

产力满足人们日益增长的物质文化需求，在公正的条件下促进人的全面发展；就是保障人民的民主权利，让国家政通人和、兴旺发达；就是维护人的尊严和自由，让每个人的智慧和力量得以迸发，成功地追求自己的幸福生活。

30 年来，中国贫困人口减少了 2 亿多，人均寿命提高了 5 岁，8，300 万残疾人得到了政府和社会的特殊关爱，这是中国保障人权的光辉业绩。九年免费义务教育的推行，农村合作医疗制度的建立，社会保障体系的完善，使学有所教、病有所医、老有所养的理想，正在变为现实。

我愿借用两句唐诗形容中国的现状："潮平两岸阔，风正一帆悬。"中国人正在努力实现现代化，这是一个古而又新的发展中大国进行的一场伟大实践。掌握了自己命运的中国人民，对未来充满信心！

我深深爱着的祖国——历经磨难而又自强不息。

我年轻时曾长期工作在中国的西北地区。在那浩瀚的沙漠中，生长着一种稀有的树种，叫胡杨。它扎根地下 50 多米，抗干旱、斗风沙、耐盐碱，生命力极其顽强。它"生而一千年不死，死而一千年不倒，倒而一千年不朽"，世人称为英雄树。我非常喜欢胡杨，它是中华民族坚韧不拔精神的象征。

千百年来，中华民族一次次战胜了天灾人祸，渡过了急流险滩，昂首挺胸地走到今天。深重的灾难，铸就了她百折不挠、自强不息的品格。中华民族的历史证明了一个真理：一个民族在灾难中失去的，必将从民族的进步中得到补偿。

此时此刻，我不禁想起在汶川地震灾区的亲身经历。去年 5 月，四川汶川发生了震惊世界的特大地震，北川中学被夷为平地，孩子们伤亡惨重。可是，时隔 10 天，当我第二次来到这里时，乡亲们已在废墟上搭起了板房教室，校园里又回荡着孩子们朗朗的读书声。当时我在黑板上，给同学们写下了"多难兴邦"几个字。地震发生以来，我7次到汶川灾区，碰到这样感人的事迹不胜枚举。我为我们中华民族这种愈挫愈奋的精神深深感动。这种伟大的精神，正是我们的民族饱经忧患而愈益坚强、生生不息的力量源泉。

经过半个多世纪的艰苦奋斗，中国有了比较大的发展，经济总量跃居世界前列，但我们仍然是一个发展中国家，同发达国家相比还有很大的差距。人口多，底子薄，发展不平衡，这种基本国情还没有从根本上得到改变。中国的人均GDP水平，排在世界100位之后，仅为英国的1/16左右。到过中国旅游的朋友，你们所看到的城市是现代的，而我们的农村还比较落后。

到本世纪中叶，中国要基本实现现代化，面临三大历史任务：既要努力实现欧洲早已完成的工业化，又要追赶新科技革命的浪潮；既要不断提高经济发展水平，又要实现社会公平正义；既要实现国内的可持续发展，又要承担相应的国际责任。中国要赶上发达国家水平，还有很长很长的路要走，还会遇到许多艰难险阻。但是，任何困难都阻挡不住中国人民前进的步伐，只要我们坚持不懈地努力奋斗，中国现代化的目标就一定能够实现。

我深深爱着的祖国——珍视传统而又开放兼容。

中华传统文化底蕴深厚、博大精深。"和"在中国古代历史上被奉为最高价值，是中华文化的精髓。中国古老的经典——《尚书》就提出"百姓昭明，协和万邦"的理想，主张人民和睦相处，国家友好往来。

"和为贵"的文化传统，哺育了中华民族宽广博大的胸怀。我们的民族，既能像大地承载万物一样，宽厚包容；又能像苍天刚健运行一样，彰显正义。

15世纪，中国著名航海家郑和七下西洋，到过三十几个国家。他带去了中国的茶叶、丝绸、瓷器，还帮助沿途一些国家剿灭海盗，真正做到了播仁爱于友邦。

国强必霸，不适合中国。称霸，既有悖于我们的文化传统，也违背中国人民意志。中国的发展不损害任何人，也不威胁任何人。中国要做和平的大国、学习的大国、合作的大国，致力于建设一个和谐的世界。

不同国家、不同民族的文化，需要相互尊重、相互包容和相互学习。今天的中国，有3亿人在学英语，有100多万青年人在国外留学。我们的电视、广播、出版等新闻传媒，天天都在介绍世界各地的文化艺术。正因为我们善于在交流中学习，在借鉴中收获，才有今天中国的繁荣和进步。

进入21世纪，经济全球化、信息网络化，已经把世界连成一体，文化的发展将不再是各自封闭的，而是在相互影响中多元共存。一个国家、一个民族对人类文化贡献的大小，越来越取决于她吸收外来文化的能力和自我更新的能力。中国将永远坚持开放兼容的方针，既珍视传统，又博采众长，用文明的方式、和谐的方式实现经济繁荣和社会进步。

……

女士们，先生们！

英国是我这次欧洲之行的最后一站。这次访问，加深了我对欧洲的了解。中欧合作已经站在一个新的历史起点上。我对中欧发展全面战略伙伴关系更加充满信心。我们之间不存在历史遗留问题，也不存在根本利害冲突。中欧合作基础坚实，前景光明。英国是最早进入现代化的国家，你们在发展经济、保护环境等方面，都有许多成功的经验。我们愿意向你们学习，加强交流与合作。

未来属于青年一代。中英关系的美好前景要靠青年去开拓。抚今追昔，我想起对中英文化交流作出重要贡献的剑桥校友李约瑟博士。他的鸿篇巨著《中国科学技术史》，在东西方两大文明之间架起了一座桥梁。继承传统、勇于创新，是剑桥大学的优秀品格。希望更多的剑桥人关注中国，用发展的眼光看中国，做中英交流的友好使者。我相信，只要中英两国青年相互学习，携手共进，一定会谱写出中英关系的崭新篇章。

谢谢大家！

实战提升
Practising & Exercise

🍃 导读 🍃

2009 年 1 月 27 日，中国国务院总理温家宝赴瑞士、德国、西班牙、英国和欧盟总部进行正式访问，并出席在瑞士达沃斯举行的世界经济论坛 2009 年年会。2 月 2 日下午，即将结束访英和访欧行程的中国总理温家宝踏雪到访剑桥大学，并发表了深情演讲，在向学生简要介绍中国改革开放的同时，敦促大家"用发展的眼光看中国"。

🍃 单词注解 🍃

fruitful ['fru:tful] *adj.* 富有成效的；收益好的
diligence ['dilidʒəns] *n.* 勤勉，勤奋
quote [kwəut] *v.* 引用；引述
claim [kleim] *n.* 主张，断言，声称
nurture ['nə:tʃə] *n.* 养育，教养，培育
absorb [əb'sɔ:b] *v.* 汲取，理解

🍃 诵读名句 🍃

With diligence and wisdom, the Chinese nation created a splendid civilization and made significantcontributions to the progress of humanity.

The argument that a big power is bound to seek hegemony does not apply to China.

In the 21st century, economic globalization and the information network have linked us all together. Different cultures live together and influence each other.

On Being Sentenced to Be Hanged
约翰·布朗：被判处绞刑时发表的讲话

John Browne/约翰·布朗

I have，may it please the court，a few words to say. *In the first place, I deny everything but what I have all along admitted—the design on my part to free the slaves.* I intended certainly to have made a clean thing of that matter，as I did last winter when I went into Missouri and there took slaves without the snapping of a gun on either side，moved them through the country，and finally left them in Canada. I designed to have done the same thing again on a larger scale. That was all I intended. I never did intend murder，or treason，or the destruction of property，or to excite or **incite** slaves to rebellion，or to make insurrection.

I have another objection；and that is，it is unjust that I should suffer such a penalty. Had I **interfered** in the manner which I admit，and which I admit has been fairly proved (for I admire the truthfulness and candor of the greater portion of the witnesses who have testified in this case)—had I so interfered in behalf of the rich，the powerful，the intelligent，the so-called great，or in behalf of any of their friends—either father, mother, brother, sister, wife or children, or any of that class—and suffered, and sacrificed what I have in this interference, it would have been all right; and every man in this court would have deemed it an act worthy of reward rather than punishment.

This court acknowledges, as I suppose, the validity of the law of God, I see a book kissed, which I suppose to be the Bible, or at least the New Testament. That teaches me that all things whatsoever I would that men should do to me I should do even so to them. It teaches me, further, to "remember them that are in bonds as bound with them". *I endeavored to act up to that instruction*. I say I am yet too young to understand that God is any respecter of persons. I believe that to have interfered as I have done—as I have always freely admitted I have done— in behalf of his despised poor was not wrong, but right. Now, if it is deemed necessary that I should forfeit my life for the furtherance of the ends of justice, and mingle my blood further with the blood of my children and with the blood of millions in this slave country whose rights are disregarded by wicked, cruel, and unjust enactments— I submit: so let it be done!

在法庭上，我只想讲几句话。首先，除了我一直承认的有计划地解放黑奴之外，我否认其他一切指控。我确实有意要帮助奴隶获得自由，去年冬天我就到过密苏里州接运黑奴，双方未发一枪就将黑奴成功运出，送至加拿大。我打算要扩大这种行动的规模。这就是我想做的一切。我从未图谋杀人、叛国、毁坏私有财产，或鼓励、煽动奴隶谋反作乱。

我还要提出一项异议，那就是：这么惩罚我是不公平的。我在法庭上所承认的我的所作所为已经得到了充分的证明（对于大部分证人所做的真实公正的发言我感到钦佩）。但是，假如我的所为侵犯那些有钱有势的人、有知识的人或那些所谓大人物的利益；或是他们的朋友、父母、兄弟、姐妹、妻子、儿女或他们所属阶级任何人的利益，并因此让他们遭到我现在所受的痛苦和牺牲，那也没什么。这法庭上的每个人都会认为我的行为不但不应受罚，反而值得奖赏。

我想，这个法庭也承认上帝的法律，我看到开庭时你们亲吻一本书，那大概是《圣经》吧，至少是《新约全书》。这本书教导我无论何事，你们愿意人怎样待你们，你们就要怎样待人，还教导我"要像自己也被囚禁那样，不忘身陷囹圄的人们"。我曾努力实践这一训条。我要说我还太年轻，不知道上帝也会待人不公。我总是坦率地承认自己所做的事情，承认我为那些被上帝遗弃的穷苦子民所做的事情：我并没有做错，相反，完全正确。现在，如果为了伸张正义，我必须献出生命，必须在这个被邪恶、残暴与不义的法制剥夺了一切权力的蓄奴国家里，把我的鲜血和我的几个孩子的鲜血以及千千万万人的鲜血流淌在一起，那就请便吧！

实战提升
Practising & Exercise

导读

1859 年，为了唤起各蓄奴州的奴隶起义，在 10 月 16 日夜晚，59 岁的布朗率领着由 22 个白人和黑人组成的队伍，进攻弗吉尼亚州的哈帕尔斯渡口，迅速占领了政府的军火库。次日黎明，惊慌的种植场奴隶主赶快集合了队伍，包围了军火库。双方展开了激烈的战斗，经过两昼夜的血战，起义者大部分牺牲，布朗的两个儿子也战死在他身旁。最后只剩下 4 个人，但仍继续战斗，直到弹尽粮绝，才负伤被俘。同年 12 月，布朗被判处死刑，在就义前，他写下遗书："我，约翰·布朗，现在坚信只有用鲜血才能洗清这个有罪国土的罪恶。过去我自以为——正如我现在也痴心妄想的一样——也许不用流很多的血就可以洗清他的罪恶。"约翰·布朗为黑奴自由解放英勇斗争的故事，促进了美国废奴力量的团结，把全国的废奴运动推向了一个新的高潮。

单词注解

incite [in'sait] v. 激励；激起

interfere [ˌintə'fiə] v. 妨碍；冲突；抵触

endeavor [in'devə] v. 努力，力图

justice ['dʒʌstis] n. 正义；公平

诵读名句

In the first place, I deny everything but what I have all along admitted—the design on my part to free the slaves.

I have another objection；and that is，it is unjust that I should suffer such a penalty.

I endeavored to act up to that instruction.

Tear Down This Wall

罗纳德·威尔逊·里根：拆掉这堵墙吧

Ronald Wilson Reagan/罗纳德·威尔逊·里根

After these four decades, then, there stands before the entire world one great and inescapable conclusion : *Freedom leads to prosperity. Freedom replaces the ancient hatreds among the nations with comity and peace. Freedom is the victor.*

And now the Soviets themselves may, in a limited way, be coming to understand the importance of freedom. We hear much from Moscow about a new policy of reform and openness. Some political prisoners have been released. Certain foreign news broadcasts are no longer being jammed. Some economic enterprises have been permitted to operate with greater freedom from state control.

Are these the beginnings of **profound** changes in the Soviet state? Or are they token gestures, intended to raise false hopes in the West, or to strengthen the Soviet system without changing it? We welcome change and openness ; for we believe that freedom and security go together, that the advance of human liberty can only strengthen the cause of world peace. There is one sign the Soviets can make that would be unmistakable, that would advance dramatically the cause of freedom and peace.

General Secretary Gorbachev, if you seek peace, if you seek prosperity for the Soviet Union and Eastern Europe, if you seek liberalization : Come here to this gate! Mr. Gorbachev, open this gate! Mr. Gorbachev, tear down this wall!

I understand the fear of war and the pain of division that afflict this continent— and I pledge to you my country's efforts to help overcome these burdens. To be sure, we in the West must **resist** Soviet expansion. So we must maintain defenses of unassailable strength. Yet we seek peace, so we must strive to reduce arms on both sides.

...

Today thus represents a moment of hope. We in the West stand ready to cooperate with the East to **promote** true openness, to break down barriers that separate people, to create a safe, freer world. And surely there is no better place than Berlin, the meeting place of East and West, to make a start.

Free people of Berlin : Today, as in the past, the United States stands for the strict observance and full implementation of all parts of the Four Power Agreement of 1971. Let us use this occasion, the 750th anniversary of this city, to usher in a new era, to seek a still fuller, richer life for the Berlin of the future. Together, let us maintain and develop the ties between the Federal Republic and the Western sectors of Berlin, which is permitted by the 1971 agreement.

And I invite Mr Gorbachev : Let us work to bring the Eastern and Western parts of the city closer together, so that all the inhabitants of all Berlin can enjoy the benefits that come with life in one of the great cities of the world.

To open Berlin still further to all Europe, East and West, let us expand the vital air access to this city, finding ways of making commercial air service to Berlin more convenient, more comfortable, and more economical. We look to the day when West Berlin can become one of the chief aviation hubs in all central Europe.

With our French and British partners, the United States is prepared to help bring international meetings to Berlin. It would be only fitting for Berlin to serve as the site of United Nations meetings, or world conferences on human rights and arms control or other issues that call for international cooperation.

There is no better way to establish hope for the future than to enlighten young minds, and we would be honored to sponsor summer youth exchanges, cultural events, and other programs for young Berhners from the East. Our French and British friends, I'm certain, will do the same. And it's my hope that an authority can be found in East Berlin to sponsor visits from young people of the Western sectors.

One final proposal, one close to my heart : Sport represents a source of enjoyment and ennoblement, and you may have noted that the Republic of Korea—South Korea has offered to permit certain events of the 1988 Olympics to take place in the North. International sports competitions of all kinds could take place in both parts of this city. And what better way to demonstrate to the world the openness of this city than to offer in some future year to hold the Olympic Games here in Berlin, East and West? In these four decades, as I have said, you Berliners have built a great city. You've done so in spite of threats—the Soviet attempts to impose the East-mark, the blockade. Today the city thrives in spite of the challenges implicit in the very presence of this wall. What keeps you here? Certainly there's a great deal to be said for your fortitude, for your defiant courage. But I believe there's something deeper, something that involves Berlin's whole look and feel and way of life—not mere sentiment. No one could live long in Berlin without being completely disabused of illusions. Something instead, that has seen the difficulties of life in Berlin but chose to accept them, that continues to build this good and proud city in contrast to a surrounding totalitarian presence that refuses to **release** human energies or aspirations. Something that speaks with a powerful voice of affirmation, that says yes to this city, yes to the future, yes to freedom. *In a word, I would submit that what keeps you in Berlin is love—love both profound and abiding.*

Perhaps this gets to the root of the matter, to the most fundamental distinction of all between East and West. The totalitarian world produces backwardness because it does such violence to the spirit, thwarting the human impulse to create, to enjoy, to worship. The totalitarian world finds even symbols of love and of worship an affront. Years ago, before the East Germans began rebuilding their churches, they erected a secular structure : the television tower at Alexander Platz. Virtually ever since, the authorities have been working to correct what they view as the tower's one major flaw, treating the glass sphere at the top with paints and chemicals of every kind. Yet even today when the sun strikes that sphere—that sphere that towers over all Berlin—the light makes the sign of the cross. There in Berlin, like the city itself, symbols of love, symbols of worship, cannot be suppressed.

As I looked out a moment ago from the Reichstag, that embodiment of German unity, I noticed words crudely spray-painted upon the wall, perhaps by a young Berliner : "This wall will fall. Beliefs become reality." Yes, across Europe, this wall will fall. For it cannot **withstand** faith ; it cannot withstand truth. The wall cannot withstand freedom.

And I would like, before I close, to say one word. I have read, and I have been questioned since I've been here about certain demonstrations against my coming. *And I would like to say just one thing, and to those who demonstrate so*. I wonder if they have ever asked themselves that if they should have the kind of government they apparently seek, no one would ever be able to do what they're doing again.

Thank you and God bless you all.

……

40 年后的今天，整个世界将面对一个伟大和无法逃避的结论：自由导致繁荣，自由使得各个国家用礼让和宽容来代替古老的憎恨。自由是胜利者！

现在苏联自己可能以有限的方式，渐渐明白了自由的重要性。我们经常从莫斯科听到一些关于改革和开放的新政策颁布，一些政治犯被释放，某些外国新闻广播不再被封锁，一些经济企业已经开始拥有了更多的自主权。

这些是苏联社会中一些深刻变化的开端吗？或者这些仅仅是用来迷惑西方的假象，使西方国家对苏联产生希望，或者是在不改国易帜的前提下加强苏联体系的实力？我们欢迎变化和开放，因为我们相信自由和安全总是相伴而行，人类自由的进步只会加强世界和平事业的发展。所以，苏联能够做的，不被人误解而且还能够显著加快自由与和平事业步伐的事只有一件。

戈尔巴乔夫总书记，如果你真的要寻找和平，真的愿为苏联和东欧寻找繁荣，真的想寻找自由，那么就请来到这扇门前吧！戈尔巴乔夫先生，打开这扇门吧！戈尔巴乔夫先生，拆掉这堵墙吧！

我理解战争的恐惧和折磨这个大陆的分割的痛苦，我向你们保证我的国家会帮助你们承担这些重荷。当然，我们西方自由世界必须抵抗苏联的扩张，因此我们必须保持强大的防御力量。然而我们从来都在寻找和平，因此我们必须努力减少双方的军备竞赛。

　　……

　　今天，象征着一个希望的时刻：我们西方准备好与东方合作，推进真正的开放，消除分裂人们的障碍，建立一个安全，更加自由的世界。当然，没有任何一个地方比柏林更适合作为东西方开始接洽和会晤的地方了。

　　柏林的自由人民们，美国今天会像过去一样，坚定地捍卫和施行1971年"四国协议"的各项规定。让我们借此机会，借本市750周年纪念日的契机，迎接一个新的时代，为将来的柏林寻找一种更加充实，更加富有的生活。让我们遵循1971年的协定，共同维系和发展民主德国和柏林西部的联系。

　　我邀请戈尔巴乔夫先生：让我们一起努力加强这座城市东、西部的联系，让所有柏林人民能够享受来自于世界上一个伟大城市的福利。

　　对欧洲、东方和西方，更加广泛地开放柏林，让我们把主要的航空线路都延伸到这里，寻找一切方法使到柏林来的商务航空路线变得更加便捷、舒适和经济。我们期待着有一天，西柏林能够成为中欧重要的航空枢纽之一。

　　美国与我们的伙伴——法国和英国，准备在柏林召开一些国际会议。只有柏林才最适合作为联合国会议的承办地，或者一些有关人权和军事控制或者其他需要国际合作的议题的世界性会议的召开地。

　　培养年轻人是建立未来希望的最好方法，我们将非常荣幸地赞助夏季青年交换项目、文化盛事和其他一些为东柏林地区年轻人服务的活动。我们的朋友们，无论是法国的还是英国的，我相信，他们也会乐于做同样的事情。我希望在东柏林能建立一个权威机构来赞助西部地区年轻人的访问活动。

最后一个建议，也是我最真心的建议：运动是娱乐和高尚品质的来源。你们应该已经注意到韩国已经允许 1988 年奥运会的一些赛事在北方举行。各种各样的国际体育赛事都能够在这个城市的两边进行。如果将来的某一天能在柏林的东西部共同举办奥运会，向世界展示这个城市的真诚，还有比这更好的办法吗？正如我所说的，在这 40 年里，柏林人民已经建起了一座伟大的城市。尽管有威胁——苏联企图建立东部边界作为阻碍——你们仍然做到了。尽管这座墙的存在构成了隐形的威胁，但是今天这座城市依然繁荣。是什么让你们身处此地？当然你们的勇气和大无畏的精神是值得赞扬的，但是我相信还有更深层次的，围绕着柏林的整体面貌、精神和生活方式——不仅仅是情感。如果不能够完全矫正幻想，那么没有人能够在柏林常住。相反，有某种力量见证了柏林所遭受的苦难生活，但依然选择接受他们，这种力量继续建设这座美好且令人骄傲的城市，使它与周围那个拒绝释放人类能量和抱负的极权主义政体形成了鲜明的对比。这种力量以坚定有力的声音诉说，这个城市是可以肯定的，将来是可以肯定的，自由是可以肯定的。总之，我要说让你们离不开柏林的是爱——深沉的爱，永恒的爱。

也许这就让我们看到了事情的根源，找到了东西方区别的根源。极权的世界必然落后，因为它对精神施以暴力，阻止人类创造、享受和崇拜的冲动。极权的世界甚至把爱和崇拜的象征看成是一种冒犯。多年以前，在东德人开始重建教堂之前，他们建立了一个世俗的建筑：在亚历山大广场上建起了电视塔。事实上从那以后，政府当局一直在努力纠正他们心中电视塔的一个主要缺点，用各种油漆和化学物质处理顶端的玻璃球。但是直到今天，当太阳照到这个球的时候——这个球体位于整个柏林的上空——阳光总会留下经过的痕迹。在柏林，像这个城市一样，爱的象征，崇拜的象征是不能被压制的。

在我刚才看 Reichstag——德国统一的化身的时候，我注意到粗糙地喷画在墙上的文字，可能是一个年轻的柏林人写的，"这座墙会倒掉的。信仰会成真的。"是的，整个欧洲都相信，这堵墙会倒掉的。因为它经不起信仰的考验；它经不起真理的拷问。这堵墙抵不住自由的呼唤。

在结束之前，我想说一句话。自从我来到这里，我读到过一些反对我来这里的文字，也被质问过。对那些人我只想说一件事，我想知道他们是否扪心自问过，是否应该拥有他们一心追寻的那种政府，如果问过的话，就没有人再这么做了。

谢谢大家，上帝会保佑你们的。

实战提升
Practising & Exercise

导读

随着苏联和西方国家紧张局势的加剧，不同地区间的通道逐渐缩小。1961 年，东西柏林的边界变成了一堵砖墙，柏林墙把千千万万的德国家庭分隔开来，许多居住在东部的德国人无法再去西部上班，许多交通工具无法再在那里行驶。多年来，很多东德人试图逃到西边去。柏林墙建成后，西柏林变成了一片孤独的、被敌视和被包围的土地。到了 20 世纪 80 年代，柏林墙已经成为冷战的最持久象征。1987 年 6 月 12 日清晨，美国总统里根抵达柏林，此时这座城市正在庆贺其 750 岁诞辰。在将东西柏林割裂 20 余年的分界线——勃兰登堡门的柏林墙前，里根发表了这个著名的演说。

单词注解

profound [prə'faund] *adj.* 深深的；深刻的

resist [ri'zist] *v.* 抵抗，反抗；抗拒

promote [prə'məut] *v.* 促进；发扬；引起

release [ri'li:s] *v.* 释放，解放

withstand [wið'stænd] *v.* 抵挡，反抗；禁得起

诵读名句

Freedom leads to prosperity. Freedom replaces the ancient hatreds among the nations with comity and peace. Freedom is the victor.

In a word, I would submit that what keeps you in Berlin is love—love both profound and abiding.

And I would like to say just one thing, and to those who demonstrate so.

Hillary Clinton Endorsement Speech
希拉里退选演说

Hillary Clinton/希拉里·克林顿

Thank you so much. Thank you all.

Well，this isn't exactly the party I'd planned，but I sure like the company.

I want to start today by saying how grateful I am to all of you——to everyone who poured your hearts and your hopes into this campaign，who drove for miles and lined the streets waving homemade signs，who scrimped and saved to raise money，who knocked on doors and made calls，who talked and sometimes argued with your friends and neighbors，who e-mailed and contributed online，who invested so much in our common enterprise. To the moms and dads who came to our events，who lifted their little girls and little boys on their shoulders and whispered in their ears，"See，you can be anything you want to be."

To the young people，like 13-year-old Ann Riddle from

Mayfield, Ohio, who had been saving for two years to go to Disney World, and decided to use her savings instead to travel to Pennsylvania with her mom and volunteer there as well. To the **veterans** and the childhood friends, to New Yorkers and Arkansans who traveled across the country, telling anyone who would listen why you supported me.

To all those women in their 80s and their 90s, born before women could vote, who cast their votes for our campaign. I've told you before about Florence Steen of South Dakota, who was 88 years old, and insisted that her daughter bring an absentee ballot to her hospice bedside. Her daughter and a friend put an American flag behind her bed and helped her fill out the ballot. She passed away soon after, and under state law, her ballot didn't count. But her daughter later told a reporter, "My dad's an ornery old cowboy, and he didn't like it when he heard mom's vote wouldn't be counted. I don't think he had voted in 20 years. But he voted in place of my mom."

To all those who voted for me, and to whom I pledged my utmost, my commitment to you and to the progress we seek, is **unyielding**. *You have inspired and touched me with the stories of the joys and sorrows that make up the fabric of our lives, and you have humbled me with your commitment to our country.*

Eighteen million of you from all walks of life——women and men, young and old, Latino and Asian, African-American and Caucasian, rich, poor and middle-class, gay and straight—you have stood strong with me. And I will continue to stand strong with you, every time, every place and every way that I can. The dreams we share are worth fighting for.

Remember—we fought for the single mom with a young daughter, juggling work and school, who told me, "I'm doing it all to better myself for her." We fought for the woman who grabbed my hand, and asked me, "What are you going to do to make sure I have health care?" and began to cry, because even though she works three jobs, she can't afford insurance.

We fought for the young man in the Marine Corps T-shirt who waited months for medical care and said, "Take care of my buddies over there—and then, will you please help take care of me?" We fought for all those who've lost jobs and health care, who can't afford gas or groceries or college, who have felt **invisible** to their president these last seven years.

...

We cannot let this moment slip away. We have come too far and accomplished too much.

Now, the journey ahead will not be easy. Some will say we can't do it. That it's too hard. That we're just not up to the task. But for as long as America has existed, it has been the American way to reject "can't-do" claims, and to choose instead to stretch the boundaries of the possible through hard work, determination and a pioneering spirit.

It is this belief, this optimism, that Senator Obama and I share, and that has inspired so many millions of our supporters to make their voices heard.

So today, I am standing with Senator Obama to say : Yes we can.

...

We'll have to work hard to get back to fiscal responsibility and a strong middle class. But on the day we live in an America whose middle class is thriving and growing again, where all Americans, no matter where they live or where their ancestors came from, can earn a decent living, we will live in a stronger America, and that is why we must elect Barack Obama our president.

We'll have to work hard to **foster** *the innovation that makes us energy—independent and lift the threat of global warming from our children's* **future**. But on the day we live in an America fueled by renewable energy, we will live in a stronger America. That's why we have to help elect Barack Obama our president.

非常感谢各位！谢谢你们！

这场聚会并不是我事先计划好的哦，但有你们的陪伴，我确实很开心。

今天我首先要说，我是多么地感谢你们大家——感谢为这次竞选倾注了激情和希望的每个人，感谢那些长途跋涉，在街上挥舞自制标语的人们，感谢那些省吃俭用，踊跃募款的人们，感谢那些挨家挨户敲门，给每个人打电话，并且和你的朋友邻居们讨论甚至争论起来的人们。感谢那些通过电子邮件和网络进行捐助的人们，感谢那些在我们的公共事业上大量投资的人们。更要感谢那些带着孩子参加我们活动的父母们，他们轻声地告诉肩膀上的孩子们："看啊，有梦想就能实现！"

我也应该感谢像安这样的年轻人，她今年刚13岁，来自俄亥俄州的梅菲尔得市，她存了两年的零花钱，准备去迪斯尼游玩，却决定将这笔钱省下来，作为和妈妈一起去宾夕法尼亚当志愿者的经费。还有那些退伍老兵，孩提时的朋友，以及纽约和阿肯色地区的人们，感谢他们不远万里来到这里，并转告他人，相信他们同你们一样支持我。

感谢那些在女性拥有选举权之前出生的：八九十岁并在竞选活动中投票的女士们。我在之前提到过的，来自南达科他州88岁的弗朗斯·斯汀，坚持让她的女儿带一张缺席选举人票到她的病床前。她女儿和朋友将国旗插在她的床头并帮她填选票。没多久她就离开了人世。根据国家法律，她的选票不能生效。后来她的女儿对记者说："我爸性子很倔，当他听说妈妈的选票无效时，马上就不高兴了。他20年都没投票了，这次算是替妈妈投了一票。"

我亲爱的选民们，我曾经承诺过的人们，我感谢你们，虽然结果不尽如人意，可很感谢你们能陪我坚持到现在，你们的快乐与悲伤激励了我，也感动了我，完整了我们的生命，你们对国家的承诺和担当使我自惭形秽。

1,800万人，来自各行各业——无论男人和女人，年轻人和老年人，拉丁裔和亚裔，非裔美国人和高加索人，富人、穷人和中产阶级的人，无论是同性恋者还是异性恋者，你们给予了我有力的支持。无论何时何地，我将尽我所能，坚定地和你们站在一起。我们拥有同样的梦想，值得我们一起为之奋斗，为之拼搏。

记住——我们奋斗，为了那个在学校和工作间不断奔波独自抚养年幼女儿的单身母亲，她说："我所做的一切都是让我这个母亲更称职"。我们奋斗，为了那个妇女，她抓住我的手问我："你打算怎样来保证我的医疗保障？"然后痛哭不已，尽管她同时打着三份工，却仍然支付不起保险费。

我们奋斗，为了那个身着海军陆战队 T 恤的年轻人。他为了医疗护理而等待了数月，他告诉我说："请照顾好我在那里的朋友，然后请你也护理一下我好吗？"我们奋斗，为了所有失去工作和没有医疗保障的人，为了所有不能支付汽油费、杂货费或学费的人，为了所有那些在过去 7 年中被他们的总统所忽略的人！

　……

现在不能再与之失之交臂了，我们走得太远，付出太多了。

然而，前方的路并非坦途。有人说，那太难了，不是我们力量所能及的，我们不可能胜任。但自打美国诞生起，我们就有一个美国式的对"不可能"说不的方式——通过辛苦工作，坚定的信念和开拓精神，不遗余力地跨域任何可能的疆域。

这种信念，这份乐观，激励了我和奥巴马；这种信念，这份乐观，激励了数以百万的你们，让支持的声音响彻太空。

所以今天，我和参议员奥巴马并肩站立，高喊："我们能"。

　……

我们将全力以赴，重掌财政责任和一个强势的中产阶级。一旦到了那天，美国出现中产阶级再次繁荣成长，不管他们或者他们的祖先来自何方，都能得到一个体面的收入，我们就生活在一个更加强大的美国里了。那就是为何我们必须帮助奥巴马成为总统的原因。

　　我们将全力以赴，扶持能源独立型创新技术，让我们的孩子远离全球变暖的威胁。一旦到了美国使用了可再生能源的那天，我们就是生活在一个更加强大的美国里。那就是为什么我们必须帮助奥巴马成为总统的原因。

实战提升
Practising & Exercise

导读

2008 年 6 月 7 日，美国民主党总统竞选人希拉里在华盛顿正式宣布停止竞选，转而支持竞争对手奥巴马。希拉里的退选演说内容可圈可点，赢得阵阵掌声。一般来说，这种承认自己失败的演说，很难讲好，既不能流露出对对手的怨恨，又不能让自己显得灰溜溜，所以演说的难度可想而知。虽然选举失败，但离开得仍然如同一个胜利者。

单词注解

veteran ['vetərən] *n.* 老兵；老手；富有经验的人

unyielding [ʌnˈjiːldiŋ] *adj.* 不屈服的；不让步的；顽固的

invisible [inˈvizəbl] *adj.* 看不见的；无形的

foster [ˈfɔstə] *v.* 养育，领养

fuel [fjuəl] *v.* 对……供给燃料；给……加油；激起

诵读名句

You have inspired and touched me with the stories of the joys and sorrows that make up the fabric of our lives, and you have humbled me with your commitment to our country.

We cannot let this moment slip away. We have come too far and accomplished too much.

We'll have to work hard to foster the innovation that makes us energy—independent and lift the threat of global warming from our children's future.

President Hu's Speech at Yale University
胡锦涛在耶鲁大学的演讲

Hu Jintao/胡锦涛

Let me begin by thanking you, Mr. Levin, for your kind invitation and the opportunity to come to Yale to meet young friends and teachers of this world-renowned university.

Coming to the Yale campus, with its distinctive academic flavor, and looking at the eager young faces in the audience, I cannot but recall my great experience studying at Tsinghua University in Beijing 40 years ago. Indeed, what happens during one's school year will influence his whole life. I still benefit greatly from the instruction and my interaction with other students.

Yale is renowned for its long history, unique way of teaching and excellence in academic pursuit. If time could go back several decades, I would really like to be a student of Yale just like you.

Yale's motto "Light and Truth," which is a calling for

human progress, represents the aspiration of every motivated young men and women. Over the past three centuries, Yale has produced a galaxy of outstanding figures, including 20 Nobel laureates and five American presidents. The words of Nathan Hale, an American hero and Yale alumnus, "I only regret that I have but one life to lose for my country," have also inspired me and many other Chinese. I sincerely hope that Yale will produce more talent and contribute further to the social and economic development of the United States and the cause of human progress.

Ladies and gentlemen, dear friends,

The Chinese and Americans have always had an **intense** interest in and cared deeply about each other. The Chinese admire the pioneering and enterprising spirit of the Americans and their proud achievement in national development. *As China develops rapidly and steady headway is made in China-US cooperation, more and more Americans are following with great interest China's progress and development.*

Understanding leads to trust. Today, I would like to speak to you about China's development strategy and its future against the backdrop of the evolution of the Chinese civilization and China's current development endeavor. I hope this will help you gain a better understanding of China.

In a history that spans more than five millennia, the Chinese nation has contributed significantly to the progress of human civilization. But its course of national development has been an arduous one. In particular in the 160 years and more since the Opium War in 1840, the Chinese people have fought courageously and unyieldingly to rid themselves of poverty and backwardness and to realize national rejuvenation, thus profoundly changing the destiny of the Chinese nation. Ninety-five years ago, the Chinese people launched the Revolution of 1911 that overthrew the feudal autocracy which had ruled China for several thousand years and opened the door to China's progress. Fifty-seven years ago, the Chinese people succeeded in winning liberation after protracted and hard struggle and founded New China in which people became their own masters. Twenty-eight years ago, the Chinese people embarked upon the historic drive of reform and opening-up and modernization and have made phenomenal progress through unremitting efforts. Between 1978 and 2005, China's GDP grew from $147.3 billion to $2.2257 trillion. Its import and export volume went up from $20.6 billion to $1.4221 trillion and its foreign exchange reserve soared from $167 million to $818.9 billion. During this period, the number of its poor rural population dropped from 250 million to 23 million. The above review of the profound changes in these 160 years shows one thing, namely, by carrying out persistent and hard struggle, the Chinese people have both changed their own destiny and advanced the cause of human progress.

On the other hand, I need to point out that, despite the success in its development, China remains the world's largest developing country, with per capita GDP ranking behind the 100th place. The Chinese people are yet to live a well-off life and China still faces daunting challenges in its development endeavor. Therefore it requires **sustained** and unremitting efforts to transform the country and make life better for its people.

In the next 15 years, we will strive to make new progress in building a moderately prosperous society in an all-round way that will benefit China's one billion and more population. We aim to raise China's GDP to $4 trillion by 2020, averaging $3, 000 per person. By then, China's economy will be better developed and its democracy will be further enhanced. More progress will be made in science and education. Its culture will be further enriched, the society will become more harmonious and the people will lead a better life.

To realize these goals, China has adopted a new concept of development in line with its national conditions and the requirement of the times. That is, to pursue a scientific outlook on development that makes economic and social development people-oriented, comprehensive, balanced and sustainable. We will work to strike a proper balance between urban and rural development, development among regions, economic and social development, development of man and nature, and domestic development and opening wider to the outside world. Greater emphasis will be put on addressing issues affecting people's livelihood, overcoming imbalances in development and resolving key problems that have occurred in the course of development. We will pursue a new path to industrialization featuring high technology, good economic returns, low resource-consumption, low environment pollution and full use of human resources. We will bring about coordinated economic, political, cultural and social development. And we will endeavor to ensure sustainable development by boosting production, improving people's lives and protecting the environment.

This concept of scientific development is based on the experience China has gained in its modernization drive and put forth in response to the trends of the times. It is also rooted in the cultural heritages of the Chinese nation.

The Chinese civilization is one that has continued uninterrupted for more than 5, 000 years. The distinct cultural tradition of the Chinese nation that developed in the long course of history has exerted a strong influence on contemporary China, just as it did on ancient China. Putting people first, keeping pace with the times, maintaining social harmony and pursuing peaceful development : these values that are being pursued in China today are derived from its tradition. But they also give expression to the progress of the times.

The Chinese civilization has always given **prominence** to the people and respect for people's dignity and value. Centuries ago, the Chinese already pointed out that "people are the foundation of a country ; when the foundation is stable, the country is in peace." Nothing is more valuable in the universe than human beings. The ancient Chinese emphasized the value of serving the people, enriching them, nourishing them, and benefiting them. We are pursuing today a people-oriented approach toward development because we believe that development must be for the people and by the people and its benefit should be shared among the people.

We care about people's value, rights and interests and freedom, the quality of their life, and their development potential and happiness index because our goal is to realize the all-around development of the people. Ensuring the right to survival and development remains China's top priority. We will vigorously promote social and economic development, protect people's freedom, democracy and human rights according to law, achieve social fairness and justice and enable the 1.3 billion Chinese people to live a happy life.

The Chinese civilization has always given prominence to unremitting self-improvement, reform and innovation. As an ancient Chinese motto puts it, "As Heaven keeps vigor through movement, a gentleman should unremittingly practice self-improvement." Throughout its 5, 000-year history, it is thanks to their perseverance, determination, stamina and innovation that the Chinese nation has grown after surviving numerous setbacks and adversity. The Chinese people have shown enterprising spirit and reform and opening-up creativity in national development and great **tenacity** in overcoming difficulties on the road to progress. And all this gives expression to the spirit of unremitting self-improvement embodied in China's cultural tradition.

The Chinese civilization has always given prominence to social harmony, unity and mutual assistance. Back in the early days of the Chinese nation, the Chinese already advocated that "harmony is most valuable." They strove for harmony between man and nature, among people and between man's body and soul, and yearned for an ideal society where "everyone loves everyone else, everyone is equal and the whole world is one community." Today, China is endeavoring to build a harmonious society. It is a society of democracy and rule of law, fairness and justice, integrity, fraternity, vitality, stability, order and harmony between man and nature. It is a society where there is unity between the material and the spirit, democracy and rule of law, fairness and efficiency, and vitality and order. The Chinese people takes the maintenance of ethnic unity and harmony as their bounden duty and the defense of the country's sovereignty and territorial integrity their sacred mission. Any act that promoted ethnic harmony and national unity will receive the warm welcome and support of the Chinese people. On the other hand, any act that undermines China's ethnic harmony and national unity will meet their strong opposition and resistance. The Chinese civilization has always given prominence to good neighborliness. The Chinese nation cherishes peace. In foreign relations, the Chinese have always believed that "the strong should not oppress the weak and the rich should not bully the poor" and advocated that "all nations live side by side in perfect harmony." The Chinese held that "one should be as inclusive as the ocean, which is vast because it admits hundreds of rivers" and called for drawing upon the strength of others. Today, China holds high the banner of peace, development and cooperation. It pursues an independent foreign policy of peace and commits itself firmly to peaceful development. It seeks to accelerate its development by upholding world peace. The world peace is, in turn, enhanced by China's development. China firmly pursues a strategy of opening-up for mutual benefit and win-win outcomes. It genuinely wishes to enter into extensive cooperation with other countries. It is inclusive and is eager to draw on the strength of other civilizations to pursue peace and development through cooperation and play its part in building a harmonious world of enduring peace and common prosperity.

Ladies and gentlemen, dear friends,

China and the United States are both countries of vast territory where many ethnic groups coexist and different cultures intermingle. Both our two peoples are hard-working and talented. Due to different historical backgrounds and national conditions, there are differences between China and the United States. But this enables us to learn from each other and draw on each other's strengths. Closer China-U.S. cooperation serves the fundamental interests of our two countries and peoples and is also of far-reaching significance for peace and development of the whole world.

Vast as it is, the Pacific Ocean has not stood in the way of exchanges and cooperation between our two peoples over the past two hundred years, and many moving episodes of mutual learning and mutual help between our two peoples who represent different civilizations have been recorded. In the 27 years since the establishment of diplomatic relations in 1979, China-U.S. relations have maintained steady momentum of growth despite twists and turns on the way, bringing tremendous benefits to both countries and peoples.

Entering the 21st century, the world has continued to undergo profound changes. Peace and development remain the calling of our times. On the other hand, factors causing instability and uncertainty are increasing and new challenges and threats are looming. Against this backdrop, the common interests between our two countries are increasing and the areas of our cooperation widening. Global peace and security now face new challenges, such as fighting international terrorism, preventing the proliferation of weapons of mass destruction, protecting the environment and human habitat and combating transnational crimes. And it is exactly in these fields that we share important strategic interests. China has a huge market and its development has generated strong demand, while the United States has advanced technology and high quality products. This has created enormous opportunities for economic and technical cooperation between our two countries. Indeed, there is a broad prospect for the growth of constructive and cooperative China—US relations in all fields.

Yesterday morning, President Bush and I had an in-depth exchange of views on China—US relations and major international and regional issues of common interest and reached broad and important agreement. We are both of the view that the two sides should approach our relations from the strategic and long-term perspective and that we should enhance dialogue, expand common ground, increase mutual trust, deepen cooperation and promote the overall growth of the constructive and cooperative China—US relations in the 21st century.

When we focus on the overall interest of China—US relations, respect and show understanding to each other, I am confident that our relations will move ahead in a healthy and steady manner, and contribute to the well-being of our two peoples and bring greater hope to people around the world.

Ladies and gentlemen, dear friends.

A composer cannot write enchanting melody with one

note, and a painter cannot paint landscape with only one color. The world is a treasure house where the unique cultural achievements created by people of all countries are displayed. The culture of a nation tells a lot about the **evolution** of the nation's understanding of the world and life, both past and present. Culture thus embodies a nation's fundamental pursuit of mind and dictates its norms of behavior. The historical process of human development is one in which different civilizations interact with and enrich each other and all civilizations in human history have contributed to human progress in their own unique way.

Cultural diversity is a basic feature of both human society and today's world and an important driving force for human progress. As history has shown, in the course of interactions between civilizations, we not only need to remove natural barriers and overcome physical isolation, we also need to remove obstacles and obstructions of the mind and overcome various prejudices and misunderstandings. Differences in ideology, social system and development model should not stand in the way of exchanges among civilizations, still less should they become excuses for mutual confrontation. We should uphold the diversity of the world, enhance dialogue and interaction between civilizations, and draw on each other's strength instead of practicing mutual exclusion. When this is done, mankind will enjoy greater harmony and happiness and the world will become a more colorful place to live in.

Ladies and gentlemen, dear friends,

Exchanges in culture and education and among young

people serve as a bridge for increasing mutual understanding between our two peoples. They are also a major driving force for the healthy and stable growth of China—US relations. Yale is a forerunner in conducting China—US educational exchanges and provides an important platform for cultural exchanges between our two countries. One hundred and fifty—six years ago, a Chinese young man named Rong Hong entered Yale Campus. Four years later, he graduated with distinction and received a bachelor of arts degree, making him the first ever Chinese graduate of an American university. Later, group after group of young Chinese followed his footsteps and studied at Yale. Over the past 20 years, Yale has accepted over 4, 000 Chinese students and undertaken more than 80 cooperation projects in culture, science and technology, and education with China. Last summer, Yale sent the first group of students to China for internships and some among them became the first foreign interns to work with China's Palace Museum. I wish to take this opportunity to express my appreciation to you, Mr. Levin, and Yale for the efforts you have made to promote exchanges between our two peoples.

To **enhance** mutual understanding between young people and educators of the two countries, I announce with pleasure here that we have decided to invite 100 Yale faculty members and students to visit China this summer. I'm sure you can look forward to an enjoyable experience in China.

Ladies and gentlemen, dear friends,

As an old Chinese saying goes : "As in the Yangtze River where the waves behind drive on those before, so a new generation always excels the last one." *Young people represent the hope and future of the world*. They are full of vitality，new ideas and creativity. I sincerely hope that the young people in China and the United States will join hands and work to enhance friendship between our two peoples，and，together with people of other countries，create a better world for all.

Thank you!

尊敬的理查德·莱文校长，同学们，老师们，女士们，先生们：

首先，我感谢莱文校长的邀请，使我有机会来到世界著名学府耶鲁大学，同青年朋友和老师们相聚在一起。

进入耶鲁大学的校园，看到莘莘学子青春洋溢的脸庞，呼吸着书香浓郁的空气，我不由回想起 40 年前在北京清华大学度过的美好时光。学生时代，对人的一生都会产生重要的影响，当年老师们对我的教诲，同学们给我的启发，我至今仍受用不尽。

耶鲁大学以悠久的发展历史、独特的办学风格、卓著的学术成就闻名于世。如果时光能够倒流几十年，我真希望成为你们中的一员。

耶鲁大学校训强调追求光明和真理，这符合人类进步的法则，也符合每个有志青年的心愿。300多年来，耶鲁大学培养出一大批杰出人才，其中包括20位诺贝尔奖获得者、5位美国总统。美国民族英雄内森·黑尔是耶鲁校友，他的名言——"我唯一的憾事，就是没有第二次生命献给我的祖国"，深深感染了我和许多中国人。我衷心祝愿贵校培养出更多英才，为美国经济社会发展、为人类进步事业作出更大贡献！

女士们、先生们、朋友们！

长期以来，中美两国人民一直相互抱有浓厚的兴趣和友好的感情。中国人民欣赏美国人民的开拓进取精神，钦佩美国人民在建设国家中取得的骄人业绩。随着中国的快速发展和中美合作的不断拓展，越来越多的美国人把目光投向中国，更加关注中国的发展进步。

了解是信任的基础。今天，我愿从中华文明历史流变和现实发展的角度，谈谈当代中国的发展战略和前进方向，希望有助于美国人民更全面、更深入地了解中国。

在5,000多年的历史长河中，中华民族为人类文明进步作出了巨大贡献，同时也走过了曲折艰辛的道路。特别是从1840年鸦片战争以来的160多年间，中国人民为摆脱积贫积弱的境遇，实现民族复兴，前仆后继，顽强斗争，使中华民族的命运发生了深刻变化。95年前，中国人民通过辛亥革命推翻了统治中国几千年的君主专制制度，为中国的进步打开了闸门。57年前，中国人民经过长期浴血奋斗实现了民族独立和人民解放，建立了人民当家作主的新中国。28年前，中国人民开始了改革开放和现代化建设的伟大历史进程，经过艰苦创业取得了举世瞩目的巨大成就，从1978年到2005年，中国国内生产总值从1，473亿美元增长到22，257亿美元，进出口总额从206亿美元增长到14，221亿美元，国家外汇储备从1.67亿美元增加到8，189亿美元，农村贫困人口由2.5亿人减少到2，300多万人。回顾这160多年来中国发生的沧桑巨变，可以说，中国人民经过艰苦探索和顽强奋斗，既改变了自己的命运，也推动了人类进步事业。

必须看到，中国尽管取得了巨大的发展成就，但仍是世界上最大的发展中国家，人均国内生产总值仍排在世界100名之后，中国人民的生活还不富裕，中国的发展还面临着不少突出的矛盾和问题。要彻底改变中国的面貌和改善中国人民的生活，需要继续持之以恒地艰苦奋斗。中国将在未来15年集中力量全面建设惠及十几亿人口的更高水平的小康社会。具体来说，就是要使中国国内生产总值到2020年达到40，000亿美元左右，人均达到3，000美元左右，使经济更加发展、民主更加健全、科教更加进步、文化更加繁荣、社会更加和谐、人民生活更加殷实。

为了实现我们的发展目标，中国根据本国国情和时代要求明确了自己的发展理念，这就是树立和贯彻以人为本、全面协调可持续发展的科学发展观，统筹城乡发展、统筹区域发展、统筹经济社会发展、统筹人与自然和谐发展、统筹国内发展和对外开放，更加注重解决民生问题，更加注重克服发展的不平衡性，更加注重解决发展中存在的突出矛盾，致力于走科技含量高、经济效益好、资源消耗低、环境污染少、人力资源优势得到充分发挥的新型工业化道路，推进经济建设、政治建设、文化建设、社会建设协调发展，努力实现生产发展、生活富裕、生态良好的文明发展格局。

科学发展的理念，是在总结中国现代化建设经验、顺应时代潮流的基础上提出来的，也是在继承中华民族优秀文化传统的基础上提出来的。

中华文明是世界古代文明中始终没有中断、连续 5，000 多年发展至今的文明。中华民族在漫长历史发展中形成的独具特色的文化传统，深深影响了古代中国，也深深影响着当代中国。现时代中国强调的以人为本、与时俱进、社会和谐、和平发展，既有着中华文明的深厚根基，又体现了时代发展的进步精神。

——中华文明历来注重以民为本，尊重人的尊严和价值。早在千百年前，中国人就提出"民惟邦本，本固邦宁"、"天地之间，莫贵于人"，强调要利民、裕民、养民、惠民。今天，我们坚持以人为本，就是要坚持发展为了人民、发展依靠人民、发展成果由人民共享，关注人的价值、权益和自由，关注人的生活质量、发展潜能和幸福指数，最终是为了实现人的全面发展。保障人民的生存权和发展权仍是中国的首要任务。我们将大力推动经济社会发展，依法保障人民享有自由、民主和人权，实现社会公平和正义，使 13 亿中国人民过上幸福生活。

——中华文明历来注重自强不息，不断革故鼎新。"天行健，君子以自强不息。"这是中国的一句千年传世格言。中华民族之所以能在 5，000 多年的历史进程中生生不息、发展壮大，历经挫折而不屈，屡遭坎坷而不馁，靠的就是这样一种发愤图强、坚韧不拔、与时俱进的精神。中国人民在改革开放中表现出来的进取精神，在建设国家中焕发出来的创造热情，在克服前进道路上的各种困难中表现出来的顽强毅力，正是这种自强不息精神的生动写照。

——中华文明历来注重社会和谐，强调团结互助。中国人早就提出了"和为贵"的思想，追求天人和谐、人际和谐、身心和谐，向往"人人相亲，人人平等，天下为公"的理想社会。今天，中国提出构建和谐社会，就是要建设一个民主法治、公平正义、诚信友爱、充满活力、安定有序、人与自然和谐相处的社会，实现物质和精神、民主和法治、公平和效率、活力和秩序的有机统一。中国人民把维护民族团结作为自己义不容辞的职责，把维护国家主权和领土完整作为自己至高无上的使命。一切有利于民族团结和国家统一的行为，都会得到中国人民真诚的欢迎和拥护。一切有损于民族团结和国家统一的举动，都会遭到中国人民强烈的反对和抗争。

——中华文明历来注重亲仁善邻，讲求和睦相处。中华民族历来爱好和平。中国人在对外关系中始终秉承"强不执弱"、"富不侮贫"的精神，主张"协和万邦"。中国人提倡"海纳百川，有容乃大"，主张吸纳百家优长、兼集八方精义。今天，中国高举和平、发展、合作的旗帜，奉行独立自主的和平外交政策，坚定不移地走和平发展道路，既通过维护世界和平来发展自己，又通过自身的发展来促进世界和平。中国坚持实施互利共赢的对外开放战略，真诚愿意同各国广泛开展合作，真诚愿意兼收并蓄、博采各种文明之长，以合作谋和平、以合作促发展，推动建设一个持久和平、共同繁荣的和谐世界。

女士们、先生们、朋友们！

中美都拥有辽阔的国土，都是多个民族并存、多种文化融合的国家，都生活着勤劳智慧的人民。中美因不同的历史背景和现实国情而存在着差异，这有利于我们相互借鉴，取长补短。中美加强合作，符合两国和两国人民的根本利益，对世界的和平与发展也具有重大影响。

200多年来，浩瀚的太平洋并未阻断中美两国人民的交流合作，中美两国人民相互学习、相互帮助，谱写了世界不同文明相互借鉴的美好篇章。1979年中美建交27年来，两国关系曾历经曲折，但总体上保持了稳定发展的大方向，给两国和两国人民带来了巨大利益。

进入21世纪，国际形势继续深刻变化。和平与发展仍然是当今时代的主题，但不稳定不确定因素在增多，新挑战新威胁在增加。在新的国际形势下，中美两国共同利益在增多，合作领域在扩大。世界和平与安全面临的新课题，特别是反对国际恐怖主义、防止大规模杀伤性武器扩散、保护人类生存环境、打击跨国犯罪等，使我们两国拥有重要的共同战略利益。中国的巨大市场和发展需求，美国的先进科技和优质产品，使两国具有巨大的经济技术合作空间。中美全面发展建设性合作关系前景广阔。

昨天上午，我同布什总统就中美关系及共同关心的重大国际和地区问题深入交换看法，达成了许多重要共识。我们都认为，双方应该坚持从战略高度和长远角度审视和处理中美关系，加强对话，扩大共识，增进互信，深化合作，全面推进21世纪中美建设性合作关系。

我相信，只要我们从中美关系发展的大局出发，彼此尊重，相互理解，两国关系就能够健康稳定地向前发展，给两国人民带来更多利益，给世界各国人民带来更大希望。

女士们、先生们、朋友们！

一个音符无法表达出优美的旋律，一种颜色难以描绘出多彩的画卷。世界是一座丰富多彩的艺术殿堂，各国人民创造的独特文化都是这座殿堂里的瑰宝。一个民族的文化，往往凝聚着这个民族对世界和生命的历史认知和现实感受，也往往积淀着这个民族最深层的精神追求和行为准则。人类历史发展的过程，就是各种文明不断交流、融合、创新的过程。人类历史上各种文明都以各自的独特方式为人类进步作出了贡献。

文明多样性是人类社会的客观现实，是当今世界的基本特征，也是人类进步的重要动力。历史经验表明，在人类文明交流的过程中，不仅需要克服自然的屏障和隔阂，而且需要超越思想的障碍和束缚，更需要克服形形色色的偏见和误解。意识形态、社会制度、发展模式的差异不应成为人类文明交流的障碍，更不能成为相互对抗的理由。我们应该积极维护世界多样性，推动不同文明的对话和交融，相互借鉴而不是相互排斥，使人类更加和睦幸福，让世界更加丰富多彩。

女士们、先生们、朋友们！

文化、教育和青年交流是中美两国人民增进相互了解和友谊的重要桥梁，也是推动中美关系健康稳定发展的重要力量。耶鲁大学是中美教育合作的先行者和文化交流的重要平台。156年前，一位名叫容闳的中国青年走进了耶鲁大学校园，4年后他以优异的成绩获得了文学学士学位，成为毕业于美国大学的第一个中国留学生。此后，一批又一批中国青年来到耶鲁大学求学。近20年来，耶鲁大学吸引了4，000多名中国留学人员，同中国文化界、科技界、教育界的合作项目超过80个。去年夏天，耶鲁大学派遣首批学生到中国实习，其中一些人成为中国故宫博物院的第一批外国实习生。借此机会，我对莱文校长和耶鲁大学为增进中美两国人民的交流所做的积极努力表示赞赏。

为增进中美两国青年以及教育界的相互了解，我高兴地宣布，中方决定邀请 100 名耶鲁大学师生今年夏天访问中国。我相信，你们的访问将是一次十分愉快的经历。

女士们、先生们、朋友们！

"长江后浪推前浪，世上新人换旧人。"青年人是世界的希望和未来，青年人有着蓬勃向上的生命活力和无穷的创造力。我衷心希望，中美两国青年携起手来，以实际行动促进中美两国人民友好，同世界各国人民一道，共创世界美好的明天。

谢谢各位。

实战提升
Practising & Exercise

导读

2006 年 4 月 21 日，中国国家主席胡锦涛访问了世界著名高等学府——美国耶鲁大学，并发表重要演讲。他强调，文明多样性是人类社会的客观现实，是当今世界的基本特征，也是人类进步的重要动力。我们应该积极维护世界多样性，推动不同文明的对话和交融，相互借鉴而不是相互排斥，使人类更加和睦幸福，让世界更加丰富多彩。

单词注解

intense [in'tens] *adj.* 强烈的，剧烈的；极度的

sustain [səs'tein] *v.* 支撑；承受，承担

prominence ['prɔminəns] *n.* 显著；杰出，卓越

tenacity [ti'næsiti] *n.* 固执；坚持，顽强

evolution [,i:və'lu:ʃən] *n.* 发展，进展

enhance [in'hɑ:ns] *v.* 提高，增加

诵读名句

As China develops rapidly and steady headway is made in China-U.S. cooperation, more and more Americans are following with great interest China's progress and development.

To realize these goals, China has adopted a new concept of development in line with its national conditions and the requirement of the times.

Young people represent the hope and future of the world.

Peace in the Atomic Age

阿尔伯特·爱因斯坦：原子能时代的和平

Albert Einstein/阿尔伯特·爱因斯坦

I am grateful to you for the opportunity to **express** my conviction in this most important political question.

The idea of achieving security through national armament is, at the present state of military technique, a disastrous illusion. On the part of the United States, this illusion has been particularly fostered by the fact that this country succeeded first in producing an atomic bomb. The belief seemed to prevail that in the end it were possible to achieve decisive military superiority.

In this way, any potential opponent would be intimidated, and security, so ardently desired by all of us, brought to us, and to all of humanity. *The maxim which we have been following during the last five years has been, in short : Security through superior military power, whatever the cost.*

The armament race between the USA and the USSR,

originally supposed to be a **preventive** measure, assumes hysterical character. On both sides, the means to mass destruction are perfected with feverish haste—behind the respective walls of secrecy. The H-bomb appears on the public horizon as a probably attainable goal.

If successful, radioactive poisoning of the atmosphere and hence annihilation of any life on earth has been brought within the range of technical possibilities. *The ghostlike character of this development lies in its apparently compulsory trend.* Every step appears as the unavoidable consequence of the preceding one. In the end, there beckons more and more clearly general annihilation.

Is there any way out of this impasse created by man himself ? All of us, and particularly those who are responsible for an attitude of the US and the USSR, should realize that we may have **vanquished** an external enemy, but have been incapable of getting rid of the mentality created by the war.

It is impossible to achieve peace as long as every single action is taken with a possible future conflict in view. The leading point of view of all political actions should therefore be : What can we do to bring about a peaceful co-existence and even loyal cooperation of the nations?

The first problem is to do away with mutual fear and distrust. Solemn renunciation of violence (not only with respect to means of mass destruction) is undoubtedly necessary.

Such renunciation, however, can only be effective if at the same time a supernational judicial and executive body is set up empowered to decide questions of immediate concern to the security of the nations. Even a declaration of the nations to collaborate loyally in the realization of such a "restricted world government" would **considerably** reduce the imminent danger of war.

In the last analysis, every kind of peaceful cooperation among men is primarily based on mutual trust and only secondly on institutions such as courts of justice and police. This holds formations as well as for individuals. And the basis of trust is loyal to give and take.

　　我非常感谢大家给我机会对这个最重要的政治问题发表见解。

　　就现如今军事技术发展的情况来看，想通过加强军备来保障国家安全的概念，只是一个会招致大祸的幻想。就美国而言，因为她率先研制出了原子弹，故她也最容易抱此幻想。而美国最终可能取得决定性的军事优势地位这种想法似乎颇受青睐。

这样，任何潜在的对手都会受到震慑，我们共同期盼的安全就会降临到我们乃至全人类身旁。近5年来我们一直恪守的座右铭，简言之就是：不惜一切代价，通过强势的军事力量保证安全。

美苏军备竞赛的初衷是为了防止战争的发生，现在却已显出狂躁的性质了。在保证安全的漂亮幌子下，双方都以狂热的速度完善其大规模破坏性武器。在公众心中，氢弹的制造似乎已经是可以达到的目标了。

如果氢弹研制成功的话，大气层可能会遭受的放射性污染，以及进而可能导致地球上所有生命灭绝，在技术上已经成为可能。这种发展的恐怖性在于它的发展显然已经成为一种无法遏止的态势。有了第一步，必然会有第二步的出现。最终，越来越明显地，必然导致全人类的灭亡。

我们还能在这个人类自己制造的死局中找到出路吗？我们所有的人，特别是那些美国和苏联的决策者们，应该明白我们也许可以战胜外界的敌人，但战争带来的那种心理状态，却是我们无法消除的。

如果每采取一次行动都考虑将来可能会发生冲突，那么和平是不可能实现的。因此，一切政治活动的首要出发点就是：为了实现国与国之间的和平共存甚至真诚合作，我们能做什么呢？

首先就是要解除双方的畏惧和猜忌。毫无疑问，庄严地声明放弃使用武力（不仅指放弃大规模的破坏性武器）是不可缺少的。

然而，要想有效地杜绝武力的使用，必须同时成立一个超越国家的司法和执行机构，赋予它权力来决定与各国安全密切相关的问题。即便是各国发表共同声明，保证精诚合作，促成这样一个"权力有限的世界政府"的成立，也会大大降低战争发生的危险。

　　总之，相互信任是人类各种和平合作的首要基础，法庭与警察机关之类的机构只是其次。个人交往如此，国家关系也是如此。而信任的建立就在于互相之间以诚相待。

实战提升
Practising & Exercise

🍃导读🍃

1945 年 8 月，美国向日本广岛和长崎投掷了两枚原子弹，导致 25 万人死亡。爱因斯坦，作为原子弹基本原理的发现者和制造原子弹的倡导者，深感痛苦和懊丧。从此，防止毁灭人类的核战争，推进世界永久和平成为他战后的首要任务。这是爱因斯坦 1950 年 2 月 12 日在美国发表的电视演说。

🍃单词注解🍃

express [iks'pres] *v.* 表达，陈述
preventive [pri'ventiv] *adj.* 预防的，防止的
vanquish ['væŋkwiʃ] *v.* 征服，击败
considerably [kən'sidərəbəli] *adv.* 相当，非常，颇

🍃诵读名句🍃

The maxim which we have been following during the last five years has been, in short: Security through superior military power, whatever the cost.

The ghostlike character of this development lies in its apparently compulsory trend.

In the last analysis, every kind of peaceful co-operation among men is primarily based on mutual trust and only secondly on institutions such as courts of justice and police.

迈向成功之路

On the road to success

Baccalaureate Address to Class of 2008
哈佛第一任女校长在毕业典礼上的讲话

Drew G. Faust/德鲁·吉尔平·福斯特

In the curious custom of this venerable institution，I find myself standing before you expected to impart words of lasting wisdom. Here I am in a pulpit，dressed like a Puritan minister—an apparition that would have **horrified** many of my distinguished forebears and perhaps rededicated some of them to the extirpation of witches. This moment would have propelled Increase and Cotton[①] into a true "Mather lather." But here I am and there you are and it is the moment of and for Veritas.

You have been undergraduates for four years. I have been president for not quite one. You have known three presidents；I one senior class. Where then lies the voice of experience? Maybe you should be offering the wisdom. Perhaps our roles could be reversed and I could，in Harvard Law School style，do cold calls

---

①Increase和Cotton是父子俩，Mather是他们的姓。Lather是愤怒的意思。
——编者注

for the next hour or so.

We all do seem to have made it to this point—more or less in one piece. Though I recently learned that we have not provided you with dinner since May 22. I know we need to wean you from Harvard in a **figurative** sense. I never knew we took it quite so literally.

But let's return to that notion of cold calls for a moment. Let's imagine this were a baccalaureate service in the form of Q & A, and you were asking the questions. "What is the meaning of life, President Faust? What were these four years at Harvard for? President Faust, you must have learned something since you graduated from college exactly 40 years ago?" (Forty years. I'll say it out loud since every detail of my life—and certainly the year of my Bryn Mawr degree—now seems to be publicly available. But please remember I was young for my class.)

In a way, you have been engaging me in this Q & A for the past year. On just these questions, although you have phrased them a bit more narrowly. And I have been trying to figure out how I might answer and, perhaps more **intriguingly**, why you were asking.

...

As I have listened to you talk about the choices ahead of you, I have heard you articulate your worries about the relationship of success and happiness—perhaps, more accurately, how to define success so that it yields and encompasses real happiness, not just money and prestige. The most remunerative choice, you fear, may not be the most meaningful and the most satisfying.

But you wonder how you would ever survive as an artist or an actor or a public servant or a high school teacher? How would you ever figure out a path by which to make your way into journalism? Would you ever find a job as an English professor after you finished who knows how many years of graduate school and dissertation writing?

The answer is : you won't know till you try. But if you don't try to do what you love—whether it is painting or biology or finance ; if you don't pursue what you think will be most meaningful, you will regret it. Life is long. There is always time for Plan B. But don't begin with it.

I think of this as my parking space theory of career choice, and I have been sharing it with students for decades. Don't park 20 blocks from your destination because you think you'll never find a space. Go where you want to be and then circle back to where you have to be.

You may love investment banking or finance or consulting. It might be just right for you. Or, you might be like the senior I met at lunch at Kirkland who had just returned from an interview on the West Coast with a **prestigious** consulting firm. "Why am I doing this?" she asked. "I hate flying, I hate hotels, I won't like this job." Find work you love. It is hard to be happy if you spend more than half your waking hours doing something you don't.

But what is ultimately most important here is that you are asking the question—not just of me but of yourselves. *You are choosing roads and at the same time challenging your own choices.* You have a notion of what you want your life to be and you are not sure the road you are taking is going to get you there.

This is the best news. And it is also, I hope, to some degree, our fault. Noticing your life, reflecting upon it, considering how you can live it well, wondering how you can do good : These are perhaps the most valuable things that a liberal arts education has equipped you to do. A liberal education demands that you live self-consciously. It prepares you to seek and define the meaning inherent in all you do. It has made you an analyst and critic of yourself, a person in this way **supremely** equipped to take charge of your life and how it unfolds. It is in this sense that the liberal arts are liberal—as in liberate—to free. They empower you with the possibility of exercising agency, of discovering meaning, of making choices. The surest way to have a meaningful, happy life is to commit yourself to striving for it. Don't settle. Be prepared to change routes. Remember the impossible expectations we have of you, and even as you recognize they are impossible, remember how important they are as a lodestar guiding you toward something that matters to you and to the world. The meaning of your life is for you to make.

I can't wait to see how you all turn out. Do come back, from time to time, and let us know.

在这所久负盛名的大学的别具一格的仪式上，我站在了你们的面前，被期待着给予一些蕴含着恒久智慧的言论。站在这个讲台上，我穿得像个清教徒教长——一个可能会吓到杰出前辈们的怪物，或许使他们中的一些人重新致力于铲除巫婆的事业上。这个时刻也许会使我们的前辈 Increase 和 Cotton 父子气得发疯。但现在，我在上面，你们在下面，此时此刻，属于真理，为了真理。

你们已经在哈佛做了四年的大学生，而我当哈佛校长还不到一年。你们认识了三个校长，而我只认识了你们这一届大四的。算起来我哪有资格说什么经验之谈？或许应该由你们上来展示一下智慧。要不我们换换位置？然后我就可以像哈佛法学院的学生那样，在接下来的一个小时内不时地冷不防地提出问题。

学校和学生们似乎都在努力让时间来到这一时刻，而且还差不多是步调一致的。我这两天才得知哈佛从 5 月 22 日开始就你们就没有晚饭吃了。虽然有比喻说"我们早晚得给你们断奶"，但没想到我们的后勤还真的早早就把"奶"给断了。

现在还是让我们回到我刚才说的提问题的事上吧。让我们设想一下这是个哈佛大学给本科生的毕业服务，是以问答的形式。你们将问些问题，比如："福校长啊，人生的价值是什么呢？我们上这四年大学是为了什么呢？福校长，你大学毕业到现在的 40 年里一定学到些什么东西可以教给我们吧？"（40 年啊，我就直说了，因为我人生中的每段细节——当然包括我在布林茅尔女子学院的一年——现在似乎都成了公共资源。但请记住在哈佛我可是"新生"。）

在某种程度上，在过去的一年里你们一直都在让我从事这种问答。仅仅从这些问题上，即使你们措辞问题都倾向于狭义，而我除了思考怎么做出回答外，更激发我去思考的，是你们为什么问这些问题。

……

在聊天时我听过你们谈到你们目前所面临的选择，我听到你们一字一句地说出你们对于成功与幸福的关系的忧虑——也许，更精确地讲，怎样去定义成功才能使它具有或包含真正的幸福，而不仅仅是金钱和荣誉。你们害怕，报酬最丰厚的选择，也许不是最有价值的和最令人满意的选择。但是你们也担心，如果作为一个艺术家或是一个演员，一个人民公仆或是一个中学老师，该如何才能生存下去？然而，你们可曾想过，如果你的梦想是新闻业，怎样才能想出一条通往梦想的道路呢？难道你会在读了不知多少年研，写了不知多少毕业论文终于毕业后，找一个英语教授的工作吗？

答案是：你不试试就永远都不会知道。但如果你不试着去做自己热爱的事情，不管是玩泥巴、生物还是金融，如果连你自己都不去追求你认为最有价值的事，你终将后悔。人生路漫漫，你总有时间去给自己留"后路"，但可别一开始就走"后路"。

我把这叫做我的关于职业选择的"泊车"理论，几十年来我一直都在向学生们"兜售"我的这个理论。不要因为怕找不到停车位而把车停在距离目的地20个路口远的地方。直接到达你想去的地方，哪怕再绕回来停，你暂时停的地方只是你被迫停的地方。

你也许喜欢做投行，或是做金融抑或做理财咨询。都可能是适合你的。那也许真的就是适合你的。或许你也会像我在Kirkland House见到的那个大四学生一样，她刚从美国西海岸一家著名理财咨询公司的面试回来。"我为什么要做这个？"她说，"我讨厌坐飞机，我讨厌住宾馆，我是不会喜欢这份工作的。"找个你热爱的工作。如果你把你一天中醒着的一大半时间用来做你不喜欢的事情，你是很难感到幸福的。

但是我在这儿说的最重要的是：你们在问那些问题——不仅是问我，而是在问你们自己。你们正在选择人生的道路，同时也在对自己的选择提出质疑。你们知道自己想过什么样的生活，也知道你们将走的道路不一定会把你们带到想去的地方。这样其实很好。某种程度上，我倒希望这是我们的错。我们一直在标榜人生，像镜子一样照出你们将来的模样，思考你们怎么可以过得幸福，探索你们怎样才能去做些对社会有价值的事：这些也许是文科教育可以给你们"装备"的最有价值的东西。文科教育要求你们要活得"明白"。它使你探索和定义你做的每件事情背后的价值。它让你成为一个经常分析和反省自己的人。而这样的人完全能够掌控自己的人生或未来。从这个道理上讲，文科——照它的字面意思——才使你们自由。（英语里文科是Liberal Art，照字面解释是自由的艺术）学文科可以让你有机会去进行理论的实践，去发现你所做的选择的价值。想过上有价值的，幸福的生活，最可靠的途径就是为了你的目标去奋斗。不要安于现状得过且过。随时准备着改变人生的道路。记住那些我们寄予你们的"过于崇高"的期待，可能你们自己也承认那些期待是有点"太高了"。不过如果想做些对于你们自己或是这个世界有点价值的事情，记住它们，它们将会像北斗星一样指引着你们。你们人生的价值将由你们去实现！

我都等不及想看看你们将来都会怎样。毕业以后，常回"家"看看，让我们了解你们的情况。

🍃导读🍃

这是哈佛 2007 年 2 月 11 日宣布，并于 7 月份正式上任的校长 Drew G. Faust 给哈佛大学 2008 年的本科毕业生做的演讲。Drew G. Faust 是哈佛历史上第一位女性校长。她自 2001 开始在哈佛的 Radcliffe 学院任教。之前的哈佛校长因为公开发表"歧视女性"的言论被迫辞职。

🍃单词注解🍃

horrify ['hɔrifai] *v.* 使恐惧，使惊惧
figurative ['figjurətiv] *adj.* 比喻的；象征的
intriguingly [in'tri:ginli] *adv.* 有趣地；有魅力地
prestigious [ˌpres'ti:dʒəs] *adj.* 有名望的，有威信的
supremely [sju:'pri:mli] *adv.* 至上地；崇高地

🍃诵读名句🍃

I think of this as my parking space theory of career choice, and I have been sharing it with students for decades.

You are choosing roads and at the same time challenging your own choices.

I can't wait to see how you all turn out. Do come back, from time to time, and let us know.

Bill Gates Harvard Commencement Speech
比尔·盖茨在哈佛毕业典礼上的演讲

Bill Gates/比尔·盖茨

President Bok，former President Rudenstine，incoming President Faust，members of the Harvard Corporation and the Board of Overseers，members of the faculty，parents，and especially，the graduates：

I've been waiting more than 30 years to say this："Dad，I always told you I'd come back and get my degree." I want to thank Harvard for this timely honor. I'll be changing my job next year...and it will be nice to finally have a college degree on my resume. I applaud the graduates today for taking a much more direct route to your degrees. *For my part，I'm just happy that the Crimson has called me "Harvard's most successful dropout."* I guess that makes me valedictorian of my own special class ... I did the best of everyone who failed.

But I also want to be **recognized** as the guy who got Steve Ballmer to drop out of business school. I'm a bad influence. That's why I was invited to speak at your graduation. If I had spoken at your orientation, fewer of you might be here today.

Harvard was just a phenomenal experience for me. Academic life was fascinating. I used to sit in on lots of classes I hadn't even signed up for. And dorm life was terrific. I lived up at Radcliffe, in Currier House. There were always lots of people in my dorm room late at night discussing things, because everyone knew I didn't worry about getting up in the morning. That's how I came to be the leader of the anti-social group. We clung to each other as a way of validating our rejection of all those social people.

Radcliffe was a great place to live. There were more women up there, and most of the guys were science-math types. That combination offered me the best odds, if you know what I mean. This is where I learned the sad lesson that improving your odds doesn't guarantee success.

One of my biggest memories of Harvard came in January 1975, when I made a call from Currier House to a company in Albuquerque that had begun making the world's first personal computers. I offered to sell them software.

I worried that they would realize I was just a student in a dorm and hang up on me. Instead they said : "We're not quite ready, come see us in a month," which was a good thing, because we hadn't written the software yet. From that moment, I worked day and night on this little extra credit project that marked the end of my college education and the beginning of a remarkable journey with Microsoft.

What I remember above all about Harvard was being

in the midst of so much energy and intelligence. It could be **exhilarating**, intimidating, sometimes even discouraging, but always challenging. It was an amazing privilege—and though I left early, I was transformed by my years at Harvard, the friendships I made, and the ideas I worked on.

...

Members of the Harvard Family : Here in the Yard is one of the great collections of intellectual talent in the world.

What for?

There is no question that the faculty, the alumni, the students, and the benefactors of Harvard have used their power to improve the lives of people here and around the world. But can we do more? Can Harvard dedicate its intellect to improving the lives of people who will never even hear its name?

Let me make a request of the deans and the professors— the intellectual leaders here at Harvard : As you hire new faculty, award tenure, review curriculum, and determine degree requirements, please ask yourselves :

Should our best minds be dedicated to solving our biggest problems?

Should Harvard encourage its faculty to take on the world's worst inequities? Should Harvard students learn about the depth of global poverty ... the prevalence of world hunger... the scarcity of clean water... the girls kept out of school ... the children who die from diseases we can cure?

Should the world's most privileged people learn about the

lives of the world's least privileged?

These are not rhetorical questions—you will answer with your policies.

My mother, who was filled with pride the day I was admitted here—never stopped pressing me to do more for others. A few days before my wedding, she hosted a bridal event, at which she read aloud a letter about marriage that she had written to Melinda. My mother was very ill with cancer at the time, but she saw one more opportunity to deliver her message, and at the close of the letter she said : "From those to whom much is given, much is expected."

When you consider what those of us here in this Yard have been given—in talent, privilege, and opportunity—there is almost no limit to what the world has a right to expect from us.

In line with the promise of this age, I want to exhort each of the graduates here to take on an issue—a complex problem, a deep **inequity**, and become a specialist on it. If you make it the focus of your career, that would be phenomenal. But you don't have to do that to make an impact. For a few hours every week, you can use the growing power of the Internet to get informed, find others with the same interests, see the barriers, and find ways to cut through them.

Don't let complexity stop you. Be activists. Take on the big inequities. It will be one of the great experiences of your lives.

You graduates are coming of age in an amazing time. As you leave Harvard, you have technology that members of my class never had. You have awareness of global inequity, which we did not have. And with that awareness, you likely also have an informed conscience that will torment you if you abandon these people whose lives you could change with very little effort. *You have more than we had ; you must start sooner, and carry on longer.*

Knowing what you know, how could you not?

And I hope you will come back here to Harvard 30 years from now and reflect on what you have done with your talent and your energy. I hope you will judge yourselves not on your professional accomplishments alone, but also on how well you have addressed the world's deepest inequities... on how well you treated people a world away who have nothing in common with you but their **humanity**.

Good luck.

布克校长, 前任校长路登斯坦, 未来的校长法斯特, 哈佛集团成员们, 督导团成员们, 全体教员、家长们, 特别是所有

毕业生们：

　　有一句话，我等了 30 年，现在终于可以说了："爸爸，我说过我会回来拿到我的学位的"。我想感谢哈佛给予我这份及时的荣誉。我明年要换份工作（注：指全力投入比尔及梅琳达基金会的慈善工作），在我的简历里写上我拥有一个学士学位，这真是不错啊。我为今天在座的各位同学感到高兴，你们拿学位比我简单多了。就我而言，我很高兴克里姆森把我叫做"哈佛最成功的辍学学生"。我猜他这么说可以让我当上我们这个特殊班级的学生代表来致词……我在失败者里面做得是最好的。

　　但是，我还要提醒大家，我使得史蒂夫·鲍默尔也从商学院退学了。我是个坏榜样。那就是我为什么被邀请来你们的毕业典礼上作演讲。如果我是在你们入学欢迎仪式上演讲的话，恐怕你们中有些人今天就不能在这里了。

　　对我来说，哈佛的求学经历是一段非凡的经历。校园生活很有趣，我常去旁听我没选修的课。哈佛的课外生活也很棒，我在 Radcliffe 过着逍遥自在的日子。每天我的寝室里总有很多人一直待到半夜，讨论着各种事情。因为每个人都知道我从不担心第二天要早起。这使得我变成了校园里那些不安分学生的头头，我们整天粘在一起，做出一种拒绝所有正常学生的姿态。

　　Radcliffe 是个过日子的好地方。那里的女生比男生多，而且大多数男生都是理工科的。这种结合为我创造了极好的机会，如果你们明白我的意思的话。可惜的是，我正是在这里学到了人生中悲伤的一课：机会大，并不等于你就会成功。

　　我在哈佛最难忘的回忆之一发生在 1975 年 1 月。那时，我从宿舍楼里给位于 Albuquerque 的一家公司打了一个电话，当时那公司已经在着手制造世界上第一台个人电脑了。我想卖给他们软件。

　　我担心他们会听出来我只是一个住在宿舍里的学生而挂掉我的电话。但他们却说："我们还没准备好，一个月后你再来找我们吧。"那是个好消息，因为那时候我们还没有开始编写那个软件。从那一刻起，我开始不分昼夜地在这项附加学分微乎其微的项目上工作，那标志着我大学教育的终结，同时也意味着我微软非凡旅途的开始。

　　不管怎样，我对哈佛的回忆主要都与充沛的精力和智力活动有关。哈佛的生活令人愉快，但也压力重重，有时甚至会感到泄气，但却总是充满了挑战。生活在哈佛是一种吸引人的特殊待遇——虽然我离得比较早，但是我在这里的经历、在这里结识的朋友、在这里产生的一些想法，永远地改变了我。

　　……

　　哈佛，这个大家庭的成员们：现在在这个院子里汇集着一批全世界最棒的智力天才。

　　为什么而相聚呢？

　　毫无疑问，哈佛的老师、校友、学生和资助者，已经用他们的能力改善了这里和世界上其他人的生活。但是我们能不能做得更多一点？哈佛的人们可以将他们的智慧，用来帮助那些甚至从来没有听到过"哈佛"这个名字的人？

　　请允许我向各位院长和教授提出一个请求——你们是哈佛的智力领袖，当你们雇用新的老师、授予终身教职、评估课程、决定学位颁发标准的时候，请问你们自己如下的问题：

　　我们最优秀的人才是否在致力于解决我们最大的问题？

　　哈佛是否鼓励她的老师去研究解决世界上最严重的不平等？哈佛的学生是否从全球那些极端的贫穷中学到了什么……

世界性的饥荒……淡水资源的缺乏……无法上学的女童……死于非恶性疾病的儿童……哈佛的学生有没有从中学到东西？

那些世界上过着最优越生活的人们是否应该了解世界上最贫困的人的生活？

这些问题并非语言上的修辞，你可以依照你自己的原则来回答。

我的母亲在我被哈佛大学录取的那一天，曾经感到非常骄傲。她从没有停止督促我，去为他人做更多的事情。在我结婚的前几天，她主持了一个新娘进我家的仪式。在这个仪式上，她高声朗读了一封关于婚姻的信，那是她写给梅林达的。当时我母亲患有很严重的癌症，但是她还是认为这是一个传递她的信息的机会，在信的最后她说："被给予的越多，人们对你的期望也就越大。"

当你考虑到在这个院子里的我们都被给予了什么的时候——才能，特权，机会——世界有权向我们索要的东西就几乎没有限制。

同这个时代的期望一样，我也要向今天各位毕业的同学提出一个忠告：你们要选择一个问题，一个复杂的问题，一个有关于人类的深刻的不平等问题，然后你们要变成这个问题的专家。如果你们能够使得这个问题成为你们职业的核心，那么你们就会非常杰出。但是，你们不必一定要去做那些大事。你可以每周抽出几小时，通过互联网得到信息，找到志同道合的朋友，发现困难所在，找到解决它们的途径。

别让那些复杂因素阻止了你。做一个行动者。承担起这个巨大的不平等。那将会成为你生命中最伟大的经历之一。

你们这些毕业生处于一个了不起的时代。当你们离开哈佛的时候，你们拥有我当年的同学从来没有过的技术，你们拥有我们没有的，即对全球不平等的感知。因为这种感知，你们可能也拥有一个更加广博的道德心，如果你不理会那些你运用很小努力就能够改变他们命运的人，你将受到良心的谴责。你们比我们拥有更大的能力；你们必须尽早开始，尽可能长地坚持下去。

知道了你们所知道的，你们怎么可能不采取行动呢？

我希望你们能在 30 年后回到这里回想你们运用自己的能力和天赋所做出的贡献。我希望你们在评判自己的时候不仅考虑到你们职业上的成就，而且包括你们为改变这个世界深刻的不平等所作出的努力以及你们如何善待那些远隔千山万水，与你们毫不相干的人们，你们与他们唯一的共同点就是同为人类。

最后，祝各位同学好运。

导读

微软创始人比尔·盖茨，是闻名于世的美国商人、亿万富豪。根据美国《福布斯》杂志的统计，比尔·盖茨一个人的财富要比全世界最贫穷的50%人口的财富总额还要多。2007年盖茨被母校邀请在毕业典礼上致词，这篇演讲语言幽默恳切，发人深省。字里行间都透露着盖茨的人格魅力和博大的爱心。

单词注解

recognize ['rekəgnaiz] v. 认出，识别
exhilarating [ig'ziləreitiŋ] adj. 令人振奋的；使人高兴的
inequity [in'ekwiti] n. 不公平
humanity [hju(:)'mæniti] n. 人性；人道；慈爱

诵读名句

For my part, I'm just happy that the Crimson has called me "Harvard's most successful dropout.

There is no question that the faculty, the alumni, the students, and the benefactors of Harvard have used their power to improve the lives of people here and around the world.

You have more than we had; you must start sooner, and carry on longer.

The Speech About Lenovo
联想董事长的演讲

Yang Yuanqing/杨元庆

Now let's discuss who we are to become—our aspirations as a company—and our 3-phase plan to achieve these aspirations. To become all that we can be.

First : Satisfying our customers

Lenovo will deliver the highest customer **satisfaction** to both businesses and individuals.

Second : Shareholder value

Lenovo will be the company people want to invest in by leading our industry in shareholder returns over the next 2, 5, and 10 years.

Third : Financial targets

Lenovo will **double** our profit within 3 years, and grow revenue faster than our industry.

Fourth : Market position

Lenovo is committed to improve our market position every year by applying long term investments where we can become No.1 or No.2 in share or profit, depending on the market.

Fifth : Is my aspirations for each of us, the people who chose to work at Lenovo.

We at Lenovo will create an inspiring culture of ethics, performance, teamwork and professional development.

Some of these might appear to be big aspirations. *I want you to know that we're committed to them, and that while I expect progress every day, every week, these aspirations will take years to fully achieve.*

Now to get this done we have a broad 3-phase plan. Phase one began on December 8th, and will continue well into the beginning of 2006.

Our second phase has also begun. And each project in phase 2 will be at least 12 to 24 months in length.

Our third phase will launch when we stand before the world as the IT **sponsor** of the Olympics in February of 2006.

...

Finally, I want to wrap up by speaking about the values of Lenovo. Those of us who came from IBM created "new" values only 18 months ago —— as part of a "Values Jam" that all IBM employees participated in. Our Lenovo colleagues have been guided for the last several years by four key values. Its no **coincidence** that the values Lenovo has worked by are so similar to the values held by PCD.

First : Serving customers

We are dedicated to the satisfaction and success of every customer.

Second : Innovative and entrepreneurial spirit

This means innovation that matters to our customers and our company created and delivered with speed and efficiency.

Third : Accuracy and truth-seeking

This means we manage our business and make decisions based on carefully understood facts.

And Fourth : Trustworthiness and integrity

Meaning trust and personal responsibility in all relationships.

I've seen first hand what each you expect of yourselves and what you can do. It's nothing short of amazing. *We have before us an extraordinary opportunity to make a difference for our customers and to succeed at this exciting new venture.*

So that's it... a short list of difficult but achievable aspirations.

A 3-phase plan of how well go from a new company to one that uses its competitiveness to **aggressively** grow.

And four clear values punctuated with the word integrity that will guide our decisions and our behavior.

This is our opportunity and our time. Let's go make the most of it.

Thank you and congratulations.

现在，我们谈一下我们公司的愿景，以及实现愿景的三个步骤。我们要成为我们能够成为的一切。

第一：服务客户

联想将为企业及个人客户提供最好的客户体验。

第二：股东利益

联想将成为投资人的选择。我们将在未来的 2 年、5 年以及 10 年内实现业界领先的股东回报。

第三：财务目标

联想将在 3 年内使利润水平翻番，并实现超出业界水平的营业额增长。

第四：市场地位

联想将在未来每年间，不断提高我们的市场地位。我们将选择投资于能令我们在利润或市场份额方面成为第一或第二的市场。

第五是我对我们，选择来到联想工作的每一名员工的愿景。

我们将创造一个注重职业道德、业绩导向、团队精神以及职业发展的公司文化。

以上提到的可能是非常宏伟的愿景。我希望你们知道我们一定要努力达到我们的目标，我希望我们每天，每星期都向着我们的目标前进。所有这些愿景需要长年的努力才能实现。

为了达成这些愿景，我们订立了三个阶段的规划。第一阶段于 2005 年 12 月 8 日已经开始，并将持续到 2006 年初。

第二阶段也已经开始，这个阶段的项目将历时 12~24 个月。

第三阶段将于 2006 年 2 月——我们以奥运会 IT 赞助商的身份面向世界的时候启动。

……

最后我想谈一下联想的核心价值观。18 个月前在全体 IBM 员工参与的"企业价值观大融合"活动中，PCD 创造了一个"新的价值观"。而联想的同事们多年来一直由四个核心价值观所指导。PCD 和联想的价值观是如此的相似，而这绝非巧合。

第一：服务客户

我们致力于实现每一个客户的满意和成功。

第二：创业创新

我们将高效地创造并实现我们客户需要的创新科技和产品。

第三：精准求实

我们将基于仔细研究的事实进行决策及管理我们的业务。

第四：诚信共享

在所有合作关系中取得信任和负起个人的责任。

我已经亲身体验了你们每一个人的愿望和能力，这令我非常惊讶。我们正面临一个令人兴奋的机遇，为我们的客户提供价值并取得成功。

关于我们的愿景我先谈到这里，虽然有很多困难但还是可以实现的。

我们的三阶段规划勾勒出了我们新公司如何运用竞争力实现迅速增长。

　　我们清晰的 4 个核心价值观点出了诚信是指导我们决策和行为的准则。

　　各位，这是属于我们的机会和时刻。让我们全力以赴投身其中吧！

　　谢谢！并再次表示祝贺。

实战提升
Practising **&** Exercise

🍃导读🍃

这是联想的新一代领导人，新董事主席杨元庆先生对员工发表的演讲。新联想已经成为全球第三大 PC 厂商，全球第五大 IT 企业，以及中国最大的 IT 企业。

🍃单词注解🍃

satisfaction [ˌsætisˈfækʃən] *n.* 满意，满足；称心

double [ˈdʌbl] *adj.* 两倍的；加倍的

sponsor [ˈspɔnsə] *n.* 发起者；主办者；倡议者

coincidence [kəuˈinsidəns] *n.* 巧合；巧事；同时发生

aggressively [əˈgresivli] *adv.* 侵略地；攻击地

🍃诵读名句🍃

We at Lenovo will create an inspiring culture of ethics，performance，teamwork and professional development.

I want you to know that we're committed to them，and that while I expect progress every day，every week，these aspirations will take years to fully achieve.

We have before us an extraordinary opportunity to make a difference for our customers and to succeed at this exciting new venture.

The Speech About IBM
IBM 总裁的演讲

Gerstiner/杰斯特尼

Good evening! It is a great honor for me to share this stage with the Lord Mayor, chief executive of Hannover, with Mr. Yang, and in a few minutes with Chancellor Kohl. I have been looking forward to this evening for a long time, because I have known for many years how important CeBIT is to the global Information Technology industry. So before I go any further I want to thank you very much for inviting me to **participate** in this important forum.

Now I have given a lot of thought as to what I would say to you this evening. On the one hand, I am here as a representative of the Information Technology industry on the event that is bigger by orders of magnitude than any other technology exhibit. *That is quite a statement in a industry that is good at many things, especially celebrating its own creations.* On the other hand, like most of you, I have spent most of my professional life as a customer of this industry. So I know that after the splash and promises comes the harsh light of morning and often the customer is left standing alone wondering what happened, or as the head of one of our most important German customers put it, "Yours is an industry that is very good at weddings and not so good at marriages."

So tonight, while I will talk about the power and potential of Information Technology, I hope the temper of my **remarks** with the perspective I had when I came to IBM five years ago, the perspective of a customer.

Now it is certainly easy to see why raw technology dominates these events. It is adoptive ; it is breathtaking ; and it is penetrating every aspect of our lives. Today there are more PCs sold annually in the world than TVs or cars. The typical luxury automobile today has 20 to 30 microprocessors in it, more computing power by far than was inside the landing-craft that took the first astronauts to the moon. Last year there were five times more E-mail messages sent than the number of pieces of paper mail delivered worldwide, 2.7 trillion E-mails. And I got more than my share. There is another way to look at what is going on. In the mid-1970s, the first super computers appeared. They were capable of about 100 million calculations per second. And they cost about one million dollars. Today the laptop computer that college students carry in their bags, packs, is twice as fast as that first super computer, and it costs less than 3, 000 dollars. The trend in data **storage** is even more impressive. In the early 80s, the standard unit of computer storage, one mega-byte, or one million bytes of information, cost about 100 dollars. Today, it is 10 cents. In two years, it will cost 2 cents.

These gains are driven by continuous advances in how we pack information into smaller and smaller spaces. If the US Library of Congress could shrink its collections of 17 million books by the same factor we just discussed，it could replace 800 kilometers of shelf space with less than 40 meters of space. These advances are going to continue and accelerate the rate microprocessors，storage，communications，memory，and all the other engines that are propelling this industry or continue to lead to the products of the faster，smaller，and less expensive，just as they have for 30 years. But as we stand here today，the opening of CeBIT，we are on the threshold of a very important change and the evolution of this industry. In many ways，this industry，a very emitory industry，is about to play out in its most important dimension. That is because the technology has become so powerful and so pervasive that its future impact on people and governments and all institutions will dwarf what has happened today.

　　各位晚上好！非常荣幸能够与汉诺威市市长、杨先生共同出席今晚的会议，非常荣幸能与科尔总理共同度过这个美好的

夜晚。我一直在盼望着今晚的到来，因为很多年以前我就知道CeBIT 对全球信息技术产业的重要性。因此在演讲之前我首先要对你们邀请我参加这个重要的会议表示衷心的感谢。

对于今晚要说的内容我想过很多。一方面，我是作为信息技术产业界的代表出席这次比其他任何技术展览会的规模都大的会议的。我们的工业是一个对很多事情都很拿手的工业，尤其善于庆祝其自己的创造发明。另一方面，和你们大多数人一样，我的绝大部分职业生涯也是作为这个产业的消费者度过的。因此，我知道一通承诺之后必将是黎明炫目的阳光。消费者常常被撇在一边，琢磨着发生了什么事，或是像我们一个非常重要的德国客户的首脑所说的那样，"你们的产业好像对结婚典礼非常在行，但对婚姻却不太懂。"

因此，虽然今晚我要谈谈信息技术的力量和潜力，但是我希望我能够像五年前刚到 IBM 时那样，站在消费者的立场上表达我的观点。

由纯技术主宰本次展览会的原因是很简单的，因为现在的纯技术是可以被接受的，是令人惊奇的，而且它已经渗透到了我们生活的各个方面。现在全世界每年销售的 PC 数量比电视机和汽车都要多。如今典型的豪华汽车中有 20 到 30 个微处理器，比那个把第一批宇航员送上月球的登月飞船的计算能力还强。去年全球发送的电子邮件数量比传统的纸邮件数量多 5 倍，达到 27，000 亿封。我的信箱容量就总是不够用。我们还可以从另外一个角度看看现在都发生了些什么事。七十年代中期出现了最初的超级计算机，计算能力是大约每秒一亿次，价格大约是一百万美元。而如今大学生的书包里装着的笔记本电脑的计算能力是那种超级计算机的两倍，价格却只有不到 3，000

美元。数据存储技术的发展趋势更是令人瞠目。八十年代初期，一个标准单位的计算机存储能力，即 1MB，或者说 1 百万字节，售价是 100 美元，而现在却只要 10 美分，再过两年只要 2 美分就够了。这种结果是在技术不断进步的推动下产生的，我们可以把信息存储到越来越小的空间。如果把这种技术用到美国国会图书馆的 1,700 万册存书上，其书架长度将由 800 公里变成不到 40 米。这种进步将继续下去，并且会加速微处理器、存储设备、通信、内存以及所有其他正在推动信息产业前进的"发动机"式的产品的发展，或者会继续创造出更快、更小、更便宜的产品。过去 30 年的情况就是如此。然而当我们今天站在这里，出席 CeBIT 的开幕式的时候，我们面对的是一场业界非常重要的变化和革命。在很多方面，信息产业将成为最重要的产业。这是因为信息技术已经变得如此强大、如此普遍，以至于未来它对人们、政府和各个机构的影响将使目前发生的事相形见绌。

实战提升
Practising & Exercise

导读
2002 年 9 月 5 日，IBM 总裁杰斯特尼作为信息技术产业界的代表发表了演说。

单词注解
participate [pɑːˈtisipeit] *v.* 参加，参与
remark [riˈmɑːk] *v.* 谈到；评论
dominate [ˈdɔmineit] *v.* 支配，统治，控制
storage [ˈstɔridʒ] *n.* 贮藏，保管
continuous [kənˈtinjuəs] *adj.* 连续的，不断的

诵读名句
That is quite a statement in a industry that is good at many things，especially celebrating its own creations.

Now it is certainly easy to see why raw technology dominates these events.

These gains are driven by continuous advances in how we pack information into smaller and smaller spaces.

The Superinvestors of Graham-and-Doddsville
格雷厄姆—多德的超级投资者们

Warren Buffett/沃伦·巴菲特

Is the Graham and Dodd "look for values with a significant margin of safety relative to prices" approach to security analysis out of date？ Many of the professors who write textbooks today say yes. *They argue that the stock market is efficient；that is，that stock prices reflect everything that is known about a company's prospects and about the state of the economy.* There are no undervalued stocks，these theorists argue，because there are smart security analysts who utilize all available information to ensure unfailingly appropriate prices. Investors who seem to beat the market year after year are just lucky. "If prices fully reflect available information，this sort of investment adeptness is ruled out，" writes one of today's textbook authors.

Well，maybe. But I want to present to you a group of investors who have，year in and year out，beaten the Standard & Poor's 500 stock index. The hypothesis that they do this by pure chance is at least worth examining. **Crucial** to this examination is the fact that these winners were all well-known to me and pre-identified as superior investors, the most recent identification occurring over fifteen years ago. Absent this condition—that is, if I had just recently searched among thousands of records to select a few names for you this morning—I would advise you to stop reading right here. I should add that all of these records have been audited. And I should further add that I have known many of those who have invested with these managers, and the checks received by those **participants** over the years have matched the stated records.

Before we begin this examination, I would like you to imagine a national coin-flipping contest. Let's assume we get 225 million Americans up tomorrow morning and we ask them all to wager a dollar. They go out in the morning at sunrise, and they all call the flip of a coin. If they call correctly, they win a dollar from those who called wrong. Each day the losers drop out, and on the subsequent day the stakes build as all previous winnings are put on the line. After ten flips on ten mornings, there will be approximately 220, 000 people in the United States who have correctly called ten flips in a row. They each will have won a little over $1, 000.

Now this group will probably start getting a little puffed up about this, human nature being what it is. They may try to be modest, but at cocktail parties they will occasionally admit to attractive members of the opposite sex what their technique is, and what **marvelous** insights they bring to the field of flipping.

Assuming that the winners are getting the appropriate rewards from the losers, in another ten days we will have 215 people who have successfully called their coin flips 20 times in a row and who, by this exercise, each have turned one dollar into a little over $1 million. $225 million would have been lost, $225 million would have been won.

By then, this group will really lose their heads. They will probably write books on "How I turned a Dollar into a Million in Twenty Days Working Thirty Seconds a Morning." Worse yet, they'll probably start jetting around the country attending seminars on efficient coin-flipping and tackling skeptical professors with, "If it can't be done, why are there 215 of us？"

By then some business school professor will probably be rude enough to bring up the fact that if 225 million orangutans had **engaged** in a similar exercise, the results would be much the same—215 egotistical orangutans with 20 straight winning flips.

…

One quick example：The Washington Post Company in 1973 was selling for $80 million in the market. At the time, that day, you could have sold the **assets** to any one of ten buyers for not less than $400 million, probably appreciably more. The company owned the Post , Newsweek , plus several television stations in major markets. Those same properties are worth $4 billion now, so the person who would have paid $400 million would not have been crazy.

Now, if the stock had declined even further to a price that made the valuation $40 million instead of $80 million, its beta would have been greater. And to people that think beta measures risk, the cheaper price would have made it look riskier. This is truly Alice in Wonderland. I have never been able to figure out why it's riskier to buy $400 million worth of properties for $40 million than $80 million. And, as a matter of fact, if you buy a group of such securities and you know anything at all about business valuation, there is essentially no risk in buying $400 million for $80 million, particularly if you do it by buying ten $40 million piles of $8 million each. Since you don't have your hands on the $400 million, you want to be sure you are in with honest and reasonably competent people, but that's not a difficult job.

You also have to have the knowledge to enable you to make a very general estimate about the value of the underlying businesses. But you do not cut it close. That is what Ben Graham meant by having a margin of safety. You don't try and buy businesses worth $83 million for $80 million. You leave yourself an **enormous** margin. When you build a bridge, you insist it can carry 30, 000 pounds, but you only drive 10, 000 pound trucks across it. And that same principle works in investing.

In conclusion, some of the more commercially minded among you may wonder why I am writing this article. Adding many converts to the value approach will perforce narrow the spreads between price and value. I can only tell you that the secret has been out for 50 years, ever since Ben Graham and Dave Dodd wrote Security Analysis , yet I have seen no trend toward value investing in the 35 years that I've practiced it. There seems to be some perverse human characteristic that likes to make easy things difficult. The academic world, if anything, has actually backed away from the teaching of value investing over the last 30 years. It's likely to continue that way. Ships will sail around the world but the Flat Earth Society will flourish. *There will continue to be wide discrepancies between price and value in the marketplace，and those who read their Graham & Dodd will continue to prosper.*

　　格雷厄姆与多德追求"价值远超过价格的安全保障"，这种证券分析方法是否已经过时？目前许多撰写教科书的教授认为如此。他们认为，股票市场是有效率的市场；换言之，股票价格已经充分反映了公司一切已知的事实以及整体经济情况：这些理论家认为，市场上没有价格偏低的股票，因为聪明的证券分析师将运用全部的既有资讯，以确保适当的价格。投资者能经年累月地击败市场，纯粹是运气使然。"如果价格完全反映既有的资讯，则这类的投资技巧将不存在。"一位现今教科书的作者如此写道。

　　或许如此！但是，我要提供一组投资者的绩效供各位参考，他们长期的表现总是超越标准普尔 500 种股价指数。即使是纯属巧合，这项假说至少也值得我们加以研究。研究的关键事实是，我早就熟识这些赢家，而且长年以来便视他们为超级投资者，最近的认知也有 15 年之久。缺少这项条件——换言之，如果我最近才从成千上万的记录中挑选几个名字，并且在今天早上提供给各位——我建议各位立即停止阅读本文。我必须说明，所有这些记录都经过稽核。我必须再说明，我认识许多上述经理人的客户，他们长年以来所收取的支票确实符合既有的记录。

在进行研究之前，我要各位设想一场全国性的掷铜板大赛。我们假定，全美国 2.25 亿的人口在明天早晨起床时都掷出一枚一美元的铜板。在早晨太阳升起时，他们都走到门外掷铜板，并猜铜板的正反。如果猜对了，他们将从猜错者的手中赢得一美元。每天都有输家遭到淘汰，奖金则不断地累积。经过十个早晨的十次投掷之后，全美国约有 2.2 万人连续十次猜对掷铜板的结果。每人所赢得的资金大约有 1，000 多美元。

现在，这群人可能会开始炫耀自己的战绩，此乃人的天性使然。他们可能保持谦虚的态度，但在鸡尾酒宴会中，他们偶尔会以此技巧吸引异性的注意，并炫耀其投掷铜板的奇异洞察力。

假定赢家都可以从输家手中得到适当的奖金，再经过十天，约有 215 个人连续 20 次猜对掷铜板的结果，每个人并赢得大约 100 万美元的奖金。输家总共付出 2.25 亿美元，赢家则得到 2.25 亿美元。

这时候，这群人可能完全沉迷在自己的成就中：他们可能开始著书立说："我如何每天早晨工作 30 秒，而在 20 天之内将一美元变成 100 万美元。"更糟糕的是，他们会在全国各地参加讲习会，宣扬如何有效地投掷铜板，并且反驳持怀疑态度的教授说，"如果这是不可能的事，为什么会有我们这215个人呢？"

但是，某商学院的教授可能会粗鲁地提出一项事实，如果2.25亿只猩猩参加这场大赛，结果大致上也是如此——有215只自大的猩猩将连续赢得20次的投掷。

……

我可以举一个简单的例子：在1973年，华盛顿邮报公司的总市值为8千万美元。在这一天，你可以将其资产卖给十位买家之一，而且价格不低于4亿美元，甚至还能更高。该公司拥有华盛顿邮报、商业周刊以及数家重要的电视台。这些资产目前的价值为4亿美元，因此愿意支付4亿美元的买家并非疯子。

现在，如果股价继续下跌，该企业的市值从8千万美元跌到4千万美元，其bate值也上升。对于用bate值衡量风险的人来说，更低的价格让他觉得风险更大。这真是仙境中的爱丽丝。我永远无法了解，用4千万美元，而非8千万美元购买价值4亿美元的资产，其风险竟然更高。事实上，如果你买进一些这样的证券，而且稍微了解所谓的企业评价，则用8千万美元的价格买进4亿美元的资产，这笔交易基本上没有风险，尤其是分别以800万美元的价格买进10种价值4,000万美元的资产，其风险更低。因为你没有4亿美元，所以你希望能够找到诚实而有能力的人，这并不困难。

另外，你必须有能够粗略地估计企业价值的知识。但是，你并不需要精密地来评估。这便是本杰明·葛拉厄姆所谓的安全边际。你不必试图以8,000万美元的价格购买价值8,300万美元的企业。你必须让自己保有相当的缓冲。架设桥梁时，你坚持载重量为3万磅，但你只准许1万磅的卡车穿梭其间。

相同的原则也适用于投资领域。

有些具备商业头脑的人可能会怀疑我撰写本文的动机：更多人皈依价值投资法，将会缩小价值与价格之间的差距。我只能够如此告诉各位，自从本杰明·格雷厄姆与大卫·多德出版《证券分析》以来，这个秘密已经流传了 50 年，在我奉行这项投资理论的 35 年中，我不曾目睹价值投资法蔚然成风。人的天性中似乎存在着偏执的特色，喜欢把简单的事情复杂化。最近 30 年来，学术界如果有任何作为的话，皆完全背离了价值投资的教训。这种现象很可能还会继续。船只将环绕地球而行。但地平之说仍会畅行无阻。在市场上，价格与价值之间还会存在着很大的差值，而奉行格雷厄姆与多德理论的人也会繁荣不绝。

🍃 导读 🍃

1984 年在庆祝格雷厄姆与多德合著的《证券分析》发行 50 周年大会上，巴菲特在哥伦比亚大学的演讲稿。在他的演讲中，回顾了 50 年来，格雷厄姆的追随者们采用价值投资策略持续战胜市场的无可争议的事实，总结归纳出价值投资策略的精髓，在投资界具有非常大的影响力。

🍃 单词注解 🍃

crucial ['kruːʃiəl] *adj.* 决定性的，重要的

participant [pɑːˈtisipənt] *n.* 关系者；参与者

marvelous ['mɑːvələs] *adj.* 令人惊叹的；非凡的；不可思议的

engaged [inˈgeidʒd] *adj.* 从事……的；忙于……的

asset ['æset] *n.* 财产，资产

enormous [iˈnɔːməs] *adj.* 巨大的，庞大的

🍃 诵读名句 🍃

They argue that the stock market is efficient ; that is , that stock prices reflect everything that is known about a company's prospects and about the state of the economy.

You also have to have the knowledge to enable you to make a very general estimate about the value of the underlying businesses.

There will continue to be wide discrepancies between price and value in the marketplace, and those who read their Graham & Dodd will continue to prosper.

Stay Hungry, Stay Foolish

苹果 CEO 乔布斯：求知若饥，虚心若愚

Steve Jobs/史蒂夫·乔布斯

I am honored to be with you today at your commencement from one of the finest universities in the world. I never graduated from college. Truth be told, this is the closest I've ever gotten to a college graduation. Today I want to tell you three stories from my life. That's it. No big deal. Just three stories.

The first story is about connecting the dots.

I dropped out of Reed College after the first 6 months, but then stayed around as a drop—in for another 18 months or so before I really quit. So why did I drop out?

It started before I was born. My **biological** mother was a young, unwed college graduate student, and she decided to put me up for adoption. She felt very strongly that I should be adopted by college graduates, so everything was all set for me to be adopted at birth by a lawyer and his wife. Except that when I popped out they decided at the last minute that they really wanted a girl. So my parents, who were on a waiting list, got a call in the middle of the night asking : "We have an unexpected baby boy ; do you want him?" They said : "Of course." My biological mother later found out that my mother had never graduated from college and that my father had never graduated from high school. She refused to **sign** the final adoption papers. She only relented a few months later when my parents promised that I would someday go to college.

And 17 years later I did go to college. But I naively chose a college that was almost as expensive as Stanford, and all of my working-class parents'savings were being spent on my college **tuition**. After six months, I couldn't see the value in it. I had no idea what I wanted to do with my life and no idea how college was going to help me figure it out. And here I was spending all of the money my parents had saved their entire life. So I decided to drop out and trust that it would all work out OK. *It was pretty scary at the time, but looking back it was one of the best decisions I ever made.* The minute I dropped out I could stop taking the required classes that didn't interest me, and begin dropping in on the ones that looked interesting.

It wasn't all romantic. I didn't have a dorm room, so I slept on the floor in friends'rooms, I returned coke bottles for the 5 ¢ deposits to buy food with, and I would walk the 7 miles across town every Sunday night to get one good meal a week at the Hare Krishna temple. I loved it. And much of what I stumbled into by following my curiosity and intuition turned out to be priceless later on. Let me give you one example :

Reed College at that time offered perhaps the best calligraphy instruction in the country. Throughout the campus every poster, every label on every drawer, was beautifully hand calligraphed. Because I had dropped out and didn't have to take the normal classes, I decided to take a calligraphy class to learn how to do this. I learned about **serif** and san serif typefaces, about varying the amount of space between different letter combinations, about what makes great typography great. *It was beautiful, historical, artistically subtle in a way that science can't capture, and I found it fascinating.*

None of this had even a hope of any practical application in my life. But ten years later, when we were designing the first Macintosh computer, it all came back to me. And we designed it all into the Mac. It was the first computer with beautiful typography. If I had never dropped in on that single course in college, the Mac would have never had multiple typefaces or proportionally spaced fonts. And since Windows just copied the Mac, its likely that no personal computer would have them. If I had never dropped out, I would have never dropped in on this calligraphy class, and personal computers might not have the wonderful typography that they do. Of course it was impossible to connect the dots looking forward when I was in college. But it was very, very clear looking **backwards** ten years later.

Again, you can't connect the dots looking forward ; you can only connect them looking backwards. So you have to trust that the dots will somehow connect in your future. You have to trust in something—your gut, destiny, life, karma, whatever. This approach has never let me down, and it has made all the difference in my life.

我今天很荣幸能和你们一起参加毕业典礼，斯坦福大学是世界上最好的大学之一。我从未从任何一所学院毕业。说实话，今天也许是在我的生命中离大学毕业最近的一天了。今天我想向你们讲述我生活中的三个故事。不是什么大不了的事情，只是三个故事而已。

第一个故事是关于如何把生命中的点点滴滴串连起来。

我在 Reed 大学读了 6 个月之后就退学了，但是在 18 个月以后——我真正作出退学决定之前，我还经常去学校。我为什么要退学呢？

故事从我出生的时候讲起。我的亲生母亲是一个年轻的、未婚的大学毕业生。她决定让别人收养我，她非常希望我能被大学毕业生收养。所以万事俱备，所有的一切都安排好了，我出生时就会被一个律师和他的妻子所收养。但是她没有料到，当我出生之后，律师夫妇突然决定他们想要一个女孩。所以我那在等待批准的申请人名单上的父母在半夜接到了一个电话："我们现在这儿有一个不小心生出来的男婴，你们想要他吗？"

他们回答道："当然！"但是我亲生母亲随后发现，我的养母从来没有上过大学，我的父亲甚至没有读过高中。她拒绝签这个收养合同。只是在几个月以后，我的父母答应她一定要让我上大学，那个时候她才同意。

在 17 岁那年，我真的上了大学。但是我很愚蠢的选择了一所几乎和斯坦福大学一样贵的学校，我工薪阶层的父母几乎把所有积蓄都花在了我的学费上面。6 个月后，我已经看不到其中的价值所在了。我对我生命中要做的一切都不知所措，我也不知道大学能否为我描绘出来。但是在那里，我几乎花光了我父母这辈子的所有积蓄。所以我决定要退学，我觉得这是个正确的决定。不能否认，我当时确实非常的害怕，但是现在回头看看，那的确是我这一生中最棒的一个决定。在我做出退学决定的那一刻，我终于可以不必去读那些令我提不起丝毫兴趣的课程了。然后我还可以去修那些看起来有点意思的课程。

但是这并不是那么浪漫。学校宿舍不让我住了，所以我只能在朋友房间的地板上面睡觉，我去捡 5 美分的可乐瓶子，仅仅为了填饱肚子，在星期天的晚上，我需要走 7 英里的路程，穿过这个城市到 Hare Krishna 寺庙（注：位于纽约 Brooklyn 下城），只是为了能吃上饭——这个星期唯一一顿好点的饭菜。但是我喜欢这样。我跟着我的直觉和好奇心走，遇到的很多东西，此后被证明是无价之宝。让我给你们举一个例子吧：

Reed 大学在那时提供也许是全美国最好的美术字课程。在这个大学里面的每个海报，每个抽屉的标签上面全都是漂亮的美术字。因为我退学了，没有受到正规的训练，所以我决定去参加这个课程，去学学怎样写出漂亮的美术字。我学到了 san serif 和 serif 字体，我学会了怎么样在不同的字母组合之中改变空格的长度，还有怎么样才能做出最棒的印刷式样。那是一种科学永远不能捕捉到的、美丽的、真实的艺术精妙，我发现那实在是太美妙了。

当时看起来这些东西在我的生命中，好像都没有什么实际应用的可能。但是十年后，当我们在设计第一台 Macintosh 电脑的时候，就不是那样了。我把当时所学的全都用在了 Mac 中。那是第一台使用了漂亮的印刷字体的电脑。如果我当时没有退学，就不会有机会去参加这个我感兴趣的美术字课程，Mac 就不会有这么多丰富的字体，以及赏心悦目的字体间距。那么现在个人电脑就不会有现在这么美妙的字体了。当然我在大学的时候，还不可能把从前的点点滴滴串连起来，但是当我十年后回顾这一切的时候，真的豁然开朗了。

需要再次说明的是，你在向前展望的时候不可能将这些片断串连起来；你只有在回顾的时候才能做到这一点，所以你必须相信这些片断会在将来的某一天能串连起来。你必须要相信某些东西：你的秉性、命运、生活、因缘。这个过程从来没有令我失望，反而让我的生命更加的与众不同。

实战提升
Practising & Exercise

导读
史蒂夫·乔布斯，苹果电脑公司 CEO。本文是史蒂夫·乔布斯 2005 年 6 月 12 日在斯坦福大学毕业典礼上的演讲。

单词注解
biological [baiə'lɔdʒikəl] *adj.* 生物的；生物学的

sign [sain] *n.* 记号，符号

tuition [tjuː'iʃən] *n.* 讲授，教学；教诲

serif ['serif] *n.* 衬线

backward ['bækwəd] *adj.* 向后的，反向的，返回的

诵读名句
It was pretty scary at the time, but looking back it was one of the best decisions I ever made.

It was beautiful, historical, artistically subtle in a way that science can't capture, and I found it fascinating.

None of this had even a hope of any practical application in my life.

China and the WTO : the 15-year Itch
中国与WTO：十五年的渴望

David Eldon/大卫·艾尔敦

Good morning Ladies and Gentlemen，

I stand before you today with a confession to make.

It relates to something that I did recently.

Exactly one month ago，I delivered a speech to another American audience. It was a gathering of the American Chamber of Commerce in Hong Kong. I talked about Hong Kong's changing role. And about how Hong Kong can compete as it becomes **increasingly** easier for foreign companies to do business in China.

On that day in March，I made several suggestions. *One of which was that when travelling overseas，government officials and business people from Hong Kong should spend more time selling Hong Kong to the sceptics. And less time speaking to the converted.*

Consequently I am here today，in front of a decidedly Hong

Kong-friendly crowd, in direct violation of my own advice. That said, I plan to redeem myself by not devoting too much time talking about Hong Kong—a topic that is well known to this audience. Rather I intend to concentrate on the less known. In particular, the implications of China's entry into the WTO. The implications for Hong Kong and the implications for foreign companies.

In doing so, I am going to focus my talk on three distinct areas of knowledge :

what we know we know;

what we know we do not know ; and

what we do not know we know.

Common knowledge

First, what we know we know. We know that China means different things to different people.

To overseas manufacturing firms or trading companies it is "the land of a billion buyers of shoes, cars and computers." To foreign companies already in China it is a place that warrants expansion. In fact, a recent survey found that nine out every 10 foreign companies operating in China plan to expand their investment in the next three years. To foreign financial institutions—particularly those interested in the provision of wealth management services—China is a market with **enormous** potential. After all it is a country with the highest rate of savings in the world. A country where reportedly more than 80 percent of the bank deposits are held in 20 percent of the accounts. To my Bank it is our birthplace. To your President it is a "strategic competitor."

Another thing we know we know and this audience in particular knows is that China's entry into the WTO means the role of Hong Kong will inevitably change.

Hong Kong was once the only gateway to the Mainland market. A vital link between East and West. Between developed and less-developed nations. Between capitalist and reforming economies. Between China and everywhere else. Today, Hong Kong no longer holds this privileged position. The reality is that Hong Kong hasn't held it for quite some time. Long before the ink was dry on China's WTO agreement, companies were choosing to bypass Hong Kong and go directly to Beijing, Shanghai and elsewhere in the Mainland. Of course, a significant number of companies were also still coming to Hong Kong to take advantage of the city's close geographic, economic, political and cultural ties to the Mainland. And as you are aware they continue to come.

We also know that China is in the midst of two transitions at one time : from a command to a market economy and from a rural to an urban society. And we know that the country faces a number of challenges : allocating incoming capital effectively ; reforming state-owned enterprises ; creating more jobs ; spreading wealth more evenly ; reducing bureaucracy ; and **eliminating** corruption. And now, living up to the commitments and the expectations of WTO membership can be added to this list.

Finally, we know that China has changed a great deal in a relatively short period of time. Thirty years ago, US President

Richard Nixon and his national security adviser Henry Kissinger made a historic journey to China. Their seven-day trip concluded with the signing of the Shanghai Communiqué inside the Grand Hall of the Jinjiang Hotel in Shanghai. A couple of weeks ago，Dr Kissinger returned to the Jinjiang to deliver a speech commemorating the events of 1972.

I do not know if Dr Kissinger took the time to explore the surrounding area. If he did，he would have possibly seen the nearby theatre that regularly plays the latest offering from Hollywood. He would have probably come across the American fast food outlets or the Italian designer clothing store just down the block. Before crossing the street，he would have likely had to wait for a line of Japanese cars to pass and perhaps even the bus emblazoned with a larger-than-life Winnie the Pooh. And if he stayed out late enough，he would have undoubtedly been able to stroll back to the hotel under the colorful neon lights advertising German cellular phones. In short，he would have definitely seen a very different China today than the one he saw 30 years ago.

Existing uncertainties

The second area I want to focus on is what we know we do not know. In other words，the uncertainties related to the further opening of China's market.

Clearly，we do not know exactly how numerous industries will evolve. And it is a lack of advanced knowledge that is prompting much speculation. In the area of financial services for example，some predict that many of China's domestic banks will have a limited life span once the market is fully opened up in five years time.

Personally, I do not share this view. I think they will be very strong competitors. Partly because they are in the advantageous position of knowing the marketplace. Partly because they have national networks that are impossible—not to mention impractical—to match. And partly because they have a strong base of customers and are becoming increasingly modern. Consider the Mainland's largest bank, the Industrial and Commercial Bank of China. It recently announced that it has more than 10, 000 corporates and 1.8 million individuals using its online banking services. But the main reason I think domestic banks in China will be strong competitors : they are very fast learners.

Another thing we know we do not know—and this specifically relates to Hong Kong—is the indirect benefits that will flow from a more open market in China.

For example, if mainland investors are allowed to invest their foreign exchange holdings in Hong Kong, the SAR's stock market would clearly benefit. Hong Kong's position as a fund raising centre for Mainland companies would also be enhanced. We know this idea is under consideration. We also know we do not know when it may happen.

Likewise, we know that if banks in Hong Kong are permitted to accept RMB deposits, the SAR's status as an international financial centre and as the premier regional financial centre will be enhanced even further. Once again we know this idea is being considered, but we do not know when it may happen.

...

At the outset of the 1972 talks, Dr Kissinger reportedly told his Chinese hosts : "The good thing about our relationship is that we want nothing from each other."

Chairman Mao is said to have promptly disagreed, noting : "If I had wanted nothing from you, I wouldn't have invited you. And if you wanted nothing from me, you shouldn't have come."

Similar sentiments apply to the WTO agreement. If China did not have something to gain, it would not have joined the WTO. Nor would it have made, as some observers suggest, commitments that are far more reaching than any **previous** membership applicant has. Likewise, foreign companies would not be flocking to and expanding their operations in China if they thought there was nothing to gain. Nor if they thought there were no profits to be made.

In closing, let me make one final observation about Hong Kong and the impact of China's entry into the WTO.

I know and I think all of you would agree that Hong Kong is well positioned to play a significant role in the post-entry period. And I know the people of Hong Kong have the capacity and the capability to respond to new challenges. *Simply put, I know that if New York is the city that never sleeps, then Hong Kong is the city that never stagnates.*

Thank you.

先生们，女士们，早上好！

今天我站在这里，要向大家坦白。

是关于最近我说过的一些话。

一个月前，我向另一些美国听众发表了讲话。那是在香港的美国商会的一次聚会上。我谈到香港的角色正在发生变化。现在外国公司在中国开展业务越来越容易，所以我也谈到了在这种情况下香港该怎样进行竞争。

就在那一天，也就是在三月份，我提出了几点建议。其中一点是香港的政府官员和商业人员在去海外时应该多花些时间向那些对香港持怀疑态度的人宣传香港，而不要花太多时间和对香港友好的人谈论香港。

所以我今天会站在这里，站在一群对香港极为友好的人面前，直截了当地违背自己提出的建议。既然这么说，我打算对自己说过的话作出补偿，不用太多的时间谈论香港——这个话题对于今天的听众来说已经非常熟悉了。我想多谈一些大家不太熟悉的东西。尤其是中国加入 WTO 所产生的影响，对香港的影响，还有对外国公司的影响。

这样，我准备集中谈论三部分的内容：

我们知道自己已经了解的事；

我们知道自己还没有了解的事；还有

我们不知道自己已经了解的事。

众所周知的内容

首先是我们知道自己已经了解的事。我们知道中国对于不同的人来说意味着不同的东西。

对于海外的制造商和贸易公司来说，中国是"有着十多亿购买鞋子、汽车和电脑的消费者的国家"。对于已经在中国的外国公司来说，在这里扩展业务是理所当然的。事实上，最近的一项调查表明，在中国运作的每十家外国公司中有九家计划在未来三年里扩大投资。对于外资的金融机构来说，尤其是那些对提供财富管理服务感兴趣的外资金融机构来说，中国是一个有着巨大潜力的市场。毕竟这是一个有着全世界最高存款率的国家。根据报道，在中国超过80%的银行存款存在20%的账户之中。对于我的银行——汇丰银行——来说，中国是我们的诞生地。对于各位总统来说，中国是"战略性的竞争对手"。

另一件我们知道自己已经了解的事，也是在座的各位听众了解的事，就是中国加入WTO意味着香港的角色肯定会发生变化。

香港曾经一度是进入中国内地市场的唯一通道。它是东西方联系的一条至关重要的纽带，联系着发达国家和欠发达的国家，联系着资本主义经济和改革之中的经济体，也联系着中国和世界各地。今天，香港已经不再拥有这一特殊地位了。事实上，香港失去这一地位已经有一段时间了。在中国加入WTO之前，各公司早就选择绕过香港，直接进入北京，上海和中国内地的其他地方。当然，也有大量公司还是到香港来，以利用这座城市与中国内地在地理，经济，政治和文化方面的紧密联系。大家也都看到，还有公司陆续到来。

我们也知道中国正同时处于两种转变之中：从计划经济到市场经济，从农业到都市社会。我们也知道这个国家正面临着一系列的挑战：有效分配涌入的资金；改革国有企业；创造更多的就业机会；更平均地分配财富；减少官僚作风；还有杜绝腐败。现在，还可以加上一条：达到 WTO 成员国的承诺和期望。

最后，我们知道中国在相对较短的时间里发生了巨大的变化。30 年前，美国总统尼克松和他的国家安全事务助理基辛格对中国进行了一次具有历史意义的访问。他们为期 7 天的访问的最后一项内容是在上海的锦江饭店小礼堂签订上海公报。就在几星期前，基辛格博士又来到锦江饭店发表讲话，纪念 1972 年的这一事件。

我不知道基辛格博士是否花时间去周围的地方看过。如果他这么做了，他可能会看到附近的一家电影院，这家电影院经常上映最新的好莱坞大片。沿着大街走，他可能会见到美式的快餐店或是意大利款式的服装店。在过马路之前，他很有可能要等着一长排日本汽车开过，甚至是画着非常显眼的小熊维尼图案的公共汽车。如果他在外面逗留到很晚，他一定会在德国移动电话广告的霓虹灯下漫步走回宾馆。总而言之，他现在一定会看到与 30 年前完全不同的一个中国。

存在的不确定因素

我想说的第二部分是我们知道自己不了解的东西。换句话说，就是有关中国市场进一步开放的不确定因素。

很明显，我们不知道到底这么多行业会怎样发展。由于对事情缺乏深入地了解而导致许多揣测。比如，在金融服务这一方面，有一些人预测，一旦市场在五年后完全开放，许多中资银行就会陆续关门。

我个人对这种看法并不赞同。我认为这些中资银行将会是非常强劲的竞争对手。这一部分是因为这些银行了解市场，处于有利地位。另一部分原因是它们有遍布全国的网络，这一点是根本无法匹敌的，更不用说赶上它们是不切实际的了。还有一部分原因是它们拥有强大的客户基础，并且正在逐步走向现代化。比如中国内地最大的银行——中国工商银行，最近这家银行宣布有超过 10，000 家企业和 180 万的个人在使用其网上银行的服务。但是我认为中资银行将成为强劲竞争对手的主要原因是：它们学习的速度非常快。

另一件我们知道自己不了解的事和香港很有关系，就是从更加开放的中国市场获得的间接利益。

比如，如果内地的投资者获准在香港投资外币股票，香港特别行政区的股票市场肯定会得到好处。香港作为内地公司募集资金的中心，地位也会提高。我们知道这一想法正在考虑之中。我们也知道我们不了解这种情况什么时候会发生。

同样地，我们知道如果香港的银行获准接受人民币存款，香港特别行政区作为国际金融中心和主要的地区性金融中心，它的地位将会更进一步提高。我们也知道这一想法正在考虑之中，但是我们不知道这种情况什么时候会发生。

……

据报道，在 1972 年对话的开始，基辛格博士就对中国的东道主说："我们之间的关系之中有一点很好，就是我们都不想从对方那里获得什么。"

据说毛主席立刻反对说："如果我什么都不想从你们那里得到，我就不会邀请你们。如果你们什么都不想从我们这里得到，你们也就不会来了。"

同样的感觉也适用于 WTO 协议。如果中国不想获得什么，就不会加入 WTO。正如一些观察家所指出的，她也就不会作出比任何以往的成员申请国影响更深远的承诺。同样地，如果外国公司认为什么都得不到，也就不会蜂拥到中国来扩展他们的业务。如果他们认为无利可图，也不会这样做。

在结束之前，我想最后再评述一下关于香港的情况和中国加入 WTO 的影响。

我知道，而且我相信各位都同意这一点，香港处于有利的位置，可以在中国入世后扮演重要的角色。我也知道，香港人有能力应付新的挑战。简单地说，我知道如果纽约是不眠的城市，那么香港就是从不停滞的城市。

谢谢大家。

实战提升
Practising & Exercise

导读

这是香港上海汇丰银行有限公司主席大卫·艾尔敦在 2002 年 4 月 25 日纽约香港协会早餐会的演讲"中国与 WTO：十五年的渴望"。

单词注解

increasingly [in'kri:siŋli] *adv.* 渐增地；越来越多地

sceptic ['skeptik] *n.* 怀疑者，怀疑论者

enormous [i'nɔ:məs] *adj.* 巨大的，庞大的

eliminate [i'limineit] *v.* 排除，消除，消灭

specifically [spi'sifikəli] *adv.* 特别地；明确地；具体地

previous ['pri:vjəs] *adj.* 先的，前的，以前的

诵读名句

One of which was that when travelling overseas, government officials and business people from Hong Kong should spend more time selling Hong Kong to the sceptics. And less time speaking to the converted.

Another thing we know we know and this audience in particular knows is that China's entry into the WTO means the role of Hong Kong will inevitably change.

Simply put, I know that if New York is the city that never sleeps, then Hong Kong is the city that never stagnates.

Carly Fiorina Remarks at Tsinghua University
惠普 CEO 卡莉·费奥瑞纳在清华大学的演讲

Carly Fiorina/卡莉·费奥瑞纳

Xie, xie. Xia wu hao. Those are the only two words of Chinese I know. That's not true, I know a third—Ni hao. I want to thank all of you for taking time out of your what I know that is a very busy study schedule to be here today. I know this is valuable time for you that you could be using to work, or study, or maybe to play Sword on line. Thank you for having me here today.

Coming from a company that has "invent" as part of our brand, as part of our signature, I sometimes begin speeches by saying that invention and innovation have been part the DNA of HP's for more than sixty years. Our scientists and engineers today generate more than 11 patents every day. We spend more than 4 billion dollars a year on R&D. So invention is part of our future as well as part of our past. *That all sounds pretty impressive until you think about China's history, and you realize that "invent" has been part of China's DNA for more than 5, 000 years.* Every schoolchild in America learns about China's many gifts to this world—from the invention of paper, to gunpowder, the wheelbarrow, the compass, acupuncture—right up to the first blast furnace and the first use of iron casting, back in the sixth century. As a company, we **actually** at HP are especially indebted to a man named Bi Sheng, who had the vision in 1045 A.D. to invent the world's first movable type, which led to its first printer—a full 300 years before Gutenberg's invention of movable type changed the Western world. So today, I want to issue a belated thank you to Bi Sheng for having the foresight to set in motion a process that would eventually lead to a 20 billion business for HP.

...

I think the technology landscape today is changing in three fundamental ways. The first big shift we see going on in technology is that all processes, and that all content are being transformed from physical and analog to digital and mobile, and virtual. There are so many examples. Just think about the simple example of what is happening in photography. Photography is going from physical to digital and now from digital to mobile and all the content is about to become virtual and available, and accessible to anyone, anywhere in any form they want. And that transformation from physical to digital, virtual, mobile will happen to every process, every industry, and every kind of content.

The second big shift we see in technology is that the demand for simplicity, for manageability, for **adaptability**. While it is true that while technology is core to everything, it is also true that technology is also still too complex, too hard to manage, and often that complexity is a barrier.

The third big shift is that it's becoming a horizontal, heterogeneous, connected world. Whether you're a CEO trying to become more **efficient**, more effective and more agile ; or a small and medium business trying to mobilize your workforce ; or you're a consumer who wants a whole bunch of separate things that you have bought in your home to work better together, it is now about horizontal connections. It's about making a heterogeneous world work together and speak a common language—and I am speaking not of just devices, but networking and connecting businesses and companies, employees and suppliers to customers.

As technology moves from the fringe to the core of people's lives and businesses, the need for technology to deliver more becomes increasingly important. I think today our consumers are no longer willing to compromise. Now, all of our customers actually want everything from technology. They want affordability and innovation and reliability and security and simplicity and manageability and connection.

Now if I were giving you a speech today on HP, I would tell you that this is a future that we are trying to create. That we see our role to accelerate the transformation from physical to digital. That as the No.1 consumer IT company in the world ; the No.1 technology company for small and medium-sized businesses, and one of the leading enterprise technology companies, we are a company, we believe, unlike any other, with market-leading positions in virtually every category in which we compete. Today we are a almost 84 billion company with 140, 000 employees in

176 countries around the world.

This school has prepared all of you for that same journey. As you work to take what you have learned here and apply it to the world around you, I hope that you will also strive to use your capabilities to create communities that are not just richer, but better; to judge success not just by the number of networks you connect, but by the number of people you connect; that you won't just help make better companies, but better communities, and a better world.

It's that same kind of thinking that brought us to China in the first place. It was 22 years ago that HP opened our first office here in China, in an old municipal factory located in Beijing. A day before the opening, there was still sawdust on the floor, and two of our engineers worked so hard to get our systems ready that they slept overnight in the building on folding cots. When we opened that building , it was the first partnership of its kind to be sponsored by the government of the People's Republic of China in conjunction with a foreign company.

That's the same wish I leave you with here today. This University, I believe, has prepared you well and taught you the lessons of character and capability. The leaders of tomorrow will be the people of your age with the drive and commitment to fulfill their own potential and to help others reach their potential.

This is a world that in fact has always been driven by the young. Galileo published his first book on gravity at age 22. The founders of HP, Bill Hewlett and Dave Packard, were in their 20's when they began the company. Bill Gates after all started Microsoft when he was 22. Or think about a lesson of one of this school's great founders —— Zhao Yuanren, one of Tsinghua's Great Four Tutors, who knew 10 European languages and dozens of Chinese dialects, who accompanied British philosopher Bertrand Russell around China and translated his English into the local dialect at each of their destinations. He was only 28 at the time.

And let us not forget that the world's very first computer programmer was a woman in her 20s. She lived more than 150 years ago. She greatly expanded on the work of her mentor, the renowned mathematician Charles Babbage, whose work on the analytical engine preceded the modern computer. Today, the computer language Ada is named for her.

Your job, your great opportunity, is to harness the forces of change swirling all around you, in whatever field you decide to enter, and to take full advantage of the possibilities at your fingertips. Leadership can take place in acts large and small, it can come not just from CEOs and Prime Ministers, but can come as well from ordinary citizens who believe in the potential of others. I hope that whatever you do, you will remember your own power and **dedicate** yourself to the cause Tsinghua has prepared you so well for : to dedicate yourself to unlock the potential in others ; to believe in the potential of yourself ; to make this era the most exciting in all of human history—and to prove, beyond a shadow of a doubt, that everything is possible.

Thank you.

　　谢谢，下午好。我只会说这两句中国话，其实我还知道第三句，你好。我要感谢大家，在你们紧张的学习之余能够参加今天的演讲会，我知道对于你们来说时间很宝贵，你们可以利用这段时间工作、学习，或者玩网络游戏，对于你们的邀请，我非常感谢。

　　我常常以介绍惠普的创新历史作为我演讲的开始。60 年来，创新和发明一直是惠普公司的精神本质，我们的工程师和科学家每天推出 11 项专利，我们每年在研发方面的投入高达 40 亿美元。创新精神不仅代表惠普的过去，也昭示着惠普的未来。HP 60 年的创新历程固然令人瞩目，但当我们想到中国灿烂的历史，想到中国五千年的发明史时，这一切就不值一提了。美国的每一个适龄儿童都知道中国已经给世界带来的贡献，比如造纸术的发明、火药的发明、指南针的发明，还有针灸，铸铁技术是六世纪的时候中国带给世界的发明。我们惠普要特别感谢毕昇先生，他在 1045 年发明了活字印刷术，比起后来德国人古腾堡的发明早了 300 多年。活字印刷术的发明改变了整个西方世界。所以我今天要特别感谢毕昇先生，他的发明给惠普公司带来了 200 亿美元的生意。

　　我认为今天技术的格局正在以三种基本方式发生变革。第一个大的变革就是所有的流程和内容都在从物理的、模拟的变成为数字的、移动的和虚拟的。这方面的例子非常多，一个简单的例子就是摄影，摄影已经从物理式的变为数字化的，从数字化的变为可移动的，与此同时，所有的内容也正在变成虚拟的，任何人都可以在任何时间、任何地方、以他们所喜欢的任何方式来使用这些内容。这种从物理到数字化、移动式、虚拟化的变革将发生在每一个流程、每一个行业和每一种类型的内容之中。

　　第二个大的科技变革是人们对于技术的简化、可管理性、可适用性的要求越来越高。技术的确是一切的核心，但是技术也的确是太复杂、太难以管理了，复杂性是一种障碍。

　　第三个大的变革是，现在世界已经变为一种横向的、异构的、相互连接的世界。不管你是一个试图提高企业效率、效果和灵活性的 CEO，还是一个想更好地利用你的员工队伍的中小企业主，又或者你是一个消费者，你希望你家里的各种各样的高科技产品之间能更好地配合，现在的关键是把它们横向地连接起来，关键是使异构的世界能够使用共同的语言。我这里谈的不仅仅是设备之间的连接，而是一个网络，它将企业、员工、供应商、客户都连接起来。

　　当技术从人们日常生活和商业社会的边缘逐渐成为核心，人们就越来越需要技术能够提供更多的东西，这种需求变得越来越重要。现在，我们的客户不愿意再妥协了，他们需要从科技中得到所有，他们需要买得起的、可靠的、安全的、简便的、可管理的技术，还有连接。

如果今天我要跟你们专门谈惠普公司的话，我就会告诉你们，这就是我们要创建的未来。我们的作用就是为了加速从物理化到数字化的转变。我们是世界上第一大 IT 消费品公司，我们也是针对中小企业的第一大科技公司，我们还是业界领先的面向大中型企业的科技公司。与其他任何公司都不一样，我们在每一个领域都占有领先地位。今天我们的营业额已经近 800 亿美元，在全球 176 个国家拥有 140, 000 名员工。

清华大学已经为你们的未来做好了准备，当你们把你们学到的知识运用到社会中时，我希望你们能尽自己所能去建设一个更加美好的社会，而不仅仅是个富裕的社会。在这个社会里，成功的标准不在于你们能连接多少网络，而在于你们能连接多少个人，希望你们不仅能够创立更好的公司，而且能够建设更美好的社区，更美好的世界。

正是本着这样的想法，惠普作为高科技外资企业第一个进入中国。22 年前，HP 在中国、在北京的一个老厂房设立了第一个办事处，开业前一天办公室的地板上还铺满了木屑，我们的两名工程师为了使系统就绪而艰苦工作，在办公楼的折叠床上过夜。我们正式开业时，惠普是由中华人民共和国政府和外国公司合资的第一家高科技企业。

今天我也想跟你们表达同样的愿望，我认为清华大学已经使你们做好了充分的准备，培养了你们的性格和能力，明天的领导人就是你们这样的年轻人，有向前的驱动力并尽自己所能去帮助其他人发挥他们的潜力。

我们所处的世界一直都是由年轻人推动前进的。伽利略在 22 岁的时候出版了他的第一本关于地心引力的书，惠普的创始人 Bill Hewlett 和 Dave Packard 在他们 20 岁的时候创立了 HP

公司，比尔·盖茨也是在他22岁的时候创立了微软公司。清华大学的四大导师之———赵元任先生，通晓十种欧洲语言和十多种中国方言，他陪同英国哲学家罗素游历中国，将罗素的思想翻译为中国方言，那一年他才28岁。

世界上第一个计算机编程员是一名女性，她当时才20岁，她生活在150年前。她极大地扩展了她的导师、著名数学家Charles Babbage的工作，她在当时就预见到现在所使用的计算机。今天的计算机语言Ada就是以她的名字命名的。

而你们要做的、你们的巨大机遇就在于，在你所决定进入的任何一个领域，都要充分利用环绕在你周围的变革的力量，都要充分利用你们所能掌握的各种机会。领导力存在于大大小小的行动之中，领导力不仅是CEO和总理才有的，普通人也有这样的能力，只要他们相信别人也有潜力可以发挥。我希望无论你们从事什么工作，你们都深信自己的能量，并且将自己献身于清华已为你们准备好的事业当中，献身于焕发别人的潜力，同时相信自己有巨大的潜力，致力于将我们现在身处的时代变成人类历史上最激动人心的时代。让我们用行动去消除怀疑，用行动证明"一切皆有可能"！

谢谢大家。

实战提升
Practising & Exercise

导读

2004 年 3 月 12 日，作为卡莉·费奥瑞纳第四次访华的最后一站，卡莉站在了清华大学的演讲台上，这块总统访华不会放过的地方，开始了题为："变革时代的领导力"的演讲。这是一位美国炙手可热的女 CEO、知名度不亚于第一夫人。她是一位集美丽、智慧、财富、权力于一身的女人。

单词注解

impressive [im'presiv] *adj.* 深刻印象的；感人的；令人钦佩的

actually ['æktʃuəli] *adv.* 实际上，真的

adaptability [ədæptə'biliti] *n.* 顺应性；适应性；适合性

efficient [i'fiʃənt] *adj.* 效率高的；有能力的，能胜任的

dedicate ['dedikeit] *v.* 以……奉献，以……供奉

诵读名句

That all sounds pretty impressive until you think about China's history, and you realize that "invent" has been part of China's DNA for more than 5, 000 years.

That great tradition of invention and innovation has certainly been carried on here at Tsinghua, where some of the finest instructors in the world today are working to train some of the finest scientists and engineers.

And let us not forget that the world's very first computer programmer was a woman in her 20s.

优雅的灵魂

Those Elegant Spirits

In Memory of the Challenger Astronauts

怀念挑战者号宇航员

Ronald Wilson Reagan/罗纳德·威尔逊·里根

We come together today to mourn the loss of seven brave Americans, to share the grief that we all feel, and perhaps in that sharing, to find the strength to bear our sorrow and the courage to look for the seeds of hope.

Our nation's loss is first a profound personal loss to the family and the friends and the loved ones of our shuttle astronauts. To those they left behind the mothers, the fathers, the husbands and wives, brothers and sisters, yes, and especially the children—all of America stands beside you in your time of sorrow.

What we say today is only an inadequate expression of what we carry in our hearts. Words pale in the shadow of grief ; they seem insufficient even to measure the brave **sacrifice** of those you loved and we so admired. Their truest testimony will not be in the words we speak, but in the way they led their lives and in the way they lost their lives with dedication, honor, and an unquenchable desire to explore this mysterious and beautiful universe.

The best we can do is remember our seven astronauts, our Challenger Seven, remember them as they lived, bringing life and love and joy to those who knew them and pride to a nation.

They came from all parts of this great country—from South Carolina to Washington State ; Ohio to Mohawk, New York ; Hawaii to North Carolina to Concord, New Hampshire. They were so different ; yet in their mission, their quest, they held so much in common.

We remember Dick Scobee, the commander who spoke the last words we heard from the space shuttle Challenger. He served as a fighter pilot in Vietnam earning many medals for bravery and later as a test pilot of advanced aircraft before joining the space program. Danger was a familiar companion to Commander Scobee.

We remember Michael Smith, who earned enough medals as a combat pilot to cover his chest, including the Navy Distinguished Flying Cross, three Air Medals, and the Vietnamese Cross of Gallantry with Silver Star in gratitude from a nation he fought to keep free.

We remember Judith Resnik, known as J. R. to her friends, always smiling, always eager to make a contribution, finding beauty in the music she played on her piano in her off-hours.

We remember Ellison Onizuka, who as a child running barefoot through the coffee fields and macadamia groves of

Hawaii dreamed of someday traveling to the Moon. Being an Eagle said, had helped him, soar to the impressive achievements of his career.

We remember Ronald McNair, who said that he learned perseverance in the cotton-fields of South Carolina. His dream was to live aboard the space station, performing experiments and playing his saxophone in the weightlessness of space. Well, Ron, we will miss Your saxophone; and we will build your space station.

We remember Gregory Jarvis. On that ill-fated flight he was carrying with him a flag of his university in Buffalo, New York—a small token he said, to the people who unlocked his future.

We remember Christa McAuliffe, who captured the imagination of the entire nation; **inspiring** us with her pluck, her restless spirit of discovery; a teacher, not just to her students, but to an entire people, instilling us all with the excitement of this journey we ride into the future.

We will always remember them, these skilled professionals, scientists, and adventurers, these artists and teachers and family men and women; and we will cherish each of their stories, stories of triumph and bravery, stories of true American heroes.

On the day of the disaster, our nation held a vigil by our television sets. *In one crucial moment our exhilaration turned to horror; we waited and watched and tried to make sense of what we had seen.* That night I listened to a call-in program on the radio; people of every age spoke of their sadness and the pride they felt in our astronauts. Across America we are reaching out, holding hands, and finding comfort in one another.

The sacrifice of your loved ones has stirred the soul of our nation and through the pain our hearts have been opened to a profound truth : The future is not free ; the story of all human progress is one of a struggle against all odds. We learned again that this America, which Abraham Lincoln called the last, best hope of man on Earth, was built on heroism and noble sacrifice. It was built by men and women like our seven star voyagers, who answered a call beyond duty, who gave more than was expected or required, and who gave it little thought of worldly reward.

We think back to the pioneers of an earlier century, the sturdy souls who took their families and their belongings and set out into the frontier of the American West. Often they met with terrible hardship. Along the Oregon Trail, you could still see the gravemarkers of those who fell on the way. But grief only steeled them to the journey ahead.

Today the frontier is space and the boundaries of human knowledge. Sometimes when—we reach for the stars, we fall short. But we must pick ourselves up again and press on despite the pain. Our nation is indeed fortunate that we can still draw on immense reservoirs of courage, character, and fortitude—that we're still blessed with heroes like those of the space shuttle Challenger.

Dick Scobee knew that every launching of a space shuttle is a technological miracle. And he said, "If something ever does go wrong, I hope that doesn't mean the end of the space shuttle program." Every family member I talked to asked specifically that we continue the program, that that is what their **departed** loved one would want above all else. We will not disappoint them.

Today we promise Dick Scobee and his crew that their dream lives on, that the future they worked so hard to build will become reality. The dedicated men and women of NASA have lost seven members of their family. Still, they, too, must forge ahead with a space program that is effective safe and efficient, but bold and committed.

Man will continue his conquest of space. To reach out for new goals and ever greater achievements that is the way we shall commemorate our seven Challenger heroes.

Dick, Mike, Judy, E1, Ron, Greg, and Christa—your families and your country mourn your passing. We bid you goodbye ; we will never forget you. For those who knew you well and loved you, the pain will be deep and enduring. A nation, too, will long feet the loss of her sons and daughters, her seven good friends. We can find **consolation** only in faith, for we know in our hearts that you who flew so high and so proud now make your home beyond the stars, safe in God's promise of eternal life.

May God bless you all and give you comfort in this difficult time.

今天，我们聚集在一起，沉痛地哀悼我们失去的七位勇士，共同分担内心的悲痛，或许在相互间的安慰中，我们能够得到承受痛苦的力量并坚定追求理想的信念。

在所有这些损失中，首先是宇航员们的家人、朋友及他们所爱着的人们所遭受的巨大的个人损失。对那些兄弟、姐妹，尤其是孩子们，在你们悲痛哀悼的日子里，所有美国人都和你们紧紧地站在一起。

今天我们所说的远远不能表达我们内心的真实情感，言语在悲伤面前显得如此苍白，它们根本无法寄托我们对我们所深深爱着的、所深深敬佩的英勇献身的人们的哀思。英雄之所以称之为英雄，并不在于我们颂赞的语言，而在于他们始终以高度的事业心、自尊心和锲而不舍地对神奇而美妙的宇宙进行探索的责任感，去实践真正的生活以至献出生命。

我们所能尽力做到的就是记住我们的七位宇航员，七位"挑战者"，记住他们活着的时候给熟悉他们的人们带来的活力、爱和欢乐，给祖国带来的骄傲。

他们来自这个伟大国家的四面八方——从南加利福尼亚州

到华盛顿州，从俄亥俄州到纽约州的莫霍克，从夏威夷州到北加利福尼亚州，再到新罕布什尔州的康科德。他们各有不同，但他们每个人的追求和肩负的使命却又是那样的一致。

我们怀念迪克·斯科比，飞船的指挥官，我们从升空的"挑战者"号听到的最后一句话就来自这位机长之口。在参加太空计划之前，他曾在越南战争中任战斗机飞行员，因过人的勇敢而赢得多枚奖章。在参加太空飞行计划之前是一名高空飞行器的试验飞行员。对机长斯科比来说，危险从来都是如影随行。

我们怀念迈克尔·史密斯，作为战斗机飞行员，他获得过的奖章足以挂满前胸，其中包括海军杰出飞行员十字勋章，三枚空军勋章，和越南政府为感激他保卫该国自由而授予的银星十字勇士勋章。

我们怀念被朋友们叫做朱蕾的朱蒂丝·蕾斯尼科。她总是对人们微笑着，总是渴望有所贡献。在工作之余，她喜欢弹钢琴，从中获得美的享受。

我们怀念埃里森·奥尼祖卡，他孩提时总爱光着脚板在夏威夷的咖啡地和布满碎石的树丛中跑来跑去，梦想有一天去月球旅行。他告诉人们，飞行员的职业帮助他鸿鹏展翅，让他创造职业生涯中那些令人难忘的业绩。

我们怀念罗纳德·麦克耐尔。他告诉人们是南加州的棉田锤炼了他坚毅的性格。他梦想着能够到空间站去生活，在失重的太空中做试验，吹奏萨克斯管。啊，罗恩，我们将永远怀念你的萨克斯管，我们也一定会建成你所梦想的空间站。

我们怀念格里高利·杰维斯，在那次不幸飞行中，他还带着他的母校——布法洛纽约州立大学的校旗。他说，这是一份小小的纪念品。纪念那些曾为他指点过未来的人们。

我们怀念科里斯塔·麦考利芙，她凝聚了整个民族的想象力，她以坚强的意志和永不停息的探索精神激励着我们。她的确是一位老师，不仅是她的学生们的老师，也是全国人民的老师，她以这次奔向未来的太空飞行作为教例，永远地激励着我们。

我们将永远怀念他们，怀念这些杰出的专家、科学家、探险家，怀念这些艺术家、教师和热爱家庭的人们。我们将珍藏他们每个人的故事，这些诉说胜利和勇敢的故事，这些真正的美国英雄们的故事。

就在灾难发生的那天，所有的美国人都关切地守候在电视机前，彻夜不眠。在那个不幸的时刻，我们欢乐的兴奋变成了恐惧的战栗。我们等待着，注视着，想弄清所发生的一切。当天夜里我收听了广播电台的访谈节目。老老少少都在诉说自己的悲哀，都为我们的宇航员感到骄傲。阴霾笼罩着整个国家，我们走出家门，手拉着手，互相安慰。

你们所热爱的人们的牺牲轰动了整个国家。在痛苦中，我们认识到了一个意义深远的真理：未来的道路并不平坦，整个人类前进的历史是与一切艰难险阻斗争的历史。我们又一次领悟到，美国——亚伯拉罕·林肯曾称之为人类在地球上最后、最美好的希望——是在英雄主义和崇高献身精神的基础上建立起来的，是由无数像我们七位宇航员那样的人，那些把全社会的责任作为自己责任的人，那些给予人民比人民期望和要求的更多的人，那些为人类做出贡献而从不企求些微报答的人建立起来的。

我们不禁回想起一个世纪前的开拓者们，那些拖儿带女，举家开发荒凉的美国西部的刚毅不屈的人们，他们常常面临着恶劣的条件。沿着俄勒冈小道，你们仍能看见那些中途倒下去的拓荒者的墓碑。但是悲痛只能使他们更加坚定前进的决心。

今天，我们面临的荒漠就是太空和人类知识的边界。我们向太空进发，虽然结果有时会不尽如人意。但我们必须把失败的悲痛抛开，重整雄风，不断前进。我们的国家的确非常幸运，因为我们依然保持着巨大的勇气、骨气和刚毅不屈的品质，我们仍然有像"挑战者"号上七位宇航员那样的英雄。

迪克·斯科比知道，每一次宇宙飞船的发射都是一个技术上的奇迹。他曾说："如果出现什么，它决不意味着太空计划的结束。"我所接触的每一位英雄的家庭成员，都特别请求我们一定要继续这项计划，这是他们失去的可爱的亲人所梦寐以求实现的计划。我们决不会令他们失望。

今天，我们向迪克·斯科比和他的队友们保证，他们的梦想没有破灭，他们努力为之奋斗的目标一定会成为现实。国家航空航天局这个大家庭中失去了七位富于献身精神的成员，但其余与他们同样的人们必定会继续前进，开展一项既安全、可行、有效，又大胆而坚定的太空计划。

人类将继续向太空进军，不断确立新的目标，不断取得新的成就。这正是我们纪念"挑战者"号上七位英雄的最好方式。

迪克、迈克、朱迪、埃尔、罗恩、雷格和科里斯塔，你们的家人和祖国都在为你们的离去而哀伤啜泣。永别了，我们会永远记住你们。对熟悉和爱你们的人们来说，痛苦将是沉痛而难以磨灭的；对一个国家来说，她的七位儿女、七位好友的离去是难以弥补的损失。我们只能从信念中寻求安慰，因为我们知道，你们已经自豪地腾飞于广袤的天际，已经在遥远的星际建立了自己的家园，安逸地享受着上帝所赐予的永生。

在这段备受煎熬的日子里，愿上帝保佑你们，并给予你们慰藉！

◥导读◢

1986 年 1 月 28 日，美国航天飞机 "挑战者" 号从肯尼迪航天中心发射 72 秒钟后在 1.5 万米的高空突然爆炸，7 名机组人员全部遇难。飞机在顷刻间炸成一团红白色火雾，飞机的残骸碎片在一小时内散落到距发射中心 9 公里的大西洋洋面。1 月 31 日，美国总统里根在休斯顿约翰逊航天中心发表了此篇演说，纪念遇难的 7 名宇航员。

◥单词注解◢

sacrifice ['sækrifais] *v.* 牺牲；献出

inspiring [in'spaiəriŋ] *adj.* 激励人心的

boundary ['baundəri] *n.* 界限，范围

departed [di'pɑ:tid] *adj.* 过去的，往昔的

consolation [,kɔnsə'leiʃən] *n.* 安慰，慰藉

◥诵读名句◢

In one crucial moment our exhilaration turned to horror；we waited and watched and tried to make sense of what we had seen.

Today the frontier is space and the boundaries of human knowledge.

Man will continue his conquest of space. To reach out for new goals and ever greater achievements that is the way we shall commemorate our seven Challenger heroes.

The Tribute of Earl Spencer
致戴安娜的悼词

Charles Edward Maurice Spenor
查尔斯·爱德华·莫瑞斯·斯宾塞

I stand before you today the representative of a family in **grief**, in a country in mourning, before a world in shock. We are all united, not only in our desire to pay our respects to Diana, but rather in our need to do so. For such was her extraordinary appeal that the tens of millions of people taking part in this service all over the world via television and radio who never actually met her, feel that they too lost someone close to them in the early hours of Sunday morning. It is a more remarkable tribute to Diana than I can ever hope to offer her today.

Diana was the very **essence** *of compassion, of duty, of style, of beauty.* All over the world she was a symbol of selfless humanity. All over the world, a standard bearer for the rights of the truly downtrodden, a very British girl who transcended nationality. Someone with a natural nobility, who was classless and who proved in the last year that she needed no royal title to continue to generate her particular brand of magic. Today is our chance to say thank you for the way you brightened our lives, even though God granted you but half a life. We will all feel cheated always that you were taken from us so young and yet we must learn to be grateful that you came along at all. *Only now that you are gone do we truly appreciate what we are now without and we want you to know that life without you is very, very difficult.*

...

Your joy for life **transmitted** wherever you took your smile and the sparkle in those unforgettable eyes. Your boundless energy which you could barely contain. But your greatest gift was your intuition and it was a gift you used wisely. This is what underpinned all your other wonderful attributes and if we look to analyse what it was about you that had such a wide appeal we find it in your instinctive feel for what was really important in all our lives.

...

And here we come to another truth about her. For all the status, the glamour, the applause, Diana remained throughout a very insecure person at heart, almost childlike in her desire to do good for others so she could release herself from deep feelings of unworthiness, of which her eating disorders were merely a symptom. *The world sensed this part of her character and cherished her for her* **vulnerability** *whilst admiring her for her honesty.* The last time I saw Diana was on July 1st, her birthday, in London, when typically she was not taking time to celebrate her special day with friends, but was guest of honour at a special charity fund raising evening. She sparkled of course, but I would rather cherish the days I spent with her in March when she came to visit me and my children at my home in South Africa.

I am proud of the fact that, apart from when she was on display meeting President Mandela, we managed to contrive to stop the ever present paparazzi from getting a single picture of her. That meant a lot to her. These were days I will always treasure. It was as if we had been transported back to our childhood, when we spent such an enormous time together—the two youngest in the family.

...

I would like to end by thanking God for the small mercies he has shown us at this dreadful time. For taking Diana at her most beautiful and **radiant** and when she had joy in her private life. Above all we give thanks for the life of a woman I am so proud to be able to call my sister, the unique, the complex, the extraordinary and irreplaceable Diana whose beauty, both internal and external, will never be extinguished from our minds.

今天，我作为一个悲恸的家庭代表，站在你们面前，站在一个受到震惊的世界面前，站在一个举国哀悼的国度里。我们团结在一起，不仅是为了向戴安娜表达我们的敬意，更是因为我们需要这样做。这就是她的魅力，全世界几千万从没有跟她会过面的民众通过电视和收音机参加这次葬礼，他们都感到在这个星期天的早晨失去了一个可亲的人。对戴安娜来说，这个殊荣比我今天希望表达的悼词要强烈和深刻得多。

戴安娜凝聚着怜悯，责任，品格和美丽。在全世界她都是无私人性的象征；是维护被践踏者的权益的旗手，是一个跨越国界的英伦姑娘。她有着自然的高贵，她是无阶级的，并且在她生命的最后一个年头已经证明，她不需要皇室的头衔仍能散发出独特的、属于她的魅力。今天我们有机会对她说，谢谢你点亮了我们的生命，尽管上帝只给予了你半个生命。每当想到你这么年轻就离开了我们，就禁不住有受骗的感觉，但想到你毕竟来过这个世界，我们又应当学会感恩。正是因为你现在的离去才使我们真正地珍惜我们现在没有的。我们想让你知道，没有你的生活是非常非常艰难的。

……

无论在哪里，你的一颦一笑，你那令人难忘的眼神，总把生命的欢愉传给别人。你旺盛不竭的精力好像超出了你身体的蕴涵。但是你最大的天赋是你的直觉，你智慧地运用了这个天赋，而你的天赋又成为你其他美好品质的基础。如果我们仔细地分析，你为什么如此有魅力，我们发现你对于所有人生命中最重要的东西有着本能的直觉。

……

这里我们可以看到她身上的另一个事实。不管社会地位怎么显赫，怎么光彩夺目，人们怎么颂扬，戴安娜内心里始终是一个缺乏安全感的人，她像孩子似的竭力为别人做点好事以解脱她内心深受贬抑、轻视的痛苦，她的厌食也是源于这种忧郁心情的一个病症。全世界都感受到了这一点，并因她的脆弱而珍惜她，同时也因为她的诚实而敬仰她。我最后一次见到戴安娜是在 7 月 1 日——她的生日会上。在伦敦，她像往常一样，并没有跟朋友们一起庆祝这个特别的日子，而是作为嘉宾出席了一个慈善募捐晚会。当然那晚她光彩夺目，但我更愿意回想今年 3 月我们相处的日子，那时她到南非来看我和我的孩子们。

我为之骄傲的一点是，除了她与曼德拉总统的公开会面之外，我们成功地阻止了无处不在的记者的偷拍。这对她非常重要。我将永远怀念那些日子。那些日子就像我们又回到了童年，有很多年我们生活在一起，我和她是家里最小的两个孩子。

……

我要感谢上帝，感谢他在这可怕的时候给予我们的一点慈悲，在戴安娜最美丽、最耀眼的时候，在她的私人生活最快乐的时候将她带走。最后，我要感谢这个我骄傲地称之为姐姐的女性的生命，感谢独特的、难解的、非凡的、无可替代的戴安娜，她的美丽，无论是内在的还是外在的，都将在我们心中永存。

❦导读❧

1997 年 8 月 31 日，36 岁的英国王妃戴安娜在巴黎撞车身亡。全球为之扼腕。一个星期后，戴安娜的弟弟斯宾塞伯爵代表家族发表了这篇发自肺腑的演讲。

❦单词注解❧

grief [gri:f] *n.* 悲痛

essence ['esns] *n.* 精华

transmit [trænz'mit] *v.* 传递

vulnerability [ˌvʌlnərəˈbiləti] *n.* 易受伤，脆弱

radiant ['reidjənt] *adj.* 光芒四射的，美艳的

❦诵读名句❧

Diana was the very essence of compassion, of duty, of style, of beauty.

The world sensed this part of her character and cherished her for her vulnerability whilst admiring her for her honesty.

Only now that you are gone do we truly appreciate what we are now without and we want you to know that life without you is very, very difficult.

The Fringe Benefits of Failure, and the Importance of Imagination

哈利·波特的缔造者 J·k·罗琳：
失败的好处和想象的重要性

J.k.Rowling/J·k·罗琳

I was convinced that the only thing I wanted to do, ever, was to write novels. However, my parents, both of whom came from impoverished backgrounds and neither of whom had been to college, took the view that my overactive imagination was an amusing personal quirk that could never pay a mortgage, or secure a pension.

They had hoped that I would take a vocational degree; I wanted to study English Literature. A compromise was reached that in retrospect satisfied nobody, and I went up to study Modern Languages. Hardly had my parents'car rounded the corner at the end of the road than I ditched German and scuttled off down the Classics corridor. I cannot remember telling my parents that I was studying Classics; they might well have found out for the first time on graduation day. *Of all subjects on this planet, I think they would have been hard put to name one less useful than Greek mythology when it came to securing the keys to an executive bathroom.*

I would like to make it clear, in parenthesis, that I do not blame my parents for their point of view. ...... I cannot criticise my parents for hoping that I would never experience poverty. They had been poor themselves, and I have since been poor, and I quite agree with them that it is not an ennobling experience. Poverty entails fear, and stress, and sometimes depression ; it means a thousand petty humiliations and hardships. Climbing out of poverty by your own efforts, that is indeed something on which to pride yourself, but poverty itself is **romanticised** only by fools.

A mere seven years after my graduation day, I had failed on an epic scale.

An exceptionally short-lived marriage had imploded, and I was jobless, a lone parent, and as poor as it is possible to be in modern Britain, without being homeless. The fears my parents had had for me, and that I had had for myself, had both come to pass, and by every usual standard, I was the biggest failure I knew.

That period of my life was a dark one. I had no idea how far the tunnel extended, and for a long time, any light at the end of it was a hope rather than a reality.

So why do I talk about the benefits of failure? Simply because failure meant a stripping away of the inessential. I stopped pretending to myself that I was anything other than what I was, and began to direct all my energy into finishing the only work that mattered to me. Had I really succeeded at anything else, I might never have found the determination to succeed in the one arena I believed I truly belonged?

I was set free, because my greatest fear had already been realised, and I was still alive, and I still had a daughter whom I **adored**, and I had an old typewriter and a big idea. And so rock bottom became the solid foundation on which I rebuilt my life.

Failure gave me an inner security that I had never attained by passing examinations. Failure taught me things about myself that I could have learned no other way. I discovered that I had a strong will, and more discipline than I had suspected; I also found out that I had friends whose value was truly above rubies.

You will never truly know yourself, or the strength of your relationships, until both have been tested by adversity. Such knowledge is a true gift, for all that it is painfully won, and it has been worth more to me than any qualification I ever earned.

...

The fact that you are graduating from Harvard suggests that you are not very well-acquainted with failure. You might be driven by a fear of failure quite as much as a desire for success. Indeed, your conception of failure might not be too far from the average person's idea of success, so high have you already flown academically.

But how much more are you, Harvard graduates of 2008, likely to touch other people's lives? Your intelligence, your capacity for hard work, the education you have earned and received, give you unique **status**, and unique responsibilities....... That is your privilege, and your burden.

If you choose to use your status and influence to raise your voice on behalf of those who have no voice ; if you choose to **identify** not only with the powerful, but with the powerless ; if you retain the ability to imagine yourself into the lives of those who do not have your advantages, then it will not only be your proud families who celebrate your existence, but thousands and millions of people whose reality you have helped transform for the better.

We do not need magic to change the world, we carry all the power we need inside ourselves already : we have the power to imagine better.

当时，我只想写小说。但是，我的父母出身贫寒，没有受过大学教育。他们认为，我那些不安分的想象力只是一种怪癖，根本不能用来还房贷、挣养老金。

他们希望我再去读个专业学位，而我想去攻读英国文学。最后，达成了一个双方都不甚满意的妥协：我改学外语。可是等到父母一走，我立刻报名学习古典文学。我不记得将这事告诉了父母。他们可能是在毕业典礼那一天才发现的。我想，在全世界的所有专业中，他们也许认为，不会有比研究希腊神话更没用的专业了，连一间宽敞的卫生间都无法换来。

我要申明，我并不责怪父母。他们只是希望我不要过穷日子，我不能批评他们。他们自己很穷，我后来一度也很穷，所以我很理解他们，贫穷是一种悲惨的经历。它带来恐惧、压力、有时还有抑郁。它意味着许许多多的羞辱和艰辛。靠自己的努力摆脱贫穷，确实让人自豪，但是只有傻瓜才会将贫穷本身浪漫化。

我毕业后只过了7年，就失败得一塌糊涂。

短命的婚姻闪电般地破裂，我还失业了，成了一个艰难的单身母亲。除了流浪汉，我是当代英国最穷的人之一，真的一无所有。我父母对我的担忧，我对自己的担忧，都变成了现实。用平常人的标准，我是我所知道的最失败的人。

那段日子是我生命中的黑暗岁月。我不知道还要在黑暗中走多久，很长一段时间中，我有的只是希望，而不是现实。

为什么我说失败是有好处的？因为失败将那些非本质的东西都剥离了。我不再伪装自己，我找到了真正的自己，我将自己所有的精力都投入到完成对我来说最重要的唯一一项工作中去了。要是我以前在其他地方成功了，那么我也许永远不会决心投身于这个我自认为真正属于我的领域。

我自由了，因为我最大的恐惧已经成为现实，而我却还依然活着，依然有一个深爱着的女儿，我还有一台旧打字机和一个大大的梦想。我生命中最低的低点，成为我重建生活的坚实基础。

失败使我的内心产生了一种安全感，以前通过考试也没有的安全感。失败让我看清自己，以前我从没认识到自己是这样的。我发现，我比自己以为的，有更强的意志和决心。我还发现，我有一些比宝石还珍贵的朋友。

只有到逆境来临的那一天，你才会真正了解你自己，了解你结识的人。这种了解是真正的财富，虽然是用痛苦换来的，但是它比我以前得到的任何证书都有用。

……

你们是哈佛毕业生的这个事实，说明你们并不很了解失败。你们也许极其渴望成功，所以非常害怕失败。说实话，你们眼中的失败，很可能就是普通人眼中的成功，毕竟你们在学业上已经很成功了。

但是，所有各位，哈佛大学 2008 届毕业生，你们对其他人的生活了解多少？你们的智慧、你们的能力、你们所受的教育，给了你们独一无二的优势，也给了你们独一无二的责任……你们的优势就是你们的责任。

你们要用自己的地位和影响，为那些被忽略的人们说话；你们不仅要看到那些有权有势者，也要看到那些无权无势者；你们要学会设想，那些条件不如你们的人们是如何生活的；那样的话，不仅你们的亲人们将为你们感到自豪，而且千千万万的人们将因为你们的帮助而生活得更好。

我们不需要改变世界的魔法，我们自己就有这样的力量：那就是我们一直在梦想着的，让这个世界变得更美好。

实战提升
Practising & Exercise

✑导读✑

2008 年 6 月 5 日，《哈里·波特》小说作者、英国女作家 J·K·罗琳来到哈佛并发表演讲。在演讲中，她几乎没有谈到哈里·波特，而是说了年轻时的一些经历。虽然 J·K·罗琳现在是仅次于女王的最富有的女人，但是她曾经有一段非常艰辛的日子，30 岁了，还差点流落街头。她更看重的是，自己从这段经历中学到的东西。

✑单词注解✑

executive [igˈzekjutiv] *adj.* 执行的；实施的；经营管理的

romanticise [rəʊˈmæntisaiz] *v.* (使) 浪漫化；(使) 传奇化

adore [əˈdɔː] *v.* 崇拜，崇敬；敬重

status [ˈsteitəs] *n.* 地位，身份

identify [aiˈdentifai] *v.* 确认；识别；鉴定

✑诵读名句✑

Of all subjects on this planet, I think they would have been hard put to name one less useful than Greek mythology when it came to securing the keys to an executive bathroom.

An exceptionally short-lived marriage had imploded, and I was jobless, a lone parent, and as poor as it is possible to be in modern Britain, without being homeless.

The fact that you are graduating from Harvard suggests that you are not very well-acquainted with failure.

A Whisper of Aids
艾滋病者私语

Mary Fisher/玛丽·费雪

In the context of an election year, I ask you, here in this great hall, or listening in the quiet of your home, to recognize that AIDS virus is not a political creature. It does not care whether you are Democrat or Republican; it does not ask whether you are black or white, male or female, gay or straight, young or old.

Tonight, I represent an AIDS community whose members have been reluctantly **drafted** from every segment of American society. Though I am white and a mother, I am one with a black infant struggling with tubes in a Philadelphia hospital. Though I am female and contracted this disease in marriage and enjoy the warm support of my family, I am one with the lonely gay man sheltering a flickering candle from the cold wind of his family's rejection.

This is not a distant threat. It is a present danger. The rate of infection is increasing fastest among women and children. Largely unknown a decade ago, AIDS is the third leading killer of young adult Americans today. But it won't be third for long, because unlike other diseases, this one travels. Adolescents don't give each other cancer or heart disease because they believe they are in love, but HIV is different ; and we have helped it along. We have killed each other with our ignorance, our prejudice, and our silence.

We may take refuge in our stereotypes, but we cannot hide there long, because HIV asks only one thing of those it attacks. Are you human? And this is the right question. Are you human? Because people with HIV have not entered some alien state of being. They are human. They have not earned cruelty, and they do not deserve meanness. They don't benefit from being isolated or treated as **outcasts**. Each of them is exactly what God made : a person ; not evil, deserving of our judgment ; not victims, longing for our pity—people, ready for support and worthy of compassion.

...

My father has devoted much of his lifetime guarding against another **holocaust**. He is part of the generation who heard Pastor Nemoellor come out of the Nazi death camps to say, "They came after the Jews, and I was not a Jew, so, I did not protest. They came after the trade unionists, and I was not a trade unionist, so, I did not protest. Then they came after the Roman Catholics, and I was not a Roman Catholic, so, I did not protest. Then they came after me, and there was no one left to protest."

The lesson history teaches is this : If you believe you are safe, you are at risk. If you do not see this killer stalking your children, look again. There is no family or community, no race or religion, no place left in America that is safe. Until we genuinely embrace this message, we are a nation at risk.

...

Someday our children will be grown. My son Max, now four, will take the measure of his mother. My son Zachary, now two, will sort through his memories. I may not be here to hear their judgments, but I know already what I hope they are. I want my children to know that their mother was not a victim. She was a messenger. I do not want them to think, as I once did, that courage is the absence of fear. I want them to know that courage is the strength to act wisely when most we are afraid. I want them to have the courage to step forward when called by their nation or their Party and give leadership, no matter what the personal cost.

I ask no more of you than I ask of myself or of my children. To the millions of you who are grieving, who are frightened, who have suffered the ravages of AIDS firsthand : Have courage, and you will find support. To the millions who are strong, I issue the **plea** : Set aside prejudice and politics to make room for compassion and sound policy.

...

To all within the sound of my voice, I appeal : Learn with me the lessons of history and of grace, so my children will not be afraid to say the word "AIDS" when I am gone. Then, their children and yours may not need to whisper it at all.

God bless the children, and God bless us all.

Good night.

借此大选年之机，我希望在座的所有人，以及安坐在家中的所有听众，都能够认识到艾滋病病毒不是一种政治产物，它不管你是民主党人还是共和党人；也不管你是黑人还是白人，男性还是女性，同性恋者还是异性恋者，青年人还是老年人。

今天晚上，我代表的是一个艾滋病者团体。那些无奈地成为这个团体成员的人们，来自美国社会的各个领域。我是一名白人母亲，但同时也代表费城医院里那些正与输液管抗争的黑人婴儿。我是一名在婚后感染了艾滋病毒的女性，家人的支持让我倍感温暖；但我同时也代表那些孤独的同性恋男子，他们在家人排斥的冷风下，苦苦守护着自己那摇曳飘忽的生命之火。

艾滋病不是遥远的威胁，而是眼前的危险。而妇女和儿童的感染率上升得最快。十年前，大多数人还没有听说过艾滋病，现在，它已经是美国年轻人群的第三大杀手了。而且它不会一直停留在第三的位置上，因为与其他疾病不同，艾滋病是具有传染性的。年轻人不会因为相爱而互相传染癌症或者心脏病，但艾滋病毒不同，我们助长了它的传播。我们因为自己的无知、偏见和缄默而相互伤害。

我们可以用老一套方法来逃避，但却躲避不了多久。因为艾滋病毒在袭击目标的时候只考虑一点：你是不是人类？这个问题很有意义。你是不是人类？艾滋病毒携带者并没有变成什么奇异物种。他们仍是人类。他们并没有变得更凶残，不应该因此而遭受刻薄的对待。孤立和鄙视对他们没有任何的帮助。他们中的每一个人都是上帝创造的人，不是等候我们判决的魔鬼，也不是渴盼我们怜悯的受害者——他们都是人，希望得到大家的支持，也值得大家的同情。

……

我父亲把生命的大部分时间贡献给了与另一场屠戮的抗争。他们那一代人都听过内莫洛神父的那段话。从纳粹集中营出来以后，神父说："他们追捕犹太人，我不是犹太人，所以，我没有抗议。他们追捕工会主义者，我不是工会主义者，所以，我没有抗议。接着，他们追捕罗马天主教徒，我不是罗马天主教徒，所以，我没有抗议。再接下来，他们追捕我，这时，已经没有可以抗议的人了。

历史的教训告诉我们：如果你认为自己是安全的，那么你已身处险境。如果你没有发现这个杀手正悄悄地走近你的孩子，那么请再仔细看一眼。在美国，没有任何一个家庭或社区，没有任何一个种族或宗教，没有任何一个地方，是安全的了。在我们能够真正确信这一点之前，我们的国家都处境危险。

……

终有一天，我们的孩子会长大成人。我四岁的儿子马克斯，将会审视他的母亲。我两岁的儿子扎卡里，也会搜寻关于母亲的记忆。我也许无法听到他们的评价了，但我已经知道我希望得到怎样的评价。我希望孩子们明白，他们的母亲并不是一个受害者，而是一个信使。我希望他们不会像我从前那样，认为勇气等于无所畏惧。我希望他们明白，真正的勇气，是一种能在最害怕的时候采取明智行为的能力。我希望他们无论付出什么样的代价都要鼓起勇气继续前进直到政府或政党重视并给予地位。

我对你们的期望与我对自己及我的孩子们的期望是一样的。数以百万计因直接受到艾滋病侵害而正伤心恐惧的人们：请拿出勇气来吧，你们一定会得到支持的。而那些广大的身体健康的人们，我请求你们：把偏见和政治成见放在一旁吧，好为同情心和明智的政策预留出空间。

......

我向所有能听见我的声音的人们呼吁：请和我一起吸取历史的教训，学会感恩。这样，当我去世之后，我的孩子们就不会害怕提及"艾滋病"这个字眼。将来，他们的孩子，你们大家的孩子，都无需再低声细语地说出这个字眼。

愿上帝保佑孩子们，愿上帝保佑我们每一个人。

晚安。

❧导读❧

1981 年，美国首先甄别出了艾滋病毒。艾滋病现已蔓延到了美国各地以及社会的各个阶层。有人认为美国有一百多万人是艾滋病毒携带者，并且已经有 50 多万人在感染艾滋病毒后死亡。目前对艾滋病还没有有效的治疗方法，但全人类都应该协力阻止艾滋病毒的扩散，对艾滋病患者给予关爱。

❧单词注解❧

draft [drɑːft] *v.* 挑选，征兵

outcast ['autkɑːst] *n.* 被驱逐者，流浪者

holocaust ['hɔləkɔːst] *n.* 大毁灭，大屠杀

plea [pliː] *n.* 恳求，请求，辩解

❧诵读名句❧

I would never have asked to be HIV positive, but I believe that in all things there is a purpose；and I stand before you and before the nation gladly.

This is not a distant threat. It is a present danger.

To all within the sound of my voice, I appeal：Learn with me the lessons of history and of grace, so my children will not be afraid to say the word "AIDS" when I am gone.

For the Children

奥黛丽·赫本：为了孩子们

Audrey Hepburn/奥黛丽·赫本

I must say that up until a year ago, before I was given the great privilege of becoming a volunteer for UNICEF, I used to be overwhelmed by a sense of desperation and helplessness when watching television and reading about the misery of the developing world's children and their mothers. If I feel less helpless today, it is because I have seen what is being done by UNICEF and many other marvelous organizations and agencies, by the churches, by governments and most of all, with very little help, by people themselves.

The effects of the monstrous burden of debt have made the poor even poorer and have fallen most heavily on the neediest, and those whom it has damaged the most have been women and children. We must do more about the alarming state in which the children in the developing world are only just surviving, especially when we know that the finances needed are minimal compared to the global **expenditure** of this world ; when we know that less than half of one percent of today's world economy would be the total required to eradicate the worst aspects of poverty and would meet their basic human needs over the next 10 years. In other words, there is no deficit in human resources. The deficit is in human will.

The question I am most frequently asked is : "What do you really do for UNICEF?" Clearly, my task is to inform, to create awareness of the needs of children. To fully understand the problems of the state of the world's children, it would be nice to be an expert on education, economics, politics, religions, traditions and cultures. I am none of these things, but I am a mother.

There is, unhappily, a need for great **advocacy** for children—children haunted by undernourishment, disease and death, and you don't have to be a financial whiz to look into so many little faces with diseases, glazed eyes to know that this is the result of critical malnutrition. One of the worst symptoms of which is Vitamin A **deficiency** that causes corneal lesions resulting in partial or total blindness followed within a few weeks by death. Every year there are as many as 500, 000 such cases in countries like Indonesia, Bangladesh, India, the Philippines, and Ethiopia. Today there are in fact millions of children at risk of going blind. Little wonder that I and many other UNICEF volunteers travel the world to raise funds before it is too late, but also to raise awareness and to combat a different kind of darkness—a darkness people find themselves in through lack of information on how easy it is to reach out and help these children.

I have known UNICEF a long time. For almost 45 years ago, I was one of the tens of thousands of starving children in war-ravaged Europe to receive aid from UNICEF immediately after our liberation that freed us from hunger, repression and constant violence, when we were reduced to near total poverty as is the developing world today. For it is poverty that is at the root of all their suffering—the not having—not having the means to help themselves. That is what UNICEF is all about, helping people to help themselves. Giving them the aid to develop, thereby allowing them to become self-reliant and live in dignity.

Unlike droughts or floods or earthquakes, the tragedy of poverty cannot easily be captured by the media and brought to the attention of the world-wide public. It is happening not in any one particular place, but in slums and shanties and neglected rural communities across two continents. It is happening not at any one particular time, but over long years of increasing poverty which have not been featured in the nightly news but which have changed the lives of many millions of people.

...

UNICEF's business is children, not the workings of the international economy. In its every-day work in over 100 developing nations UNICEF is brought up against a face of today's international economic problems which is not seen in the corridors of financial power, not reflected in the statistics of debt service ratios, not seated at the conference tables of debt negotiations. It is in the face of a child. It is the young child whose growing mind and body is susceptible to permanent damage from even temporary **deprivation**. The human brain and body are formed within the first five years of life and there is no second chance. It is the young child whose individual development today and whose social contribution tomorrow are being shaped by the economics of now. It is the young child who is paying the highest of all prices.

...

There is so much we cannot do. We cannot give the children back their parents，but we can return to them the most basic of human rights，the right to health，to tenderness，to life. Thank you.

就在一年前，当我有幸成为联合国儿童基金会的一名志愿者之前，每当在电视上或者报纸上看到发展中国家的那些母亲和儿童遭遇的、令人难以置信的悲剧时，我常常会感到特别的

绝望和无助。现在当我再看到这样的故事时，已经觉得不那么无助了。因为现在我知道联合国儿童基金会以及另外一些组织、机构、教会、政府都在努力帮助他们，而更多时候，他们自己在以自己微薄的力量努力进行着自助。

在发展中国家，沉重的债务负担使得穷人更加贫困，而最贫困的人负担则最重。受伤害最大的莫过于妇女和儿童。我们必须为那些处于危险状态的发展中国家的儿童们做更多的事情，他们中的一些人现在处于仅仅能够活命的状况。尤其是我们要明白这样一个事实——他们所需的财力上的帮助相对于全世界的花销来说，只是小小的一部分；我们也明白，拿出不到世界经济0.5%的力量，就足以根除地球上最贫穷的情况，能让这些人们在今后十年获得基本的生存需求。换句话说，人类的资源不存在不充足的问题，不充足的是人们的意愿。

人们最常问我的一个问题是：你究竟为联合国儿童基金会做了些什么？很明显，我的职责是通过自己的努力，使社会了解和意识到儿童的需要。如果我是一位教育家、经济学家、政治家、宗教学家或者文化专家的话，我将能更深刻地了解当今世界上的儿童问题。尽管我不是上述任何一种专家，但是，我是一位母亲。

非常遗憾的是，现在儿童事业仍需要很大的支持，许多儿童处在营养不良、疾病和死亡的威胁之中。你不用知道确切的数字，只要看看那些瘦小的脸庞和生病中的呆滞的眼神，你就会明白他们生活在怎样的处境中。这些都是严重营养不良病症的表现。导致这种病最重要的因素就是缺乏维生素A，这会导致眼角膜受损甚至于部分或完全失明，几周之内可能就会死去。在印度尼西亚、孟加拉国、印度、菲律宾和埃塞俄比亚等国，每年会发生 50 万之多的此类病例。今天，实际上有上百万的儿童正在遭受失明的威胁。毫无疑问，我和基金会的其他志愿者在全世界旅行，不只是尽最大力量寻求社会对基金会的资金支持，同时也在向那些地区的人们普及最基本的医疗知识，来抗击另一种黑暗，而这种儿童们被困其中的黑暗正是因为人们缺少必要的救助常识导致的。

我很久之前就知道联合国儿童基金会。大约 45 年前，在刚刚被战火蹂躏完的欧洲，我是几万名饥饿的儿童中的一员，需要联合国儿童基金会的援助。战争结束，我们从饥饿、压迫和持久的暴力中解脱了出来。但是我们当时几乎赤贫，就像现在发展中国家那样。贫穷是一切苦难的根源，贫穷导致缺乏帮助自己的手段。这就是联合国儿童基金会要做的：使人们拥有能够帮助自己的能力，给予他们发展的援助，借此使他们能够自立自尊地活着。

与干旱、洪水或者地震等自然灾害不同，贫困并不会常常被媒体关注，因此在世界范围内也得不到社会的注意。贫穷问题不只在特定的地方发生，它在两个大陆的贫民窟、棚户区和被忽视的农村地区广泛地存在。贫穷问题也不只在特定的时间发生，很多年以来，贫困人口一直持续增长。尽管贫困问题并没有上电视台的晚间新闻，但是却威胁着上百万人的生存。

......

联合国儿童基金会的工作是为了儿童，而不是为了国际经济。联合国儿童基金会正在全球超过 100 个发展中国家开展工作。在这些工作中，联合国儿童基金会遇到了一些国际经济问题，这些问题不会在金融巨子的走廊中看到，不会在债券汇率的数据中反映出来，也不会在债务谈判桌上发现，这些问题出现在儿童的面庞上。这些问题包括：儿童们正在发育的身心正在受到哪怕是暂时性的贫困的伤害。人类大脑和身体的发育情况，在 5 岁之前就奠定了基础，而且不会有第二次发育的机会。儿童们今天的个人发展以及明天对于社会的贡献，都在隐性地被当前的经济情况所塑造。儿童们也正在付出最昂贵的代价。

……

有很多事情我们的确无能为力。我们无法使孩子们辞世的父母重返他们的身边，但我们可以使孩子们享受人权的基本保障，使他们能够拥有健康和生命的权利，享受人类的关爱。

谢谢！

❧导读❧

1989 年 6 月 13 日，奥黛丽发表了这篇演说。晚年的奥黛丽与联合国儿童基金会（UNICEF）紧密相连。她不愿让纠缠自己一生的忧郁再降临到下一代的身上。索马里是奥黛丽为 UNICEF 服务的最后一站。她和助手等了差不多一年时间，才募到足够多的捐款。1991 年的索马里之行成为奥黛丽的天鹅之歌。她成功地进去了，却在旅途中突感腹痛如绞。被送到洛杉矶医院后，医生确诊她患有结肠癌。到了第二年，奥黛丽已经虚弱到无法亲自领取颁给她的电影演员终生成就奖。特雷莎修女得知奥黛丽病情凶险后，号召所有修女彻夜为她祈祷。

❧单词注解❧

expenditure [iks'penditʃə] *n.* 支出，开支，费用

advocacy ['ædvəkəsi] *n.* 主张，提倡

deficiency [di'fiʃənsi] *n.* 缺乏，匮乏

deprivation [ˌdepri'veiʃən] *n.* 剥夺，失去

❧诵读名句❧

The effects of the monstrous burden of debt have made the poor even poorer and have fallen most heavily on the neediest, and those whom it has damaged the most have been women and children.

Unlike droughts or floods or earthquakes, the tragedy of poverty cannot easily be captured by the media and brought to the attention of the world-wide public.

There is so much we cannot do.

Blowing in the Wind
鲍勃·迪伦：随风而飘

Bob Dylan/鲍勃·迪伦

How many roads must a man walk down

Before you call him a man?

How many seas must a white dove sail

Before she sleeps in the sand?

How many times must the cannon balls fly

Before they're forever banned?

The answer，my friend，is **blowing** in the wind，

The answer is blowing in the wind.

How many times must a man look up

Before he can see the sky?

How many ears must one man have

Before he can hear people cry?

How many deaths will it take till he knows

That too many people have died?

The answer, my friend, is blowing in the wind,

The answer is blowing in the wind.

How many years can a mountain **exist**

Before it's washed to the sea?

How many years can some people exist

Before they're allowed to be free?

How many times can a man turn his head,

Pretending he just doesn't see?

The answer, my friend, is blowing in the wind,

The answer is blowing in the wind.

一个男人要走过多少路，

才能称他是男子汉？

一只白鸽要飞过多少海里，

才能在沙丘安眠？

炮弹要在天空飞翔多少次，

才能永远销声匿迹？

这答案，我的朋友，正随风而飘，

这答案正随风而飘。

一个人要仰望多少次，

才能看到蓝天？

一个人要有多少只耳朵，

才能听到人们的哭泣？

要有多少死亡才能使他了解，

已有太多的人死去？

这答案，我的朋友，正随风而飘，

这答案正随风而飘。

一座山要矗立多少年，

才能被海水冲没？

一些人要生存多少年，

才能被给予自由？

一个人要回头多少次，

才不会假装他什么都没看见？

这答案，我的朋友，正随风而飘，

这答案正随风而飘。

导读

鲍勃·迪伦，1941 年生于明尼苏达州的德卢斯，在明尼苏达大学学习一年后，他登上了音乐舞台。他被公认为 20 世纪 60 年代最有影响的歌手，他创作过反战歌曲、爱情歌曲、民歌和摇滚歌曲，他的歌声影响了几代年轻人。《随风而飘》是美国民权运动的非正式颂歌，在反越战运动中也很流行。

单词注解

blow [bləu] *v.* 吹，刮

exist [ig'zist] *v.* 生存；生活

pretend [pri'tend] *v.* 佯装；假装

诵读名句

How many roads must a man walk down

Before you call him a man?

How many times must the cannon balls fly

Before they're forever banned?

How many ears must one man have

Before he can hear people cry?

Heal the Kids
迈克尔·杰克逊：拯救儿童

Michael Jackson/迈克尔·杰克逊

Thank you, thank you dear friends, from the bottom of my heart, for such a loving and spirited welcome, and thank you, Mr. President, for your kind invitation to me which I am so honored to accept. I also want to express a special thanks to you Shmuley, who for 11 years served as Rabbi here at Oxford. You and I have been working so hard to form Heal the Kids, as well as writing our book about childlike **qualities**, and in all of our efforts you have been such a supportive and loving friend. And I would also like to thank Toba Friedman, our director of operations at Heal the Kids, who is returning tonight to the alma mater where she served as a Marshall Scholar, as well as Marilyn Piels, another central member of our Heal the Kids team.

...

Tonight, I come before you less as an icon of pop, and more as an icon of a generation, a generation that no longer knows what it means to be children.

...

Today, it's a universal calamity, a global catastrophe. Childhood has become the great casualty of modern-day living. All around us we are producing scores of kids who have not had the joy, who have not been accorded the right, who have not been allowed the freedom, or knowing what it's like to be a kid. Today children are constantly encouraged to grow up faster, as if this period known as childhood is a burdensome stage, to be endured and ushered through, as **swiftly** as possible. And on that subject, I am certainly one of the world's greatest experts. Ours is a generation that has witnessed the abrogation of the parent-child covenant.

...

About 12 years ago, when I was just about to start my Not-Bad tour, a little boy came with his parents to visit me at home in California. He was dying of cancer and he told me how much he loved my music and me. His parents told me that he wasn't going to live, that any day he could just go, and I said to him : "Look, I am going to be coming to your town in Kansas to open my tour in three months. I want you to come to the show. I am going to give you this jacket that I wore in one of my videos." His eyes lit up and he said : "You are gonna give it to me?" I said "Yeah, but you have to promise that you will wear it to the show." I was trying to make him hold on. I said : "When you come to the show I want to see you in this jacket and in this glove" and I gave him one of my rhinestone gloves. I never usually give the rhinestone gloves away. And he was just in heaven. But maybe he was too close to heaven, because when I came to his town, he had already died, and they had buried him in the glove and jacket. He was just 10 years old. God knows, I know, that he tried his best to hold on. But at least when he died, he knew that he was loved, not only by his parents, but even by me, a near stranger, I also loved him. And with all of that love he knew that he didn't come into this world alone, and he certainly didn't leave it alone.

...

Ladies and gentlemen, love is the human family's most precious legacy, its richest bequest, its golden **inheritance**. And it is a treasure that is handed down from one generation to another. Previous ages may not have had the wealth we enjoy. Their houses may have lacked electricity, and they squeezed their many kids into small houses without central heating. But those homes had no darkness, nor were they cold. They were lit bright with the glow of love and they were warmed snugly by the very heat of the human heart. Parents, undistracted by the lust for luxury and status, accorded their children primacy in their lives.

...

I would therefore like to propose tonight that we install in every home a Children's Universal Bill of Rights, the tenets as follows:

The right to be loved, without having to earn it;

The right to be protected, without having to deserve it;

The right to feel valuable, even if you came into the world

with nothing ;

The right to be listened to without having to be interesting ;

The right to be read a bedtime story without having to compete with the evening news or EastEnders ;

The right to an education without having to dodge bullets at schools ;

The right to be thought of as adorable even if you have a face that only a mother could love.

Friends, the foundation of all human knowledge, the beginning of human consciousness, must be that each and every one of us is an object of love. Before you know if you have red hair or brown, before you know if you are black or white, before you know of what religion you are a part, you have to know that you are loved.

If you enter this world knowing you are loved and you leave this world knowing the same, then everything that happens in-between can he dealt with. A professor may degrade you, but you will not feel **degraded** ; a boss may crush you, but you will not be crushed ; a corporate gladiator might vanquish you, but you will still triumph. How could any of them truly prevail in pulling you down? For you know that you are an object worthy of love. The rest is just packaging. But if you don't have that memory of being loved, you are condemned to search the world for something to fill you up. But no matter how much money you make or how famous you become, you will still fell empty.

What you are really searching for is unconditional love and unqualified acceptance. And that was the one thing that was denied to you at birth. Friends, let me paint a picture for you. Here is a typical day in America—six youths under the age of 20 will commit suicide；12 children under the age of 20 will die from firearms—remember this is a day, not a year. Three hundred and ninety-nine kids will be arrested for drug abuse, and 1,352 babies will be born to teen mothers. This is happening in one of the richest and most developed countries in the history of the world. Yes, in my country there is an **epidemic** of violence that parallels no other industrialized nation. These are the ways young people in America express their hurt and their anger. But I don't think that there is not the same pain and anguish among their counterparts in the UK. Studies in this country show that every single hour, three teenagers in the UK inflict harm upon themselves, often by cutting or burning their bodies or taking an overdose. This is now they have chosen to cope with the pain of neglect and emotional agony.

In Britain, as many as 20% of families will only sit down and have dinner together once a year. Once a year! And what about the time-honored tradition of reading your kid a bedtime story? Research from the 1980s showed that children who are read to, had far greater literacy and significantly outperformed their peers at school. And yet, less than 33% of British children aged two to eight have a regular bedtime story read to them. You may not think much of that until you take into account that 75% of their parents did have that bedtime story when they were at the same age. Clearly, we do not have to ask ourselves where all of this pain, anger and **violent** behavior come from. It is self-evident that children are thundering against the neglect, quaking against the indifference and crying out just to be noticed. The various children protection agencies in the US say that millions of children are victims of maltreatment in the form of neglect, in the average year. Yes, neglect. *In rich homes, privileged homes, they are wired to the hilt with every electronic gadget.* Homes where parents come back, but they're not really at home, because their heads are still at the office. And their kids? Well, their kids just make do with whatever emotional crumbs they get. And you don't get much from endless TV, computer games and videos. These hard, cold numbers which for me, wrench the soul and shake the spirit, should indicate to you why I have devoted so much of my time and resources into making our new Heal the Kids initiative a colossal success. Our goal is simple—to recreate the parent and child bond, to renew its promise and to light the way forward for all the beautiful children who are destined one day to walk this earth. But since this is my first public lecture, and you have so warmly welcomed me into your hearts, I feel that I want to tell you more. We each have our own story, and in that sense statistics can become personal. They say that parenting is like dancing. You take one step, your child takes another. I have discovered that getting parents to rededicate themselves to their children is only half the story. The other half is preparing the children to reaccept their parents.

　　谢谢，谢谢各位亲爱的朋友，对大家如此热烈的欢迎，我由衷地表示感谢。谢谢主席，对您的盛意邀请，我感到万分荣幸。同时，我特别地感谢犹太教律法家史马里，感谢您 11 年来在牛津大学所做的工作。您和我一起努力建立"拯救儿童"这个机构，就如我们写关于儿童素质的书一样辛苦，但您自始至终都如朋友一样给了我莫大的支持和关爱。我还要感谢"治愈儿童之家"的理事托巴·弗里德曼，她将于今晚返回母校。她曾经作为马歇尔计划中的一个学者在这里工作过。当然还要感谢我们"治愈儿童之家"的另一位核心成员玛里琳·皮耶尔。

　　……

　　今晚，我不想以一个流行偶像的身份出现在大家面前，我更愿意代表一代人，一代不了解作为孩子有什么意义的见证人站在这里。

　　……

　　现在，这已经成为全世界的灾难。人的童年已经成了现代生活的巨大的牺牲品。我们使周围的许多孩子失去了欢乐，没有享受到他们相应的权利，孩子们不曾获得自由，而我们还自以为是地认为孩子就应该是这样的。现在，大人们经常鼓励孩子们成长得快一些，好像这个叫做童年的时代是一个累赘的人生阶段，并且我们不厌其烦地想着法儿让它尽可能地快些结束。在这个问题上，我无疑是世界上最专业的人士之一了。我们这一代亲历了废除亲子盟约。

......

大概 12 年前，在我开始我的"真棒"巡演之际，一个小男孩和他的父母一起来到我在加利福尼亚的家看我。当时他正遭受着癌症的威胁。他告诉我他非常喜欢我和我的音乐。他的父母告诉我他活不了多久了，说不定哪一天就会离开。我就对他说："你瞧，3 个月之后我就要到你住的城市堪萨斯州去，开始我的巡回演出；我希望你能来看我的演出；我还要送给你一件我在一部录影带里穿过的夹克。"他眼睛一亮，说："你要把它送给我？"我说："是的，不过你必须答应我穿着它来看我的演出。"我想尽力让他坚持住，就对他说："我希望在我的演唱会上看见你穿着这件夹克，戴着这只手套。"于是，我又送了一只镶着莱茵石的手套给他。一般来说，我绝不会将我的莱茵石手套送人。但他就要去天堂了。也许他离天堂实在太近，我到他的城市时，他已经走了。人们埋葬他时，给他穿上那件夹克并戴上了那只手套。他只有 10 岁。上帝知道，我知道，他曾经多么努力地坚持活下去。但至少在他离开时，他知道自己是被深爱着的，不仅被他的父母深爱着，甚至还被几乎是陌生人的我深爱着。拥有了这些爱，他知道他不是孤独地来到这个世界，也不是孤独地离开的。

......

女士们，先生们，爱是人类家庭中最珍贵的财产，是最贵重的馈赠，是最无价的传统，是我们应该代代相传的财富。以前，我们或许没有现在富有，房子里可能没有电，很多孩子挤在没有取暖设施的狭小房间里。但这些家庭里没有黑暗，也没有寒冷。他们点燃了爱之光，贴紧的心让他们感到了温暖。父母不会为各种享受和欲望分心，他们将孩子作为生活中最重要的东西。

......

为此，我建议今晚我们为每个家庭建立一部儿童权利条约，这些条例如下：

不必付出就可以享受被爱的权利

不必乞求就可享有被保护的权利；

即使来到这个世界时一无所有，也要有被重视的权利；

即使不引人注目也有被倾听的权利；

不需要与晚间新闻和电视剧斗争就能在晚上睡觉前听故事的权利；

不需要躲避子弹就可以在学校受教育的权利；

哪怕你长了个只有妈妈才会爱的脸蛋，也要有被人尊重的权利。

朋友们，人类所有知识的创立与人类意识的萌发必然需要我们每一个人都成为被爱的对象。在你知道自己的头发是红色还是棕色，弄清自己是白人还是黑人，搞明白自己信仰哪个宗教之前，你应该首先知道自己是被爱着的。

如果你降临或离开这个世界时都感觉到被爱，那么你就能应对在这期间所发生的任何事情了。教授可能给你打低分，可你不认为自己应该得低分；老板可能排挤你，可你不会被排挤掉；公司里的对手可能会击败你，可你却仍能胜利。他们怎么能真正战胜你击倒你呢？因为你知道你是值得被爱的，其他的只是一层包装罢了。可是，如果你没有被爱的记忆，那么你就无法在这个世上找到能够让你感到充实的东西。无论你多有钱，无论你多么有名，你仍然会觉得空虚。

你真正寻找的只是无条件的爱和完全的包容。而这些在你们诞生时就被拒绝给予。朋友们，让我给大家描述一下这样的情景，在美国每天都有 6 个不满 20 岁的青年自杀，12 个 20 岁以下的孩子死在枪口之下。请注意这是一天，而不是一年。另外还有 399 个年轻人因为服用毒品而被捕，1，352 个婴儿被十几岁的妈妈生下来；这些都发生在这个世界上最富有、最发达的国家。是的，在我的国家里充斥着暴力，在这一方面，其他的工业化国家望尘莫及。而这只是美国年轻人宣泄自己所受的伤害和愤怒的途径。那么，难道英国就没有同样的烦恼痛苦吗？调查表明英国每小时都会有 3 个十几岁的孩子自残，经常割烫自己的身体或者服用过量药剂。现在这是他们用来发泄被忽视的痛苦和烦恼情绪的方法。

在英国，20% 的家庭一年只能聚在一起吃一次晚饭，一年才一次！昔日在孩子睡前讲故事的优良传统到哪儿去了？20 世纪 80 年代的研究发现，晚上睡前听故事的孩子比在校学习的同龄人有更强的识读能力和动手能力。然而，在英国只有不到 33% 的 2~8 岁的孩子享受家长固定地在晚上睡前讲故事的待遇。如果我们意识到，75% 的家长在他们的那个年龄在睡前都是听着故事成长起来的；那么大家可能对此就不会如此漠然了。显然，我们没有问过自己这些痛苦、愤怒和暴力从何而来。不言而喻，孩子们憎恨被忽略，害怕受冷漠，他们强烈要求得到父母的关注。在美国，各个儿童保护机构表明，平均每年，有千万儿童成为了被忽视和受冷漠的受害者。是的，是受到了忽视。在富有的家庭和拥有特权的家庭里成长的孩子，完全受到了现代电子用品的束缚。父母回到家中，可是他们的心并没有真正回家，他们仍然想着办公室的事情。那么孩子们呢？啊，他们只好以他们所能得到的一些感情的碎屑勉强过活吧。在无休止的电视、电脑游戏和录像带上又能得到多少呢！这些扭曲灵魂、震撼心灵的又冷又硬的数字正好可以让大家明白，我为什么要花这么多时间和精力来支援新的一届"治愈儿童之家"，并努力促使这项事业获得巨大成功。我们的目的很简单，就是要重建父母儿女之间的融洽关系，重新许下我们的承诺，去点亮所有有一天会来到这个世界的美丽孩子们前进的道路。由于这是我第一次公开演讲，而你们能真心欢迎我，所以我想和你们聊很多。我们每个人都有自己的故事，因此从这种意义上讲，那些统计数字就变得与我们个人相关了。常言道，抚养孩子就像跳舞。你走一步，你的孩子跟一步。而我发觉养育孩子时，你对孩子的付出只是事情的一半，而另一半就是让孩子重新接受父母。

🍃导读🍃

2001 年 3 月 6 日晚，迈克尔·杰克逊在牛津大学作了一场慈善演讲。目的是为了宣传由他捐资设立的儿童慈善机构"治愈儿童之家"。他通过恳切和真诚的言语传达着一个愿望，那就是唤起更多的人们对儿童的关爱，并将爱传达给所有的孩子。迈克尔·杰克逊很少做公开演讲，因此这是一场难得的演讲。这篇演讲语言精美而不失真诚，充满劝慰的话语又不乏醒世之辞。

🍃单词注解🍃

quality ['kwɔliti] *n.* 质，质量

swiftly [swiftli] *adv.* 迅速地，敏捷地

inheritance [in'heritəns] *n.* 继承物；遗产；遗赠

degraded [di'greidid] *adj.* 被降级职的；堕落的；已失名誉的

epidemic [,epi'demik] *adj.* 流行性，传染的

violent ['vaiələnt] *adj.* 激烈的；猛烈的；强烈的

🍃诵读名句🍃

Tonight, I come before you less as an icon of pop, and more as an icon of a generation, a generation that no longer knows what it means to be children.

What you are really searching for is unconditional love and unqualified acceptance. And that was the one thing that was denied to you at birth.

In rich homes, privileged homes, they are wired to the hilt with every electronic gadget.

光辉的信念
Glorious Mind

A Message to Garcia
致加西亚的信

Elbert Hubbard/阿尔伯特·哈伯德

In all this Cuban business there is one man stands out on the horizon of my memory like Mars at perihelion.

When war broke out between Spain and the United States, it was very necessary to communicate quickly with the leader of the Insurgents. Garcia was somewhere in the mountain fastnesses of Cuba—no one knew where.No mail or telegraph message could reach him. The President must secure his co-coperation，and quickly. What to do!

Some said to the President，"There's a fellow by the name of Rowan who will find Garcia for you，if anybody can."

Rowan was sent for and given a letter to be **delivered** to Garcia. How the " fellow by the name of Rowan" took the letter, sealed it up in an oilskin pouch，strapped it over his heart，in four days landed by night off the coast of Cuba from an open boat，disappeared into the jungle，and in three weeks came out on the other side of the Island, having traversed a hostile country on foot and delivered his letter to Garcia—are things I have no special desire now to tell in detail. The point that I wish to make is this : McKinley gave Rowan a letter to be delivered to Garcia ; Rowan took the letter and did not ask, "Where is he at? "

By the Eternal! *There is a man whose form should be cast in deathless bronze and the statue placed in every college of the land.* It is not book-learning young men need, nor instruction about this and that, but a stiffening of the vertebrae which will cause them to be loyal to a trust, to act promptly, concentrate their energies : do the thing— "Carry a message to Garcia."

General Garcia is dead now, but there are other Garcias. No man who has endeavored to carry out an enterprise where many hands were needed, but has been well-nigh appalled at times by the imbecility of the average man—the inability or unwillingness to concentrate on a thing and do it.

Slipshod assistance, foolish inattention, dowdy indifference, and half-hearted work seem the rule ; and no man succeeds, unless by hook or crook or threat he forces or bribes other men to assist him ; or mayhap, God in His goodness performs a miracle, and sends him an Angel of Light for an assistant.

...

We have recently been hearing much maudlin sympathy expressed for the "downtrodden denizens of the sweat-shop" and the "homeless wanderer searching for honest employment", and with it all often go many hard words for the men in power.

Nothing is said about the employer who grows old before his time in a vain attempt to get frowsy ne'er-do-wells to do intelligent work ; and his long, patient striving after "help" that does nothing but loaf when his back is turned.

In every store and factory there is a constant weeding-out process going on. The employer is constantly sending away"help" that have shown their incapacity to further the interests of the business, and others are being taken on.No matter how good times are, this sorting continues;only, if times are hard and work is scarce , the sorting is done finer—but out and forever out the incompetent and unworthy go.It is the **survival** of the fittest. Self-interest prompts every employer to keep the best—those who can carry a message to Garcia.

I know one man of really brilliant parts who has not the ability to manage a business of his own, and yet who is absolutely worthless to anyone else, because he carries with him constantly the insane suspicion that his employer is oppressing, or intending to oppress him.He cannot give orders, and he will not receive them. Should a message be given him to take to Garcia, his answer would probably be, "Take it yourself!" Of course, I know that one so **morally** deformed is no less to be pitied than a physical cripple ; but in our pitying let us drop a tear, too, for the men who are striving to carry on a great enterprise, whose working hours are not limited by the whistle, and whose hair is fast turning white through the struggle to hold in line dowdy indifference, slipshod imbecility, and the heartless ingratitude which, but for their enterprise, would be both hungry and homeless.

Have I put the matter too strongly? Possibly I have ; but when all the world has gone a slumming I wish to speak a word of sympathy for the man who succeeds—the man who, against great odds, has directed the efforts of others, and having succeeded, finds there's nothing in it : nothing but bare board and clothes. I have carried a dinner-pail and worked for day's wages, and I have also been an employer of labor, and I know there is something to be said on both sides. There is no excellence, perse, in poverty ; rags are no recommendation ; and all employers are not rapacious and high-handed, any more than all poor men are **virtuous**. My heart goes out to the man who does his work when the "boss" is away, as well as when he is at home. And the man who, when given a letter for Garcia, quietly takes the missive, without asking any idiotic questions, and with no lurking intention of chucking it into the nearest sewer, or of doing aught else but deliver it, never gets " laid off, nor has to go on a strike for higher wages.

Civilization is one long, anxious search for just such individuals.

Anything such a man asks shall be granted. He is wanted in every city, town and village—in every office, shop, store and factory. *The world cries out for such, he is needed and needed badly—the man who can "Carry a Message to Garcia" .*

So who will send a letter to Garcia?

在所有与古巴有关的事情中，有一个人常常令我无法忘怀。

美西战争爆发以后，美国必须马上与反抗军首领加西亚将军取得联系。加西亚将军隐藏在古巴辽阔的崇山峻岭中——没有人知道确切的地点，因而无法送信给他。但是，美国总统必须尽快地与他建立合作关系。怎么办呢？

有人对总统推荐说："有一个名叫罗文的人，如果有人能找到加西亚将军，那个人一定就是他。"

于是，他们把罗文找来，交给他一封信——写给加西亚的信。关于那个名叫罗文的人，如何拿了信，将它装进一个油纸袋里，打封，吊在胸口藏好，如何用 4 天的时间乘坐一条敞篷船连夜抵达古巴海岸，穿入丛林，如何在 3 个星期之后，徒步穿越一个危机四伏的国家，将信交到加西亚手上——这些细节都不是我想说明的，我要强调的重点是：美国总统将一封写给加西亚的信交给了罗文，罗文接过信后，并没有问："他在哪里？"

像罗文这样的人，我们应该为他塑造一座不朽的雕像，放在每一所大学里。年轻人所需要的不仅仅是学习书本上的知识，也不仅仅是聆听他人的种种教诲，更需要的是一种敬业精神，能够立即采取行动，全心全意去完成任务——把信送给加西亚。

加西亚将军已不在人世，但现在还有其他的"加西亚"。没有人能经营好这样的企业——虽然需要众多人手，但是令人吃惊的是，其中大部分人碌碌无为，他们要么没有能力，要么根本不用心。

懒懒散散、漠不关心、马马虎虎的工作态度，对于许多人来说似乎已经变成常态。除非苦口婆心、威逼利诱地强迫他们做事，或者，请上帝创造奇迹，派一名天使相助，否则，这些人什么也做不了。

……

最近，我们经常听到许多人对那些"收入微薄而毫无出头之日"以及"但求温饱却无家可归"的人表示同情，同时将那些雇主骂得体无完肤。

但是，从没有人提到，有些老板如何一直到白发苍苍，都无法使那些不求上进的懒虫勤奋起来；也没有人谈及，有些雇主如何持久而耐心地希望感动那些当他一转身就投机取巧、敷衍了事的员工，使他们能振作起来。

在每家商店和工厂，都有一些常规性的调整过程。公司负责人经常送走那些无法对公司有所贡献的员工，同时也吸纳新的成员。无论业务如何繁忙，这种整顿一直在进行着。只有当经济不景气，就业机会不多的时候，这种整顿才会有明显的效果——那些无法胜任工作、缺乏才干的人，都被摒弃在工厂的大门之外，只有那些最能干的人，才会被留下来。为了自己的利益，每个老板只会留住那些最优秀的职员——那些能"把信送给加西亚"的人。

我认识一个十分聪明的人，但是却缺乏自己独立创业的能力，对他人来说也没有丝毫价值，因为他总是偏执地怀疑自己的老板在压榨他，或者有压榨他的意图。他既没有能力指挥他人，也没有勇气接受他人的指挥。如果你让他"送封信给加西亚"，他的回答极有可能是："你自己去吧。"我知道，与那些四肢残缺的人相比，这种思想不健全的人是不值得同情的。相反，我们应该对那些用毕生精力去经营一家大企业的人表示同情和敬意：他们不会因为下班的铃声而放下工作；他们因为努力去使那些漫不经心、拖拖拉拉、被动偷懒和不知感恩的员工有一份工作而日增白发。许多员工想都不愿想，如果没有老板们付出的努力和心血，他们将挨饿和无家可归。

我是不是说得太严重了？不过，即使整个世界变成一座贫民窟，我也要为成功者说几句公道话——他们承受了巨大的压力，引导众人的力量，终于取得了成功。但是他们从成功中又得到了什么呢？一片空虚，除了食物和衣服以外，一无所有。我曾为了一日三餐而为他人工作，也曾当过老板，我深知两方面的种种酸甜苦辣。贫穷是不好的，贫苦是不值得赞美的，衣衫褴褛更不值得骄傲；但并非所有的老板都是贪婪者、专横者，就像并非所有的穷人都是善良者一样。我钦佩那些无论老板在不在办公室都努力工作的人，我敬佩那些能够把信交给加西亚的人。他们静静地把信拿去，不会提任何愚笨的问题，更不会随手把信丢进水沟里，而是全力以赴地将信送到。这种人永远不会被解雇，也永远不会为了要求加薪而罢工。

文明，就是孜孜不倦地寻找这种人才的一段长久过程。

这种人无论有什么样的愿望都能够实现。在每个城市、村庄、乡镇，以及每个办公室、商店、工厂，他们都会受到欢迎。世界上急需这种人才，这种能够把信送给加西亚的人。

谁将把信送给加西亚？

导读

100 多年前的一个傍晚，出版家阿尔伯特·哈伯德与家人喝茶时受儿子的启发，创作了一篇名为《致加西亚的信》的文章，刊登在《菲士利人》的杂志上。杂志很快就告罄，纽约中心铁路局的乔治·丹尼尔一次要求订购 10 万册以书籍方式印刷的《致加西亚的信》，用来在车站发放。到 1915 年作者逝世为止，《致加西亚的信》的印数高达 40,000,000 册，创造了一个作家有生之年单本图书销售量的历史记录。

单词注解

deliver [di'livə] *v.* 投递；传送；运送
survival [sə'vaivəl] *n.* 幸存；残存
morally ['mɔrəli] *adv.* 道德上；有道德地
virtuous ['və:tjuəs] *adj.* 有道德的；善良的；正直的

诵读名句

There is a man whose form should be cast in deathless bronze and the statue placed in every college of the land.

Civilization is one long, anxious search for just such individuals.

The world cries out for such, he is needed and needed badly—the man who can "Carry a Message to Garcia".

Mother Teresa's Nobel Prize Acceptance Speech
特雷莎嬷嬷：诺贝尔获奖感言

Mother Teresa/特雷莎嬷嬷

......

Let us thank God for the opportunity that we all have together today, for this gift of peace that reminds us that we have been created to live for peace, and Jesus became man to bring that good news to the poor. He being God became man in all things like us except sin, and he **proclaimed** very clearly that he had come to give the good news. The news was peace to all of good will and this is something that we all want—the peace of heart—and God loved the world so much that he gave his son—it was a giving—it is as much as if to say it hurt God to give, because he loved the world so much that he gave his son, and he gave him to Virgin Mary, and what did she do with him?

As soon as he came in her life—immediately she went in haste to give that good news, and as she came into the house of her cousin, the child—the unborn child—the child in the womb of Elizabeth, leapt with joy. He was that little unborn child, was the first messenger of peace. He recognised the Prince of Peace, he recognised that Christ has come to bring the good news for you and for me. And as if that was not enough—it was not enough to become a man—he died on the cross to show that greater love, and he died for you and for me and for that leper and for that man dying of hunger and that naked person lying in the street not only of Calcutta, but of Africa, and New York, and London, and Oslo and insisted that we love one another as he loves each one of us. And we read that in the Gospel very clearly—love as I have loved you—as I love you—as the Father has loved me, I love you—and the harder the Father loved him, he gave him to us, and how much we love one another, we, too, must give each other until it hurts. It is not enough for us to say : I love God, but I do not love my neighbour. St. John says you are a liar if you say you love God, and you don't love your neighbour. How can you love God whom you do not see, if you do not love your neighbour whom you see, whom you touch, with whom you live. *And so this is very important for us to realise that love, to be true, has to hurt. It hurt Jesus to love us, it hurt him.* And to make sure we remember his great love he made himself the bread of life to satisfy our hunger for his love. Our hunger for God, because we have been created for that love. We have been created in his image. We have been created to love and be loved, and then he has become man to make it possible for us to love as he loved us. He makes himself the hungry one— the naked one—the homeless one—the sick one—the one in prison—the lonely one—the unwanted one—and he says : You did it to me. Hungry for our love, and this is the hunger of our poor people. This is the hunger that you and I must find. It may be in our own home.

...

The other day I received 15 dollars from a man who has been on his back for twenty years, and the only part that he can move is his right hand. And the only companion that he enjoys is smoking. And he said to me : I do not smoke for one week, and I send you this money. It must have been a terrible sacrifice for him, but see how beautiful, how he shared, and with that money I bought bread and I gave to those who are hungry with a joy on both sides, he was giving and the poor were receiving. This is something that you and I—it is a gift of God to us to be able to share our love with others. And let it be as it was for Jesus. Let us love one another as he loved us. Let us love Him with undivided love. And the joy of loving Him and each other— let us give now—that Christmas is coming so close. Let us keep that joy of loving Jesus in our hearts. And share that joy with all that we come in touch with. And that **radiating** joy is real, for we have no reason not to be happy because we have no Christ with us. Christ in our hearts, Christ in the poor that we meet, Christ in the smile that we give and the smile that we **receive**. *Let us make that one point : that no child will be unwanted, and also that we meet each other always with a smile, especially when it is difficult to smile.*

...If we could only remember that God loves me, and we have an opportunity to love others as he loves me, not in big things, but in small things with great love, then Norway becomes a nest of love. And how beautiful it will be that from here a centre for peace has been given. That from here the joy of life of the unborn child comes out. If you become a burning light in the world of peace，then really the Nobel Peace Prize is a gift of the Norwegian people. God bless you!

感谢上帝赐给我们机会，让我们大家今天聚在一起，和平奖的获得告诉我们，我们生来就是要为和平而生存，它也告诉我们，基督除了没有原罪外，他和我们简直没有两样，他明确地告诉大家，他给众人带来了一个喜讯。这个喜讯就是所有善良的人所期盼的和平的愿望，也是我们都欲得到的———一颗维护和平的心。上帝是如此热爱我们这个世界，他不惜将自己的儿子都贡献出来，当然，这对他是件非常痛苦的事情；上帝是忍受着何等的痛苦，才将自己的儿子贡献给我们这个世界啊。然而，当他将自己的独生子送给少女玛利亚时，她又是如何对待基督呢？

当他闯入她的生活时，她很快将这个喜讯传播给世人。当她走进她的表亲家时，表亲伊丽莎白[1]未出世的孩子已经在她的腹中欢跃。这个孩子便是第一个为我们带来和平讯息的使者。

①伊丽莎白为圣母玛利亚的表妹。

他，这个名叫约翰的未出生的孩子认出了和平之子，和平之子就是基督，他当时还在玛利亚的腹中。他把和平带给你，带给我。但是作为男子汉的他仍嫌做得不够，他用被钉死在十字架上的悲壮行动，来向我们表示他对我们伟大的爱，他是为你，为我，为那些身患麻风病，为那些因饥饿而将死的人，为那些赤裸着身体横卧在加尔各答和其他城市的大街上的穷人，为在非洲、纽约、伦敦和奥斯陆的穷人而献身。他用他的死来劝告我们相互同情、相互爱戴。福音书中讲得非常清楚："像我爱你们一样去爱；像我的父亲爱我一样去爱。我爱你们。"他的父亲正是因为深深地爱着他，才把他贡献出来。我们彼此间也应该互相爱戴，应该像上帝对待他儿子那样，彼此将爱心贡献出来。如果我们说："我爱上帝，但是不爱我的邻居"，这是远远不够的。圣约翰说："如果你说只爱上帝，不爱邻居，那么你就是一个说谎的人。"如果连每日相见，彼此接触，和你住在一起的邻居都不爱的话，那你怎么能爱一个看不见的上帝呢？所以，对我们来说，重要的是去认识爱的含义。爱是实实在在的，是痛苦的。基督忍受了极大的痛苦来爱我们，爱使他受难。我们一定要牢牢地记住他的爱。他将自己变成面包来让我们充饥，就是让我们满足对上帝的饥渴，因为我们生来就是要体验这种爱，我们生来就是要爱别人，被别人爱。基督之所以变成一个男子汉来爱我们，就是要我们尽可能地像他爱我们那样去爱别人。他故意把自己扮成一个饥饿的人、一个衣不蔽体无家可归的人、一个病人或者一个犯人，或者一个孤独的人、被遗弃的人。他对我们说："是你们拯救了我。"他渴求我们对他的爱，就如同穷人们渴求我们对他们的爱是一样的。我们一定要了解这种饥渴，也许这样的饥渴恰好发生在我们自己的家里。

......

前几天，我从一个瘫痪 20 年的病人那里收到 15 美元的捐款。这个人全身只有右手能动。他唯一的嗜好就是吸烟。这个人对我说："我一星期没有吸烟，现在我把省下来的钱交给你们。"这样的贡献对他来说一定是经历了非常痛苦的煎熬，但是他为分担拯救贫困人们的行动是多么高尚啊。我用这笔钱为那些正在挨饿的穷人们买了面包，使捐赠者和接受捐赠的人都感到了快乐。上帝赐给我们每个人的礼物是要我们互相爱戴。我们都可以用上帝的礼物做我们能做到的事情。让我们为了基督施与他人爱心吧。让我们像他爱我们一样互相爱戴。让我们用无私的爱去爱他。让我们在圣诞节即将到来之际，为我们彼此献出我们的爱。让我们的心中保持对基督的爱，和所有我们接触过的人共同分享他的爱。传播到大众中间的欢欣是实实在在的，因为我们和基督在一起，没有什么理由不使我们欢欣鼓舞。基督存在于我们的心中，他就在我们所遇到的穷人中间。基督是我们送给他人的微笑和他人带给我们的微笑。愿我们拥有一个共同的观点，决不遗弃任何一个孩子；无论面对什么样的恶劣环境，我们都要保持微笑。

......我们只要记着上帝是爱我们的，我们就会像他爱我们那样去爱他人。不为大事而爱，只为琐细的小事而爱。从细微的小事中体现博大的爱。我们要以挪威为中心，将爱传播到整个世界，让战争远离我们。如此，那些待出生的婴儿就会欢叫着来到人间。我们把自己变成传播世界和平的火种，挪威的诺贝尔和平奖将会真正是献给和平的厚礼。

愿上帝保佑你们。

实战提升
Practising & Exercise

✍导读✍

特雷莎嬷嬷于 1979 年获得了诺贝尔和平奖。她的获奖可谓名至实归，因为正是特雷莎嬷嬷的诸多善言善举，使这个世界变得更加温暖、更加美丽。她让我们见面时彼此微笑致意，因为微笑是爱的开端。她的演讲素朴感人，处处流露着博爱。她将爱心不断地延伸，把和平传给世人，让他们理解了爱，也同时成为和平和爱心的传递者。

✍单词注解✍

proclaim [prə'kleim] v. 宣布，宣告

contemplative ['kɔntempleitiv] n. 僧人，修女，敛心默祷者

receive [ri'si:v] v. 收到，接到

radiating ['reidieit] adj. 显露的，散发的

✍诵读名句✍

And so this is very important for us to realise that love, to be true, has to hurt. It hurt Jesus to love us, it hurt him.

I believe that we are not real social workers. We may be doing social work in the eyes of the people, but we are really contemplatives in the heart of the world.

Let us make that one point : that no child will be unwanted, and also that we meet each other always with a smile, especially when it is difficult to smile.

Socrates' Defense
苏格拉底：申辩

Socrate/苏格拉底

Men of Athens, this reputation of mine has come of a certain sort of wisdom which I possess. If you ask me what kind of wisdom, I reply, such wisdom as may perhaps be attained by every man, for to that extent I am inclined to believe that I am wise; whereas the persons of whom I was speaking have a superhuman wisdom, which I may fail to describe, because I have it not myself; and he who says that I have, speaks falsely, and is taking away my character. And here, O men of Athens, I must beg you not to interrupt me, even if I seem to say something extravagant. For the word which I will speak is not mine. I will refer you to a witness who is worthy of credit; that witness shall be the God of Delphi, he will tell you about my wisdom, if I have any, and of what sort it is.

You must have known Chaerephon; he was early a friend of mine, and also a friend of yours, for he shared in the recent exile of the people, and returned with you. Well, Chaerephon, as you know, was very **impetuous** in all his doings, and he went to Delphi and boldly asked the **oracle** to tell him whether, as I was saying, I must beg you not to interrupt, he asked the oracle to tell him whether any one was wiser than I was, and the Pythian prophetess answered, that there was no man wiser. Chaerephon is dead himself ; but his brother, who is in court, will confirm the truth of what I'm saying.

Why do I mention this? Because I am going to explain to you why I have such an evil name. When I heard the answer, I said to myself, "What can the god mean? And what is the interpretation of his riddle? For I know that I have no wisdom, small or great. What then can he mean when he says that I am the wisest of men? And yet he is a god, and cannot lie ; that would be against his nature. " After long consideration, I thought of a method of trying the question. I reflected that if I could only find a man wiser than myself, then I might go to the god with a refutation in my hand. I should say to him, "Here is a man who is wiser than I am ; but you said that I was the wisest." Accordingly I went to one who had the reputation of wisdom, and observed him, his name I need not mention ; he was a politician whom first among I selected for examination, and the result was as follows : When I began to talk with him, I could not help thinking that he was not really wise, although he was thought wise by many, and still wiser by himself ; and thereupon I tried to explain to him that he thought himself wise, but was not really wise ; and the consequence was that he hated me, and his enmity was shared by several who were present. So I left him, saying to myself, as I went away : Conceit of man, although I do not suppose that either of us knows anything really beautiful and good, I am better off than he is, for he knows nothing, and thinks that he knows ; I neither know nor think that I know. In this latter particular, then, I seem to have slightly the advantage of him.

Then I went to another who had still higher pretensions to wisdom, and my conclusion was exactly the same, whereupon I made another enemy of him, and of many others besides him. Then I went to one man after another, being not unconscious of the enmity which I **provoked**, and I **lamented** and feared this : but necessity was laid upon me, the word of God, I thought, ought to be considered first. And I said to myself, I must go to all who appear to know, and find out the meaning of the oracle. And I swear to you, Athenians, by the dog I swear, for I must tell you the truth, the result of my mission was just this : I found that the men most in repute were all but the most foolish ; and that others less esteemed were really wiser and better.

I will tell you the whole of my wanderings and of the "Herculean" labors, as I may call them, which I endured only to find at last the oracle irrefutable. After the politicians, I went to the poets, tragic, dithyrambic and all sorts. And there, I said to myself, you will be instantly detected ; now you will find out that you are more ignorant than they are. Accordingly, I took them some of the most elaborate passages in their own writings, and asked what the meaning of them was, thinking that they would teach me something. Will you believe me? I am almost ashamed to confess the truth, but I must say that there is hardly a person present who would not have talked better about their poetry than they did themselves. Then I knew that not by wisdom do poets write poetry, but by a sort of genius and inspiration ; they are like diviners or soothsayers who also say many fine things, but do not understand the meaning of them. The poets appeared to me to be much in the same case; and I further observed that upon the strength of their poetry they believed themselves to be the wisest of men in other things in which they were not wise. *So I departed, conceiving myself to be superior to them for the same reason that I was superior to the politicians.*

At last I went to the artisans; I was conscious that I knew nothing at all, as I may say, and I was sure that they knew many fine things; and here I was not mistaken, for they did know many things of which I was ignorant, and in this they certainly were wiser than I was. But I observed that even the good artisans fell into the same error as the poets; because they were good workmen, so they thought that they also knew all sorts of high matters, and this defect in them overshadowed their wisdom; and therefore I asked myself on behalf of the oracle, whether I would like to be as I was, neither having their knowledge nor their ignorance, or like them in both; and I made answer to myself and to the oracle that I was better off as I was.

This inquisition has led to my having many enemies of the worst and most dangerous kind, and has given occasion also to many calumnies. And I am called wise, for my hearers always imagine that I myself possess the wisdom which I find wanting in others: but the truth is, O men of Athens, that God only is wise; and by his answer he intends to show that the wisdom of men is worth little or nothing; he is not speaking of Socrates, he is only using my name by way of illustration, as if he said, O men, he is the wisest, who, like Socrates, knows that his wisdom is in truth worth nothing. And so I go about the world, obedient to the god, and search and make enquiry into the wisdom of any one, whether citizen or stranger, who appears to be wise ; and if he is not wise, then I show him that he is not wise ; and my occupation quite absorbs me, and I have no time to give attention to any public matter of interest or to any concern of my own, but I am in utter poverty by reason of my devotion to the god.

　　雅典的公民们，我无非是由于具有某种智慧而获得了智者的名声。我所指的是什么样的智慧呢？我想是人类的智慧。在这个意义上我的确可以算作有智之人。或许我刚才提到的那些天才们有超人的智慧，但我实在无法说明。我对这种超人的智慧自然是一无所知，谁说我有这种智慧就是说谎，就是有意中伤。雅典的公民们，即便是我的申辩显得放肆，也请不要打断我，因为我将要向你们讲述的并不是我自己的意见，而是引述一位无可指责的权威的话。我将请德尔菲的神为我所具有的智慧作证。

你们当然都认识开瑞丰。自幼他就是我的至交，他也是你们的朋友，在前几年的"放逐和复辟"中，他始终是和你们站在一起的。你们知道他是什么样的人，他对于他所从事的每项工作都那么热心。我在前面说过，雅典的公民们，请不要打断我。有一天，他去德尔菲向神请教这样一个问题：是否有人比我聪明。回答说，没有。开瑞丰已经死了，上述情况可以由他的兄弟来证实，此刻他就在法庭上。

请想一想我向你们说这些话的目的吧。我是想对你们解释清楚强加于我的坏名声是怎么来的。当我听了神谕后，我对自己说："神的旨意是什么呢？他为什么不讲明白呢？我只是充分意识到自己毫无智慧，那么他说我是世界上最聪明的人又是什么意思呢？神按其本性来说是不会说谎的。"在对神谕迷惑了一段时间以后，我终于强迫自己以下述方法去证实神谕的真理性。我去访问了一位具有极高智慧声誉的人，因为我想，只有在这里我才有可能成功地对神谕作出反证，向神圣的权威指出："你说我是最聪明的人，但这里有人比我更聪明。"我全面地考察了这个人。我在这里不提他的名字，在我考察他时，他是我们城邦的政治家之一。经过交谈，我的印象是，虽然在很多人看来，特别是他自己认为，他很聪明，但事实上他并不聪明。当我试图向他指出他只是自认为聪明而并非真正聪明时，他和在场的其他很多人都表现出了对我的憎恨。离开他后，我反复思量："我确实比这个人聪明。很可惜我们谁都没有任何值得自夸的知识，但他对不知之物自认为有知，而我则非常自觉地意识到自己的无知。无论如何，在这点上我比他聪明，起码我不以我所不知为知。"

此后，我去访问了一个在智慧方面声誉更高的人，我又得出了同样的结论，我也同样遭到他本人和其他很多人的憎恨。从那以后，我访问了很多人，都感到悲哀和恐惧，因为我这样做并不受欢迎。但我强迫自己把神圣的使命放在首位。既然我试图揭示神谕的含义，我决意遍访每一个有智慧声誉的人。雅典的公民们，指犬为誓，我必须对你们坦率地说，我的印象是：当我遵照神的命令调查时，我发现，智慧声誉最高的人几乎完全无知，智慧声誉低于他们的人却颇有实际知识。

我愿你们想象一下我为确证神谕的真理性而踏上的，像朝圣一样的艰难路途。当我遍访了政治家后，我又去访问诗人、戏剧家、抒情诗人和其他各种人，相信在他们那里可以暴露我自己的无知。我在他们那里列举我所能想到的，他们的最好的作品，紧紧围绕他们写作的目的提问题，希望能借此机会扩充自己的知识。雅典的公民们，我不愿把真相告诉你们，可我又必须告诉你们事实的真相。毫不夸张地说，听了诗人们的回答，我感到，任何一个旁观者都能比诗的作者们更好地解释这些作品。这样，我很快就对诗人们也做出了评判，并不是聪明才智，而是本能和灵感，使他们创作出了诗歌。就像你们所见到的，先知和预言家传达神谕时，一点儿都不知道他们所说的话的含义。在我看来，显然诗人们在写诗时也是这样。我还注意到这样一个事实，他们是诗人，所以就自以为无所不知，而实际上他们对其他学科完全无知。这样，我怀着在离开政治家们时同样的优越感放弃了对诗人们的拜访。

最后，我又去访问熟练的手艺人。我很清楚，我对技术一窍不通，因而我相信我能从他们身上得到给人以深刻印象的知识。对他们的访问的确没令我失望，他们懂得我所不懂的事，在这方面他们比我聪明。但是，雅典的公民们，这些从事专门职业的人看来有着同诗人们同样的缺点，我是指他们自恃技术熟练，就声称他们完全通晓其他学科的知识，不管这些学科多么重要。我感到，他们的这一错误使他们的智慧黯然失色。于是，我使自己成为神谕的代言人，自问是保持我原来的样子，既没有像他们那样的智慧，也没有像他们那样的愚蠢好呢，还是像他们那样智慧和愚蠢同时具备的好？最后我回答我自己和神说：神谕说，我还是保持过去的样子好。

雅典的公民们，我遵循神谕，对人们进行调查的后果，引起了大家对我的敌对情绪，一种既强烈又持久的敌对情绪，它导致了很多恶意的中伤，包括把我描述成一个到处炫耀自己智慧的人。由于在某个特定的问题上，我成功地难住了一个自认为聪明的人，旁观者们就断定我对这个问题无所不通。但雅典的公民们，事实并非如此，真正的智慧只属于神。他借助上述神谕启迪我们，人类的智慧没什么价值，或者根本没有价值。在我看来，神并不是认为苏格拉底最聪明，而只是以我的名字为例告诫我们，"你们当中像苏格拉底那样聪明的人也意识到自己的智慧是微不足道的。"所以，我到处奔波，秉承神的意旨，检验每一个我认为有智慧的人，不管他是公民还是侨民。如果，他并不智慧，我就给神当助手，指出他并不智慧。这个工作使我非常忙碌，没有时间参加任何公务，连自己的私事也没工夫管，我一贫如洗，就是因为事神不懈的缘故。

导读

苏格拉底，古希腊哲学家。曾自喻为"牛虻'，一只时刻叮咬国家这只硕大的骏马，以让她能够精神焕发的牛虻。可要知道，被这样不停叮咬的滋味是不好受的，尽管可能很多人都懂得它的好处。最终也正是由于这种牛虻精神，公元前 399 年，三个雅典公民，墨勒图斯、安尼图斯和吕孔对苏格拉底提出公诉，指控他危害社会。苏格拉底被控告犯有"教唆青年和怠慢神灵"两条罪状，而流传百万的演讲《申辩》也因此而诞生了。

单词注解

impetuous [im'petjuəs] *adj.* 鲁莽的，急躁的；轻率的

oracle ['ɔrəkl] *n.* 神谕

provoke [prə'vəuk] *v.* 刺激，挑逗，诱发

lament [lə'ment] *v.* （为……）悲痛，哀悼

诵读名句

I will tell you the whole of my wanderings and of the "Herculean" labors, as I may call them, which I endured only to find at last the oracle irrefutable.

So I departed, conceiving myself to be superior to them for the same reason that I was superior to the politicians.

This inquisition has led to my having many enemies of the worst and most dangerous kind, and has given occasion also to many calumnies.

Farewell Address to Congress
老兵永不死亡

Douglas MacArthur/道格拉斯·麦克阿瑟

Mr. President, Mr. Speaker, and Distinguished Members of the Congress,

I stand on this rostrum with a sense of deep humility and great pride. Humility in the wake of all those great American architects of our history who have stood here before me. Pride in the reflection that this home of legislative debate represents human liberty in the purest form yet devised. Here are centered the hopes and aspirations and faith of the entire human race. I do not stand here as advocate of any **partisan** cause, for the issues are fundamental and reach quite beyond the realm of partisan consideration. They must be resolved on the highest plane of national interest, if our cause is to prove sound and our future protected. I trust, therefore, that you will do me the justice of receiving that which I have to say as solely expressing the considered viewpoint of a fellow American. *I address you with neither rancor nor bitterness, in* *the fading twilight of life, with but one purpose in mind : to serve my country.*

The issues are global, and so interlocked that to consider the problems of one sector, oblivious to those of another is but to cause disaster for the whole. While Asia is commonly referred to as the gateway to Europe, it is no less true that Europe is the gateway to Asia, and the broad influence of the one cannot fail to have its impact upon the other. There are those who claim our strength is inadequate to protect on both fronts, that we cannot divide our effort. I can think of no greater expression of defeatism. If a potential enemy can divide his strength on two fronts, it's for us to counter his efforts.

Beyond pointing out these general truisms, I shall confine my discussion to the general areas of Asia. Before one may objectively assess the situation now existing there, he must comprehend something of Asia's past and the revolutionary changes which have marked her course up to the present. Long exploited by the so-called colonial powers, with little opportunity to achieve any degree of social justice, individual dignity or higher standard of life, such as guided our own noble administration of the Philippines. The peoples of Asia found their opportunity in the war just passed to throw off the shackles of colonialism, and now see the dawn of new opportunity : a heretofore unfelt dignity and the self-respect of political freedom. Mustering half of the earth's population and sixty percent of its natural resources, these peoples are rapidly **consolidating** a new force, both moral and material,

Glorious mind

光辉的信念

263

with which to raise their living standard and the adaptations of the design of modern progress to their own distinct cultural environments. Whether one adheres to the concept of colonization or not, this is the direction of Asian progress and it may not be stopped. It is a corollary to the shift of the world economic frontiers as the whole epicenter of world affairs rotates back toward the area whence it started. In this situation, it becomes vital that our own country orient its policies in constancy with this basic evolutionary condition rather than pursue a course blind to the reality that the colonial era is now past and the Asian peoples covet the right to shape their own free destiny. What they seek now is friendly guidance, understanding and support, not imperialist directions.

It was my constant effort to preserve them and end the savage conflict honorably and with the least loss of time and in minimum sacrifice of life. Its growing bloodshed has caused me the deepest anguish and anxiety. *Those gallant men will remain often in my thoughts and my prayers, always.*

I am closing my fifty-two years of military service. When I joined the army even before the turn of the century, it was the fulfillment of all my boyish hopes and dreams. The world has turned over many times since I took the oath on the plain at WestPoint, and the hopes and dreams have long since vanished. But I still remember the **refrain** of one of the most popular barrack ballads of that day which proclaimed most proudly that old soldiers never die, they just fade away. And like the old soldier of that ballad, I now close my military career and just fade away. *An old soldier who tried to do his duty as God gave him the light to* *see that duty.*

Good-bye.

　　总统先生、议长先生和尊敬的国会议员们：

　　我怀着十分谦卑而又十分骄傲的心情站在这演讲台上。我谦卑，是因为在我之前，许多美国历史上伟大的建筑师都曾经在这里发过言；我骄傲，是因为今天我们的立法辩论代表着经思考的最纯粹的人类解放。这是全人类的希望、热情和信仰的所在。我并不是作为任何一个党派的拥护者站在这里讲话的，因为这些问题至关重要，超越了党派的界线。如果我们需要证实我们的动因是正确的，如果要保障我们的未来，我们就要从符合国家最高利益的角度解决这些问题。我相信，当我说完这些话之后，仅仅是为了表达一个美国普通公民经过深思熟虑而得出的观点，你们会公平地接受它。在我生命之暮年做这个告别演说，我无怨无悔，在我心中只有一个目的：为我的祖国服务。

这些问题是全球性而且环环相扣的，任何的顾此失彼都会给全局造成灾难。亚洲被普遍认为是通往欧洲的门户，同样的，欧洲也是通往亚洲的大门，二者息息相关。有人认为我们的力量不足以同时保住两个阵地，因为我们不能分散我们的力量。我想，这是我听到的最悲观的失败主义论调了。如果我们潜在的敌人能够把他的力量分在两条线上，那我们就必须与之抗衡。

除了指出这些大家已经明白的问题外，我将把讨论集中在亚洲地区。在客观地估计那里的现状之前，我们必须了解亚洲的过去，了解导致她今天这种局势的革命性的变化。长期遭受所谓殖民主义势力的剥削使亚洲人民没有机会获取任何程度的社会平等、个人尊严，也无法提高生活水平，就像被我们的菲律宾贵族政府所统治的那样。亚洲人民在战争中找到了机会，得以摆脱殖民主义的枷锁，而且现在有更多的、新的契机摆在他们面前：政治独立带来了以前从未感受过的尊严和自尊。亚洲拥有世界一半的人口和 60% 的自然资源，她的人民正迅速地巩固着一个新兴的力量，包括精神和物质两方面，借此提高他们的生活水平，协调现代化的进步和他们特有的文化环境。不管你是不是坚持殖民的观点，这才是亚洲前进的方向，没有人能够阻止她的脚步。这一点是世界经济防线转移、国际事务中心回归原点的必然结果。在这种情况下，我们国家在政治上必须与基本的革命形势一致，而不能无视殖民时代已经过时、亚洲人民渴望开创自己的自由生活的现实，这十分重要。他们现在需要的是友好的指引、理解和支持，而不是专制的指挥。

我坚持保全他们，并希望能用最少的时间、最小的牺牲体面地结束这场野蛮的冲突。越来越多的流血让我感到极度的痛苦和焦虑。那些勇敢的人的形象在我的脑海中挥之不去，我将永远为他们祈祷。

我将结束 52 年的军旅生涯。我在世纪之交前就已参军，它实现了我孩童时所有的希望和梦想。自从我在西点的草坪上宣誓以来，这个世界已经经历了多次转变，童年的希望和梦想早已消失得无影无踪。但我依然记得当年那首流行的军歌的歌词：一个老兵永不死亡，他只是淡出舞台。就像歌中的老兵一样，我结束了我的军旅生涯，只是淡出了人生舞台。一个力图按照上帝指引的方式完成他的职责的老兵。

再见。

实战提升
Practising & Exercise

导读

1944 年 12 月，麦克阿瑟被授予五星级上将军衔。1951 年，他与家人回到美国。在这次演讲中，他以一句歌词"一个老兵永不死亡，他只是淡出舞台"来宣告自己军旅生涯的结束。

单词注解

partisan [pɑːtiˈzæn] *n.* 拥护者
appease [əˈpiːz] *v.* 使安静、平息
consolidate [kənˈsɔlideit] *v.* 巩固、加强
refrain [riˈfrein] *v.* 克制

诵读名句

I address you with neither rancor nor bitterness，in the fading twilight of life，with but one purpose in mind：to serve my country.

Those gallant men will remain often in my thoughts and my prayers，always.

An old soldier who tried to do his duty as God gave him the light to see that duty.

The Road to Success
安德鲁·卡内基：成功之路

Andrew Carnegie/安德鲁·卡内基

It is well that young men should begin at the beginning and occupy the most **subordinate** positions. Many of the leading businessmen of Pittsburgh had a serious responsibility thrust upon then at the very threshold of their career. They were introduced to the broom, and spent the first hours of their business lives sweeping out the office. I notice we have janitors and janitresses now in offices, and our young men unfortunately miss that **salutary** branch of a business education. But if by chance the professional sweeper is absent any morning, the boy who has the genius of the future partner in him will not hesitate to try his hand at the broom. The other day a fond fashionable mother in Michigan asked a young man whether he had ever seen a young lady sweep in a room so grandly as her Priscilla. He said no, he never had, and the mother was **gratified** beyond measure, but then said he, after a pause, "What I should like to see her do is sweep out a room." It does not hurt the newest comer to sweep out the office if necessary. I was one of those sweepers myself.

Assuming that you have all obtained employment and are fairly started, my advice to you is "aim high". I would not give a fig for the young man who does not already see himself the partner or the head of an important firm. Do not rest content for a moment in your thoughts as head clerk, or foreman, or general manager in any concern, no matter how extensive. Say to yourself, "My place is at the top." Be king in your dreams.

And here is the prime condition of success, the great secret : concentrate your energy, thought, and capital exclusively upon the business in which you are engaged. Having begun in one line, resolve to fight it out on that line, to lead in it, adopt every improvement, have the best machinery, and know the most about it.

The concerns which fail are those which have scattered their capital, which means that they have scattered their brains also. They have investments in this, or that, or the other, here, there, and everywhere. "Don't put all your eggs in one basket." is all wrong. *I tell you "put all your eggs in one basket, and then watch that basket."* Look round you and take notice, men who do that not often fail. It is easy to watch and carry the one basket. It is trying to carry too many baskets that breaks most eggs in this country. He who carries three baskets must put one on his head, which is apt to tumble and trip him up. One fault of the American businessman is lack of concentration.

To **summarize** what I have said : Aim for the highest, never enter a bar room ; do not touch liquor, or if at all only at meals ; never speculate ; never indorse beyond your surplus cash fund ;

make the firm's interest yours ; break orders always to save owners ; concentrate ; put all your eggs in one basket, and watch that basket ; expenditure always within revenue ; lastly be not impatient, for as Emers on says, "no one can cheat you out of ultimate success but yourselves."

　　年轻人应该从头开始，从底层做起，这是很好的一件事情。匹兹堡许多出类拔萃的企业家在刚入行时，都承担过一个重要的职责：他们手持扫帚，在清扫办公室中开始了他们的创业生涯。我注意到，现在的办公室都配置了保洁，我们的年轻人很不幸地失去了企业教育中有益的一环。但是，假如某一天早上，专职的清洁工偶尔没来，那么具有未来合伙人潜质的小伙子就会毫不犹豫地拿起扫帚。有一次，密歇根一位溺爱孩子的时髦母亲问一个年轻人，是否见过有哪个年轻女士像她的普里茜拉那样潇洒地在屋子里扫地。年轻人回答说从来没有见过，那位母亲高兴坏了。可是他停了一下又说："我想见到的是她在屋子外头打扫。"必要时，让新来的员工在办公室外扫扫地对他们并没有坏处。我自己就曾经是那些扫地人中的一员。

当确定你获得录用并有了一个公平的起点时，我的忠告是："确定远大的目标。"对于那些还未把自己看成大公司未来的合伙人或者老板的人们，我是无话可说的。不管公司有多大，永远把自己看成这家公司的首席雇员、领班或者总经理。告诉自己："我的位置在最高层。"在你的梦想中，你应该是一流的。

通往成功之路的基本条件和重大秘密是：把你的精力、思想和资本全部集中于你所从事的事业之上。投身于哪一行，就得决心在这一行做出一番事业，做这一行的领导人物，采纳每一点建议，采用最好的设备，尽力精通专业知识。

一些公司的失败，就在于其资金的分散，以及因此而导致的精力的分散。他们这也投资，那也投资，到处投资。"不要把所有的鸡蛋放在同一个篮子里"这句话大错特错了。我要告诉你们的是："把所有的鸡蛋都放在同一个篮子里，然后看紧它。"观察周围并仔细留神，做到了这一点，你就不会失败。照管和携带一个篮子是很简单的。就是因为人们总是试图提很多的篮子，从而打破了这个国家大部分的鸡蛋。一次提着三个篮子的人，就得把一个篮子顶在头上，这个篮子很容易掉下来并把他绊倒。美国商人的一个缺点就是不能专注一事。

我所说的话总结起来就是：要目标远大；不要涉足酒吧；不要喝酒，或者仅在用餐时喝一点；不要做投机买卖；不要签署支付超过储备的现金利润的款项；把公司的利益看成是你自己的；只有基于帮助货主的目的才能取消订单；要专注；要把所有的鸡蛋放在同一个篮子里，并且照管好它；消费永远小于收入；最后，要保持耐心，因为正如爱默生所说的："只有你们自己，才能销蚀掉你们本来能够实现的最终的成功。"

导读

本篇是美国钢铁大王安德鲁·卡内基于 1885 年 6 月 23 日对柯里商业
学院毕业生的演讲。他幼时家贫，靠个人奋斗发迹，是"美国梦"的典
型代表，晚年热心于图书馆事业和慈善事业。

单词注解

subordinate [sə'bɔ:dənit] *adj.* 次要的；隶属的
salutary ['sæljutəri] *adj.* 有益的，有利的
gratify ['grætifai] *v.* 使高兴，使满意
exclusive [iks'klu:siv] *adj.* 排外的；除外的；全部的
summarize ['sʌməraiz] *v.* 总结，概述，概括

诵读名句

Assuming that you have all obtained employment and are fairly
started，my advice to you is "aim high"．

And here is the prime condition of success，the great secret：
concentrate your energy，thought，and capital exclusively upon the
business in which you are engaged.

I tell you "put all your eggs in one basket，and then watch that
basket."

Courage

马克·吐温：勇气

Mark Twain/马克·吐温

In the matter of courage we all have our limits. There never was a hero who did not have his **bounds**. *I suppose it may be said of Nelson and all the others whose courage has been advertised that there came times in their lives when their bravery knew it had come to its limit.*

I have found mine a good many times. Sometimes this was expected— often it was unexpected. I know a man who is not afraid to sleep with a rattle-snake，but you could not get him to sleep with a safety-razor.

I never had the courage to talk across a long, narrow room. I should be at the end of the room facing all the audience. If I attempt to talk across a room I find myself turning this way and that，and thus at **alternate** periods I have part of the audience behind me. You ought never to have any part of the audience behind you；you never can tell what they are going to do.

I'll sit down.

在勇气问题上，人人都有极限。从来就没有胆大包天的英雄好汉。我想，可以说，纳尔逊和所有那些被大量宣传的勇士一生中都有勇气达到极限的时候。

我就多次发现自己的勇气到了极限。有时是意料之中的——经常是出乎意料的。我认识一个人，此君不怕与响尾蛇同寝，可你无法让他与安全剃刀共眠。

我从来就没有勇气在狭长房间的中央发表讲话。我得站在房间的一头，面对全体听众。如果我试图站在房间中央讲话，我就会不断地转身，这样，就不断有部分听众在我背后。你们永远不能让自己背后有听众；你们永远不知道他们要干什么。

我得坐下了。

实战提升
Practising **&** Exercise

🍂导读🍂

1908 年 4 月 18 日，在一次纽约市美术家、漫画家和幽默作家的聚会上，马克·吐温发表了这一简短演说。讲话风趣幽默，又令人回味无穷。

🍂单词注解🍂

bound [baund] *n.* 边界，界限，界线
bravery ['breivəri] *n.* 勇敢，无畏精神
alternate [ɔːl'təːnit] *adj.* 交替的，同隔的

🍂诵读名句🍂

I suppose it may be said of Nelson and all the others whose courage has been advertised that there came times in their lives when their bravery knew it had come to its limit.

I have found mine a good many times.

I never had the courage to talk across a long，narrow room.

John Davison Rockefeller/小约翰·洛克菲勒

They are the principles on which my wife and I have tried to bring up our family. They are the principles in which my father believed and by which he governed his life. They are the principles，many of them，which I learned at my mother's knee.

They point the way to usefulness and happiness in life，to courage and peace in death.

If they mean to you what they mean to me，they may perhaps be helpful also to our sons for their guidance and inspiration.

Let me state them：

I believe in the **supreme** worth of the individual and in his right to life，liberty and the pursuit of happiness.

I believe that every right implies a responsibility；every opportunity，an obligation；every possession，a duty.

I believe that the law was made for man and not man for the law ; that government is the servant of the people and not their master.

I believe in the dignity of labor, whether with head or hand ; that the world owes no man a living but that it owes every man an opportunity to make a living.

I believe that thrift is essential to well ordered living and that economy is a prime requisite of a sound financial structure, whether in government business or personal affairs.

I believe that truth and justice are **fundamental** to an **enduring** social order.

I believe in the sacredness of a promise. That a man's word should be as good as his bond, that character—not wealth or power or position—is of supreme worth.

I believe that the rendering of useful service is the common duty of mankind and that only in the purifying fire of sacrifice is the dross of selfishness consumed and the greatness of the human soul set free.

I believe in an all-wise and all-loving God, named by whatever name, and that the individual's highest fulfillment, greatest happiness and widest usefulness are to be found in living in harmony with His will.

I believe that love is the greatest thing in the world ; that it alone can overcome hate ; that right can and will triumph over might.

These are the principles, however formulated, for which all

good men and women throughout the world，irrespective of race or creed，education social position or occupation，are standing，and for which many of them are suffering and dying.

These are the principles upon which alone a new world recognizing the brotherhood of man and the fatherhood of God can be established.

这些信条是我和我的夫人在教育儿女时尽力所依照的原则。它们是先父深信不疑的处世立身的原则。其中很多都是我在母亲膝前所学到的原则。

这些信条指出了一条活得快乐有用、死得勇敢安详的道路。

如果这些信条对各位的意义和对我的意义一样的话，那么它们或许也有助于我们的子女从中获得引导和启发。

让我说出这些信条：

我相信个人的价值至高无上，每个人都有生存的权利、自由的权利和追求幸福的权利。

我相信每一项权利都意味着一种责任，每一次机遇都意味着一项义务，每一种占有都意味着一种职责。

我相信法律是为人而制订的，但人却不是为法律而造就的；我相信政府是人民的仆人，而非人民的主人。

我相信无论脑力劳动还是体力劳动都是值得人们尊敬的；世界不会给任何人提供免费的午餐，但它却给每个人一次谋生的机会。

我相信勤俭是井然有序的生活之必需，而节俭是健全的金融机制之根本，无论政府、商务或个人事务皆是如此。

我相信真理和公正对社会的长治久安至关重要。

我相信诺言是神圣的，一言既出，如同契约；我相信具有至高无上价值的是个人品质，而不是财富、权势或地位。

我相信提供有用的服务是人类共同职责，只有在牺牲的炼火中，自私的渣滓才能被消除，人类高尚的灵魂才能发挥出来。

我相信全能全知、大慈大悲的上帝——不管用怎样的称呼；而个人最大的成就、最大的幸福、最大的作为，都必须在和上帝的意志和谐一致的生活中才能找到。

我相信爱是世界上最伟大的事物；唯有爱才能克服仇恨；我相信公理能够而且必将战胜强权。

不管如何表述，上述就是全世界一切善良的人们所信奉的原则，不论其种族、信仰、教育、地位或职业如何，而为了这些原则，许多人正在饱受煎熬，甚至献出生命。

唯有在这些信条的基础上，才能建立起人人亲如兄弟，上帝亲如父辈的新世界。

✎导读✎

本篇为 1941 年 7 月 8 日联合服务组织广播节目的一部分，在战争烽火和法西斯势力肆虐之时产生了积极的影响。

✎单词注解✎

supreme [sjuːˈpriːm] *adj.* 最高的，至高无上的

fundamental [ˌfʌndəˈmentl] *adj.* 基本的，根本的

enduring [inˈdjuəriŋ] *adj.* 持久的，持续的

triumph [ˈtraiəmf] *n.* 胜利

✎诵读名句✎

They point the way to usefulness and happiness in life，to courage and peace in death.

I believe that every right implies a responsibility；every opportunity，an obligation；every possession，a duty.

I believe that love is the greatest thing in the world；that it alone can overcome hate；that right can and will triumph over might.

English Friendship for America
英国人对美国的友情

Charles Dickens/查尔斯·狄更斯

Gentlemen,

I cannot do better than take my cue from your distinguished President, and refer in my first remarks to his remarks in connection with the old, natural, association between you and me. When I received an invitation from a private association of working members of the press of New York to dine with them today, I accepted that compliment in grateful remembrance of a calling that was once my own, and in loyal sympathy towards a brotherhood which, in the spirit, I have never quitted. *To the wholesome training of severe newspaper work, when I was a very young man, I constantly refer my first successes ; and my sons will hereafter testify to their father that he was always steadily proud of that ladder by which he rose.* If it were otherwise, I should have but a very poor opinion of their father, which, perhaps, upon the whole, I have not. Hence, gentlemen, under any circumstances, this company would have been exceptionally interesting and gratifying to me. But whereas I supposed that like the fairies'pavilion in the "Arabian Nights," it would be but a mere handful, and I find it turn out like the same elastic pavilion, capable of comprehending a multitude, so much the more proud am I of the honor of being your guest ; for you will readily believe that the more widely representative of the press in America my entertainers are, the more I must feel the good-will and the kindly sentiments towards me of that vast institution.

Gentlemen, I henceforth charge myself, not only here but on every suitable occasion whatsoever and wheresoever, to express my high and grateful sense of my second reception in America, and to bear my honest testimony to the national generosity and magnanimity. Also, to declare how astounded I have been by the amazing changes that I have seen around me on every side. Nor am I believe me so arrogant as to suppose that in twenty five years there have been no changes in me, and that I had nothing to learn and no extreme impressions to correct when I was here first.

Gentlemen, the transition from my own feelings towards and interest in America to those of the mass of my countrymen seems to be a natural one ; but, whether or not, I make it with an express object. I was asked in this very city, about last Christmas time, whether an American was not at some disadvantage in England as a foreigner. The notion of an American being regarded in England as a foreigner at all, of his ever being thought of or spoken of in that character, was so uncommonly **incongruous** and absurd to me, that my gravity was, for the moment, quite overpowered. As soon as I was restored, I said that for years and years past I hoped I had had as many American friends and had received as many American visitors as almost any Englishman living, and that my unvarying experience, fortified by theirs, was that it was enough in England to be an American to be received with the readiest respect and recognition anywhere. Hereupon, out of half-a-dozed people, suddenly spoke out two, one an American gentleman, with a cultivated taste for art, who, finding himself on a certain Sunday outside the walls of a certain historical English castle, famous for its pictures, was refused admission there. According to the strict rules of the establishment on that day, but who, on merely representing that he was an American gentleman, on his travels, had, not to say the picture gallery, but the whole castle, placed at his immediate disposal. The other was a lady, who, being in London, and having a great desire to see the famous reading-room of the British Museum, was assured by the English family with whom she stayed that it was unfortunately impossible, because the place was closed for a week, and she had only three days there. Upon that lady's going to the Museum, as she assured me, alone to the gate, self-introduced as an American lady, the gate flew open, as it were, magically. I am unwillingly bound to add that she certainly was young and exceedingly pretty. Still, the porter of that institution is of an obese habit, and, according to the best of my observation of him, not very impressible.

Now, gentlemen, I refer to these trifles as a collateral

assurance to you that the Englishmen who shall humbly strive,
as I hope to do, to be in England as faithful to America as to
England herself, have no previous conceptions to contend
against. Points of difference there have been, points of
difference there are, points of difference there probably
always will be between the two great peoples. But broadcast
in England shown the sentiment that those two peoples are
essentially one, and that it rests with them jointly to uphold
the great Anglo-Saxon race, to which our president has
referred, and all its great achievements before the world.
And if I know anything of my countrymen and they give me
credit for knowing something—if I know anything of my
countrymen, gentlemen, the English heart is stirred by the
fluttering of those Stars and Stripes, as it is stirred by no other
flag that flies except its own. If I know my countrymen, in
any and every relation towards America, they begin, not as
Sir Anthony Absolute recommended that lovers should begin,
with "a little aversion." but with a great liking and a profound
respect ; and whatever the little sensitiveness of the moment,
or the little official passion, or the little official policy now, or
then, or here, or there, may be, take my word for it, that
the first enduring, great, popular consideration in England is a
generous construction of justice.

Finally, gentlemen, and I say this subject to your
correction, I do believe that from the great majority of
honest minds on both sides, there cannot be absent the
conviction that it would be better for this globe to be riven
by an earthquake, fired by a comet, overrun by an iceberg,
and abandoned to the Arctic fox and bear, than that it should

present the spectacle of these two great nations, each of which has, in its own way and hour, striven so hard and so successfully for freedom, ever again being arrayed the one against the other. Gentlemen, I cannot thank your President enough or you enough for your kind reception of my health, and of my poor remarks, but, believe me, I do thank you with the utmost **fervor** of which my soul is capable.

先生们，

我最好是像你们杰出的主席那样，首先谈谈他提到的关于我们之间为时已久的自然交往。当我接到纽约新闻界人士邀我今天与他们共进晚餐的邀请时，我怀着对我曾从事过的职业的愉快回忆，和我在内心从未抛弃过的对报界同仁的真诚关心，接受了这一好意。我经常把早年的成功归因于，我年轻时曾在严格的新闻工作中受到的有益的锻炼，今后我的儿子们会证实，他们的父亲始终以他借以登上成功的梯子而感到骄傲。如果情况并非如此，我就会得到他们很差的评价，但基本上我是不会得到那种评价的。所以，诸位，不管怎样，这样的聚会都会令我感到分外有趣和愉快。不过，我原以为这次聚会会像《天方夜谭》里仙女们的帐篷一样，只有巴掌那么大，但我发现它就像那顶会伸缩的帐篷，容纳了一大群人，我为有幸成为你们的客人而倍感高兴。因为你们很快就会相信：我的款待者在美国新闻界的代表性越广，我所感受到的他们对我的友情和感情就越深。

先生们，从今以后，我要给自己规定这样一项责任：不仅在这里，而且在任何一个适宜的场合，我都要表达我对第二次访美时所受到的款待的分外感激之情，并提供我对这个国家的慷慨、高尚行为的诚实见证，同时也要告诉大家，我是如何为我所看到的各方面惊人变化而震惊。请相信我，我决不会自负到认为自己在 25 年里没有变化，并且觉得没有什么可以学习的东西，没有什么足以纠正我首次访美时观感的强烈印象。

先生们，我自己对美国的感情和兴趣，看来可以很自然地转变为我对同胞们的感情和兴趣。但是，无论如何，我是出于一种公开的目的来进行这方面的工作的。好像是去年圣诞节，就在纽约，有人问我：美国人，作为一个在英国的外国人，会不会处于某种不利地位。把在英国的美国人视为外国人，并以这种眼光去看待他、谈论他，在我看来是非常不恰当和荒谬的。因此在那次谈话中，我表现得过于严肃。在恢复了平常后说，多年来我一直希望像任何一个活着的英国人一样，拥有众多的美国朋友，接待那么多的美国来访者，并且希望他们的经验会使我更加相信：美国人在英国处处都会充分地感受到英国人发自内心的尊重和关怀。对于这一点，我可以立即举出两个人的例子。其中之一是一位很有艺术修养的美国绅士。某个星期日，他来到一座以收藏名画而著名的英国古城堡的城墙外。根据英国对于星期日的严格规定，那天是不允许进入城堡的。但是在他说明自己是一个正在旅行的美国绅士以后，不要说画廊，就连整个城堡都让他参观了。另一个例子讲的是一位美国女士，她在伦敦非常想看一看著名的不列颠博物馆的阅览室。她借住的那家人告诉她，很遗憾这事办不到，因为博物馆停止开放一星期，而她在伦敦只能逗留 3 日。这位女士后来告诉我，她独自走到博物馆门前，自我介绍来自美国，大门就神奇般地敞开了。我不情愿但又不得不补充一句，她当时很年轻，而且特别漂亮。不过，博物馆看门人是个大胖子，而且据我认真观察，他还是一个不易被打动的人。

　　先生们，我在这里顺便提到这些小事是为了向你们肯定：正如我所希望的那样，英国人对美国人就像对英国本国人一样的诚恳，他们本来就没有什么敌对的观念。在这两个伟大的民族之间，尽管过去、现在和将来都会有不一致的地方，然而在英国广泛地传播着、洋溢着这样一种感情：这两个伟大的民族实质上是一家人，他们共同肩负着高举盎格鲁—撒克逊旗帜的责任（这一点我们的主席已经谈到了），还要把她的一切成就展现在世人面前。如果我对我的同胞们还是有所了解的话——他们相信我是了解一些情况的——如果我对我的同胞们有所了解，先生们，尽管除了我们自己国家的旗帜外，我们的心不为其他任何飘动的旗帜而激动，但英国人的心已经为星条旗的飘扬而激动了。如果我了解我的同胞，我知道他们并不像安东尼·艾布索列特爵士所说到的恋人们的惯常表现那样，起初是"略带厌恶"、却又满怀好感与尊敬来对待他们同美国的一切关系；不论曾经有过什么样的小情绪，也不论现在、将来、这里、那里会有什么样的小小的官僚脾气和官僚政策，请相信我的话，构建一种宽容的公正态度才是全体英国人一直以来的首要想法。

先生们，我最后讲一个问题并请大家予以指正。我完全相信，在大西洋两岸众多的、诚实的、有思想的人中，可能会有这样一种看法：让地球被地震震碎，被彗星烧毁，被冰山撞翻，把它扔给北极的狐狸和熊，也比这两个通过各自的方式和时机而成功地争取到自由的、伟大的民族对立起来的景象好。先生们，对于主席和你们大家如此友好、亲切的对待我的健康问题和我的拙劣言辞，我感激不尽。请相信，我的确是以我最大的热情来感谢你们的。

实战提升
Practising & Exercise

🍃导读🍃
1864 年 4 月 18 日，英国批判现实主义作家查尔斯·狄更斯在纽约市举办的告别宴会上发表的演说。

🍃单词注解🍃
incongruous [in'kɔŋgruəs] *adj*. 不协调的，不一致的
collateral [kə'lætərəl] *n*. 担保物，抵押物
rive [raiv] *v*. 撕裂，劈开
fervor ['fə:və] *n*. 热烈，热情

🍃诵读名句🍃
To the wholesome training of severe newspaper work, when I was a very young man, I constantly refer my first successes; and my sons will hereafter testify to their father that he was always steadily proud of that ladder by which he rose.

Gentlemen, the transition from my own feelings towards and interest in America to those of the mass of my countrymen seems to be a natural one.

Now, gentlemen, I refer to these trifles as a collateral assurance to you that the Englishmen who shall humbly strive, as I hope to do, to be in England as faithful to America as to England herself, have no previous conceptions to contend against.

Retirement Speech

迈克尔·乔丹：退役演说

Michael Jordan/迈克尔·乔丹

I am here to announce my retirement from the game of basketball. It won't be another announcement to baseball or anything to that nature.

Mentally, I'm **exhausted**, I don't feel I have a challenge. Physically, I feel great. The last time in 1993 I had other agendas. I felt that I wanted to play baseball and I felt that at my age, it was a good opportunity and time to do it. And with the death of my father, and I was basically trying to deal with that.

Actually I talked to Jerry last year once the season ended and I told Jerry at that time, mentally, I was a little exhausted. I didn't know if I would play next year. I wanted to put him on awareness so that he could possibly prepare going into next season. And Jerry, once we had our conversation, wanted me to take time as I did in 1993 to make sure that it was the right decision because it was going to be the final decision.

I retired the first time when Phil Jackson was the coach. And I think that even with Phil being the coach I would have had a tough time, mentally finding the challenge for myself, although he can somehow present challenges for me. I don't know if he could have presented the challenge for me to continue on to this season. *Even though middle way of this season I wanted to continue to play a couple more years, but at the end of this season I was mentally drained and tired. So I can't say that he would have restored that.*

I will support the Chicago Bulls. I think the game itself is a lot bigger than Michael Jordan. I've been given an opportunity by people before me, to name a few, Kareem Abdul Jabbar, Doctor J, Eljohn Baylor, Jerry West. These guys played the game way before Michael Jordan was born and Michael Jordan came on the heels of all that activity. Mr Stern and what he's done for the **league**, gave me an opportunity to play the game of basketball. *I played it to the best I could play it, I tried to enhance the game itself. I've tried to be the best basketball player that I could be.*

我在这里宣布从篮坛退役，而且这次退役后不会再去从事棒球或其他类似的运动。

　　由于心理上很疲惫，我感到自己非常缺乏挑战力。体力倒还不错。上次我在 1993 年退役时有别的打算，我想去打棒球，并且觉得当时的年龄是打棒球的好时机。但是父亲去世了，我不得不全力处理这件事。

　　事实上，去年赛季刚结束时，我和杰里谈过一次。我告诉他我在精神上有些疲惫，不知道下一年还能不能打。我想让他意识到这一点，以便为下一赛季做准备。有一次我和杰里谈过这个问题，他让我像 1993 年那样，好好考虑，以便作出明智的决定，因为这将是最后的决定。

　　我第一次退役时的教练是费尔·杰克逊。我那时觉得即使是费尔当教练，我的日子也不会好过。我要在精神上给自己寻找挑战，尽管他有时也会给我一些挑战，但我不知道他能否给我足够的挑战让我继续打完这个赛季。在赛季中间的时候，我还想过再打几年，但当赛季结束时，我从内心感到彻底地枯竭和疲惫。所以我想他没法帮我恢复精力。

　　我会支持芝加哥公牛队。我觉得这项运动本身比乔丹重要得多。我的前辈给了我很多机会，比如卡里姆·阿卜杜尔·贾巴尔、J博士、埃尔金·贝勒、杰里·韦思特。这些人早在乔丹出生前就活跃在赛场上了，乔丹是踩着他们的脚步来的。斯特恩先生及其为联盟所做的一切给了我打篮球的机会。我尽了自己的所能，努力地推动篮球事业的发展，也尽了最大的努力成为最好的球员。

实战提升
Practising & Exercise

🍃导读🍃

美国时间 2003 年 4 月 16 日晚上，北京时间 2003 年 4 月 17 日上午，NBA 历史上最伟大的球员——迈克尔·乔丹，打完了他最后一场 NBA 比赛。在费城，在第一联合中心球馆，永远告别了 NBA 赛场。

🍃单词注解🍃

exhausted [ig'zɔ:stid] *adj.* 耗尽的，用完的
mentally ['mentəli] *adv.* 心理上；精神上
league [li:g] *n.* 同盟，联盟
enhance [in'hɑ:ns] *v.* 提高，增加

🍃诵读名句🍃

Actually I talked to Jerry last year once the season ended and I told Jerry at that time, mentally, I was a little exhausted.

Even though middle way of this season I wanted to continue to play a couple more years, but at the end of this season I was mentally drained and tired. So I can't say that he would have restored that.

I played it to the best I could play it, I tried to enhance the game itself. I've tried to be the best basketball player that I could be.

威廉·福克纳：接受诺贝尔奖时的演说

William Faulkner/威廉·福克纳

I feel that this award was not made to me as a man, but to my work—a life's work in the **agony** and sweat of the human spirit, not for glory and least of all for profit, but to create out of the materials of the human spirit something which did not exist before. *So this award is only mine in trust.* It will not be difficult to find a **dedication** for the money part of it commensurate with the purpose and significance of its origin. But I would like to do the same with the acclaim too, by using this moment as a **pinnacle** from which I might be listened to by the young men and women already dedicated to the same **anguish** and travail, among whom is already that one who will some day stand here where I am standing.

Our tragedy today is a general and universal physical fear so long **sustained** *by now that we can even bear it.* There are no longer problems of the spirit. There is only the question : "When will I be blown up?" Because of this, the young man or woman writing today has forgotten the problems of the human heart in conflict with itself which alone can make good writing. Because only that is worth writing about, worth the agony and the sweat.

He must learn them again. He must teach himself that the basest of all things is to be afraid ; and teach himself that forget it forever, leaving no room in his workshop for anything but the old verities and truths of the heart, the old universal truths lacking which any story is ephemeral and doomed—love and honor and pity and pride and compassion and sacrifice.

Until he does so, he labors under a curse. He writes not of love but of lust, of defeats in which nobody loses anything of value, of victories without hope and, worst of all, without pity or compassion. His griefs grieve on no universal bones, leaving no scars. He writes not of the heart but of the glands.

Until he relearns these things, he will write as though he stood among and watched the end of man. I decline to accept the end of man. It is easy enough to say that man is immortal simply because he will endure : that when the last ding-dong of doom has clanged and faded from the last worthless rock hanging tideless in the last red and dying evening, that even then there will still be one more sound : that of his puny inexhaustible voice, still talking. I refuse to accept this. I believe that man will not merely endure, he will prevail. He is immortal, not because he alone among creatures has an inexhaustible voice, but because he has a soul, a spirit capable of compassion, and sacrifice, and endurance. The poet's, the writer's duty is to write about these things. It is his privilege to help man endure by lifting his heart, by reminding him of the courage and honor and hope and pride and compassion and pity and sacrifice which have been the glory of his past. *The poet's voice need not merely be the record of man, it can be one of the props, the pillars to help him endure and prevail.*

　　我感到这个奖项不是授予我个人而是授予我的工作的——它是对我呕心沥血、毕生从事的人类精神探索的工作的肯定。我从事这项工作，既非为虚名，更非为浮利，而是为了从人的精神素材中创造出一些前所未有的东西。因此，我只是这份奖金的保管者而已。要做出与这份奖赏最初的目的和意义相符，又与其奖金等价的贡献并非难事，但我还愿意利用这个难得的机会，向那些可能听到我的讲话并已献身于同一艰苦事业的男女青年讲几句。他们中一定有人有一天也会站到我现在站着的地方。

　　人类今天的悲剧是人们普遍存在一种生理上的恐惧，这种恐惧存在已久，以至于我们已经习惯了背负这种恐惧。现在不存在精神上的问题，唯一的问题是："我什么时候会被炸得粉身碎骨？"正因如此，今天从事写作的男女青年已经遗忘了人类内心深处的冲突，而这本身就能成为好的作品。因为这是唯一值得去写、值得为之呕心沥血的题材。

　　他一定要重新思考这些问题。他必须使自己明白世间最可鄙的事情莫过于恐惧；他必须要使自己永远忘却恐惧，在他的工作室里除了心底深处永恒的真理之外，任何别的东西都没有容身之地。缺少这些永恒的普遍真理，任何小说都只能是昙花一现，注定要失败。这些真理就是：爱、荣誉、怜悯、尊严、同情与牺牲。

　　若是他做不到这一点，他的工作就是白费功夫。他写的不是爱情而是情欲；他写的失败是不值得一提的失败；他写的胜利没有希望，更可悲的是没有怜悯或同情的胜利；他写的悲伤不是为普遍的逝者而悲伤，所以留不下深刻的心灵烙印；他写的不是灵魂而是器官。

　　在他重新认识到这一点之前，他的写作就犹如他眼睁睁地看着世界末日的来临而束手无策一般。我不同意人类末日的说法。说人是不朽的，因为他能忍受巨大的苦痛，说当厄运的最后一次钟声在没有潮水冲刷的，映在末日最后一抹余晖里的，最后一块无用礁石旁渐渐消失时，还会有一个声音，那就是人类微弱但不倦的声音。说这些都很容易，但是我不能接受这种说法。我相信人类不仅能忍受，更拥有战胜一切的力量。人类之所以不朽，不是因为万物中唯有他有着不知疲倦的声音，而是因为他有灵魂，有充满同情、勇于牺牲和善于忍耐的精神。而把这些写出来就是诗人和作家的责任。诗人和作家有一种特权，那就是去鼓舞人的斗志、使人们记住曾经有过的光荣——人类曾有过的勇气、荣誉、希望、尊严、同情、怜悯与牺牲的精神——去升华人们的心灵，达到最终的永恒。诗人的声音不应仅仅是人类的记录，而应成为人类得以永存和胜利的力量。

导读

福克纳于 1949 年获诺贝尔文学奖。这是福克纳在 1949 年诺贝尔文学奖获奖时所作的演说。瑞典著名的发明家和化学家诺贝尔在 1895 年 11 月 27 日写下遗嘱，捐献全部财产设立基金，每年把利息作为奖金，授予"一年来对人类做出最大贡献的人"。这便是诺贝尔奖的由来。根据他的遗嘱，瑞典政府于同年建立"诺贝尔基金会"，负责把基金的年利息按五等分，其中一份授予"在文学方面创作出具有理想倾向的最佳作品的人"。这就是诺贝尔文学奖，由瑞典文学院颁发。另外四个奖项为物理、化学、生理或医学及和平奖。

单词注解

agony ['ægəni] *n.* 极大的痛苦

dedication [ˌdedi'keiʃən] *n.* 献身精神，奉献精神

pinnacle ['pinəkl] *n.* 顶点，极致

anguish ['æŋgwiʃ] *n.* 极度痛苦

sustained [səs'teind] *adj.* 持久的，持续的

诵读名句

So this award is only mine in trust.

Our tragedy today is a general and universal physical fear so long sustained7 by now that we can even bear it.

The poet's voice need not merely be the record of man, it can be one of the props, the pillars to help him endure and prevail.

The Origin of the Universe
史蒂芬·威廉·霍金：宇宙的起源

Stephen William Hawking/史蒂芬·威廉·霍金

According to the Boshongo people of central Africa, in the beginning there was only darkness, water, and the great god Bumba. One day Bumba, in pain from a stomach ache, **vomited** up the sun. The sun dried up some of the water, leaving land. Still in pain, Bumba vomited up the moon, the stars, and then some animals : the leopard, the crocodile, the turtle, and, finally man.

This creation myth, like many others, tries to answer the questions we all ask. Why are we here? Where did we come from? The answer generally given was that humans were of comparatively recent origin, because it must have been obvious, even at early times, that the human race was improving in knowledge and technology. So it can't have been around that long, or it would have progressed even more. For example, *The Book of Genesis* placed the creation of the world at 9 am on October the 23th, 4, 004 BC. On the other hand, the physical surroundings, like mountains and rivers, change very little in a human life time. They were therefore thought to be a **constant** background, and either to have existed for ever as an empty landscape, or to have been created at the same time as the humans.

Not everyone however, was happy with the idea that the universe had a beginning. For example, Aristotle, the most famous of the Greek philosophers, believed the universe had existed forever. Something **eternal** is more perfect than something created. He suggested, the reason we see progress was that floods, or other natural disasters, had repeatedly set civilization back to the beginning. The motivation for believing in an eternal universe was the desire to avoid invoking divine intervention, to create the universe, and set it going. Conversely, those who believed the universe had a beginning, used it as an argument for the existence of God, as the first cause, or prime mover of the universe.

If one believed that the universe had a beginning, the obvious question was : What happened before the beginning? What was God doing before He made the world? Was He preparing Hell for people who asked such questions? The problem of whether or not the universe had a beginning, was a great concern to the German philosopher, Immanuel Kant. He felt there were logical contradictions, or Antinomies, either way. If the universe had a beginning, why did it wait an infinite time before it began? He called that the thesis. On the other hand, if the universe had existed forever, why did it take an infinite time to reach the present stage? He called that the antithesis. Both the thesis, and the antithesis, depended on Kant's **assumption**, along with almost everyone else, that time was Absolute. That is to say, it went from the infinite past, to the infinite future, independently of any universe that might or might not exist in this background.

This is still the picture in the mind of many scientists today. However in 1915, Einstein introduced his revolutionary General Theory of Relativity. In this, space and time were no longer Absolute, no longer a fixed background to events. Instead, they were dynamical quantities that were shaped by the matter and energy in the universe. They were defined only within the universe, so it made no sense to talk of a time before the universe began.

If the universe was essentially unchanging in time, as was generally assumed before the 1920s, there would be no reason that time should not be defined arbitrarily far back. Any so-called beginning of the universe, would be artificial, in the sense that one could extend the history back to earlier times. Thus it might be that the universe was created last year, but with all the memories and physical evidence, to look like it was much older. This raises deep philosophical questions about the meaning of existence. I shall deal with these by adopting what is called the positivist approach. In this, the idea is that we interpret the input from our senses in terms of a model we make of the world. One can not ask whether the model represents reality, only whether it works. A model is a good model if it first, interprets a wide range of observations, in terms of a simple and elegant model. And second, if the model makes definite predictions that can be tested，and possibly **falsified** by observation.

...

We do not yet have a good theoretical understanding of the observations that the expansion of the universe is accelerating again，after a long period of slowing down. Without such an understanding，we can not be sure of the future of the universe. Will it continue to expand forever? Is inflation a law of Nature? Or will the universe eventually **collapse** again? *New observational results and theoretical advances are coming in rapidly. Cosmology is a very exciting and active subject.* We are getting close to answering the age old questions. Why are we here? Where did we come from?

Thank you！

根据中非 Boshongo 人的传说，世界太初只有黑暗、水和伟大的 Bumba 上帝。一天，Bumba 胃痛发作，呕吐出太阳。

太阳灼干了一些水，留下土地。他仍然胃痛不止，又吐出了月亮和星辰，然后吐出一些动物，豹、鳄鱼、乌龟，最后是人。

这个创世纪的神话，和其他许多神话一样，试图回答我们大家都想问的问题：为何我们在此？我们从何而来？一般的答案是，人类的起源是发生在比较近期的事。人类正在知识上和技术上不断地取得进步。这样，它不可能存在那么久，否则的话，它应该取得更大的进步。这一点甚至在更早的时候就应该很清楚了。例如，《创世纪》把世界的创生定于公元前4004年10月23日上午9时。另一方面，诸如山岳和河流的自然环境，在人的生命周期里改变甚微。所以人们通常把它们当作不变的背景。要么作为空洞的风景已经存在了无限久，要么是和人类在相同的时刻被创生出来。

但是并非所有人都喜欢宇宙有个开端的思想。例如，希腊最著名的哲学家亚里士多德，相信宇宙已经存在了无限久的时间。某种永恒的东西比某种创生的东西更完美。他提出我们之所以看到发展处于这个情形，那是因为洪水或者其他自然灾害，不断让文明回复到萌芽阶段。信仰永恒宇宙的动机是想避免求助于神意的干涉，以创生宇宙并起始运行。相反的，那些相信宇宙具有开端的人，将开端当作上帝存在的论据，把上帝当作宇宙的第一原因或者原动力。

如果人们相信宇宙有一个开端，那么很明显的问题是，在开端之前发生了什么？上帝在创造宇宙之前在做什么？他是在为那些诘问这类问题的人准备地狱吗？德国哲学家伊曼努尔·康德十分关心宇宙有无开端的问题。他觉得，不管宇宙有无开端，都会引起逻辑矛盾或者二律背反。如果宇宙有一个开端，为何在它起始之前要等待无限久。他将此称为正题。另一方面，如果宇宙已经存在了无限久，为什么它要花费无限长的时间才达到现在这个阶段。他把此称为反题。无论正题还是反题，都是基于康德的假设，几乎所有人也是这么办的，那就是，时间是绝对的，也就是说，时间从无限的过去向无限的将来流逝。时间独立于宇宙，在这个背景中，宇宙可以存在，也可以不存在。

直至今天，在许多科学家的心中，仍然保持这样的图景。然而，1915 年爱因斯坦提出他的革命性的广义相对论。在该理论中，空间和时间不再是绝对的，不再是事件的固定背景。相反的，它们是动力量，宇宙中的物质和能量确定其形状。它们只有在宇宙之中才能够定义。这样谈论宇宙开端之前的时间是毫无意义的。

如果宇宙随时间本质上不变，正如 20 世纪 20 年代之前一般认为的那样，就没有理由阻止在过去任意早的时刻定义时间。人们总可以将历史往更早的时刻延展，在这个意义上，任何所谓的宇宙开端都是人为的。于是，情形可以是这样，这个宇宙是去年创生的，但是所有记忆和物理证据都显得它要古老得多。这就产生了有关存在意义的高深哲学问题。我将采用所谓的实证主义方法来对付这些问题。在这个方法中，其思想是，我们按照我们构造世界的模型来解释自己感官的输入。人们不能询问这个模型是否代表实在，只能问它能否行得通。首先，如果按照一个简单而优雅的模型可以解释大量的观测；其次，如果这个模型作出可能被观察检验，也可能被证伪的明确预言，这个模型即是一个好模型。

……

我们观察到，宇宙的膨胀在长期的变缓之后，再次加速。

对此理论还不能理解清楚。缺乏这种理解，对宇宙的未来还无法确定。它会继续地、无限地膨胀下去吗？暴胀是一个自然定律吗？或者宇宙最终会再次坍缩吗？新的观测结果，理论的进步正迅速涌来。宇宙学是一个非常激动人心和活跃的学科。我们正慢慢接近这个古老问题的答案：我们为何在此？我们从何而来？

　　谢谢各位。

导读

2006 年 6 月 19 日，世界科学大师斯蒂芬·霍金教授参加在人民大会堂举行的国际弦理论大会开幕式，并作"宇宙的起源"主题讲座。霍金，现任英国剑桥大学应用数学及理论物理学系教授，当代最重要的广义相对论和宇宙论家，是本世纪享有国际盛誉的伟人之一，被称为在世的最伟大的科学家，还被称为"宇宙之王"。

单词注解

vomit ['vɔmit] *v.* 喷出；吐出

constant ['kɔnstənt] *adj.* 固定的，不变的

eternal [i(:)'təːnl] *adj.* 永久的，永恒的；无穷的

assumption [ə'sʌmpʃən] *n.* 假定，设想

falsify ['fɔːlsi,fai] *v.* 篡改；伪造；歪曲

collapse [kə'læps] *v.* 崩溃，瓦解

诵读名句

If one believed that the universe had a beginning, the obvious question was：What happened before the beginning?

If the universe was essentially unchanging in time, as was generally assumed before the 1920s, there would be no reason that time should not be defined arbitrarily far back.

New observational results and theoretical advances are coming in rapidly. Cosmology is a very exciting and active subject.

The Secret of Success

《钻石宝地》之致富的奥秘

Russell. H. Conwell/拉塞尔·H·康维尔

The best thing can do is to illustrate by actual facts well-known to you all. A. T. Stewart，a poor boy in New York，had $I.50 to begin life on. He lost 87.5 cents of that on the very first venture. How fortunate that young man who loses the first time he **gambles**. That boy said，"I will never gamble again in business，" and he never did. How came he to lose 87.5 cents? You probably all know the story how he lost it—because he bought some needles，threads，and buttons to sell which people did not want，and had them left on his hands，a dead loss. Said the boy，"I will not lose any more money in that way." Then he went around first to the doors and asked the people what they did want. Then when he had found out what they wanted he **invested** his 62.5 cents to supply a known demand. Study it wherever you choose—in business，in your profession，in your housekeeping，whatever your life，that one thing is the secret of success.You must first know the demand. *You must first know what people* need, and then invest yourself where you are most needed. A. T. Stewart went on that principle until he was worth what **amounted** afterward to forty millions of dollars, owning the very store in which Mr. Wanamaker carries on his great work in NewYork. His fortune was made hy his losing something, which taught him the great lesson that he must only invest himself or his money in something that people need. When will you salesmen learn it? When will you manufacturers learn that you must know the changing needs of humanity if you would succeed in life?*Apply yourselves, all you Christian people, as manufacturers or merchants or workmen to supply that human need. It is a great principle as broad as humanity and as deep as the Scripture itself.*

The best illustration I ever heard was of John Jacoh Astor. You know that he made the money of the Astor family when he lived in New York. He came across the sea in debt for his fare. But that poor hoy with nothing in his pocket made the fortune of the Astor family on one principle. Some young man here tonight will say, "Well they could make those fortunes over in New York but they could not do it in Philadelphia!" My friends, did you ever read that wonderful book of Riis, **wherein** is given his **statistical** account of the records taken in 1889 of 107 millionaires of New York. If you read the account you will see that out of the 107 millionaires only seven made their money in New York. Out of the l07 millionaires worth ten million dollars in real estate then, 67 of them made their money in towns of less than 3, 500 inhabitants. The richest man in this country today, if you read the real estate values, has never moved away from a town of 3, 500 inhabitants. *It makes not so much difference where you are as who you are. But if you cannot get rich in Philadelphia you* *certainly cannot do it in New York.*

　　我所能做的、证明这个道理的最佳方式，就是给你们讲一个众所周知的实例。斯图亚特是纽约的一个穷孩子，他最开始谋生的时候，只有 1.5 美元。做第一笔生意时，他就赔了 87.5 美分。第一次冒险就失败的年轻人是多么幸运啊！他说："我再也不会在生意上冒险了。"他确实也做到了。他是怎么损失这 87.5 美分的呢？你们可能都知道这个故事——因为他买了一些针、线和纽扣，卖给那些不需要的人，结果都压在手里，成了废物。他说："我再也不会像这样糟蹋钱了。"然后他就挨家挨户地问人们需要什么。当他弄清楚之后，就用剩下的 62.5 美分来满足人们的需求。无论你选择做什么——做生意、上班、做家务，生活中的任何事，都要认真地研究，这就是成功的秘诀。你必须首先了解需求，知道人们需要什么，然后投身到最需要你的领域中去。斯图亚特先生一直都遵循这个原则，后来他赚了 4，000 万美元；现在，在纽约他所开的商店里，沃纳梅克先生正在继续着他那伟大的事业。他的财富是从损失中得来的，他也从中吸取到了一个重要的教训：必须要把资金和精力投入到人们的需要之中去。推销员们，你们什么时候才能领会到这一点呢？制造商们，你们什么时候才能明白，如果想成功，就一定要了解人们不断变化的需求？所有的人，所有的基督徒，无论是制造商、商人，还是工人，都应满足人们的需要。这个伟大的原则就像《圣经》的经文一样意义深远，它适用于全人类。

　　我所知道的最好的例子，是关于约翰·雅各布·阿斯特的。你们知道，他在纽约时，为阿斯特家族创造了巨额财富。他当初是借钱买船票漂洋过海而来的，但这个身无分文的穷孩子，凭着一个原则，创造了阿斯特家族的奇迹。今晚在场的某个年轻人会说："他们在纽约能创造财富，但在费城就做不到！"朋友们，你们读过里斯写的那本精彩的书吗？书中记载了 1889 年纽约的 107 个百万富翁的数据资料。如果你们看过这些记录就会发现，在这 107 个富翁中，只有 7 位是在纽约发家的。这 107 个百万富翁都拥有超过 1,000 万美元的不动产，其中 67 人是在不足 3,500 人的小镇上发家的。如果你读一读这些不动产的数据的话，就会发现，这个国家现在最富有的人，毕生都没有离开过只有 3,500 户居民的小镇。这就说明，你是谁，或者你在哪里，并不是那么重要；如果你在费城赚不到钱的话，在纽约你也同样赚不到。

实战提升
Practising & Exercise

导读

拉塞尔·H·康维尔，美国著名律师、作家、演讲大师。《钻石宝地》是根据他在家乡费城的一次著名演讲整理而成。自问世以来，一直畅销不衰。其中所倡导的关于自我与梦想的观点影响了无数的读者，帮助许多寻梦的美国人实现了自己的愿望。

单词注解

gamble ['gæmbl] v. 赌博；打赌

invest [in'vest] v. 投（资）；耗费，投入

amount [ə'maunt] n. 总数；总额

wherein [(h)wɛər'in] adv. 在何处；在哪方面，在哪一点上

statistical [stə'tistikəl] adj. 统计的；统计学的

诵读名句

You must first know what people need, and then invest yourself where you are most needed.

Apply yourselves, all you Christian people, as manufacturers or merchants orworkmen to supply that human need It is a great principle as broad as humanity and as deep as the Scripture itself.

It makes not so much difference where you are as who you are. But if you cannot get rich in Philadelphia you certainly cannot do it in New York.

You Get an Office Full of Crackerjacks
乔治·H·洛里默：让身边的员工成为精英

George H. Lorimer/乔治·H·洛里默

Health is like any inheritance—you can spend the interest in work and play, but you mustn't break into the principal. Once you do, and it's only a matter of time before you've got to place the **remnants** in the hands of a doctor as receiver.

It's a mighty simple thing, though, to keep in good condition because about everything that makes for poor health has to get into you right under your nose.

Bad health hates a man who is friendly with its enemies. More men die from worry than from overwork, more stuff themselves to death than die of starvation. If the human animal reposed less confidence in his stomach and more in his legs, the streets would be full of healthy men walking down to business. Remember that a man always rides to his grave, he never walks there.

When I was a boy, the only doubt about the food was

whether there would be enough of it. I dwell on this matter of health, because when the stomach and liver aren't doing good work, the brain can't.

A good many men will say that it's none of your business what they do in their own time, but you want to make it your business, so long as it affects what they do in your time. For this reason, you should never hire men who drink after office hours. It may have been the case once that when you opened up a bottle for a customer he opened up his heart, but booze is a mighty poor salesman nowadays. Most of the men who mixed their business and their drinks have failed.

Naturally, when you expect so much from your men, they have a right to expect a good deal from you. If you want them to feel that your interests are theirs, you must let them see that their interests are yours. There are a lot of fellows in the world who are working just for glory, but they are **mostly** poets, and you needn't figure on finding many of them out at the Stock Yards. *Praise goes a long way with a good man, and some employers stop there.*

Of course, the world is full of horses who won't work except with the whip, but that's no reason for using it on those who will.

A lot of people think that adversity and bad treatment is the test of a man, and it is—when you want to develop his strength；but prosperity and good treatment is a better one when you want to develop his weakness. By keeping those who show their appreciation of it and firing those who don't, you get an office full of crackerjacks.

The men who stay in the office and plan are the brains of your business ; those who go out and sell are its arms ; and those who fill and **deliver** the orders are its legs. There's no use in the brains scheming and the arms gathering in, if the legs are going to deliver the goods with a kick.

拥有健康就如同拥有了一笔宝贵的财产——你可以在工作和闲暇之余尽情享用这笔财产提供给你的"利息"。不过，你千万不要打破必须遵守的规则，否则去医生那里"报到"不过是个时间问题罢了。

相信不必多说，所有人都明白健康的重要性，因为你所做的每一件有损健康的事情都会"找上门来"。

没有健康的身体就如同你整日与敌人为伴一样。许多人都因为忧虑而并非操劳过度而离开了人世；越来越多的人因为暴饮暴食而非饥饿而离开人世。如果人类少信点胃，多信点腿，那么大街上应该挤满了步行去上班的人。要知道。乘车去找死神的人总会比徒步前行的人快得多。

在我小时候，食物让我引发的思考只局限于它们能否将我的肚子填饱。而我现在之所以会提及健康问题，是因为我知道当我们的胃不能正常工作时，我们的大脑往往也无法正常思考。

也许别人认为你无权过问他们在工作之余都做了哪些事情，但一旦他们在生活中所做的事情影响了你们的工作状态，你就必须把这件事当成自己的事情来处理。由此，永远不要雇用那些酗酒成性的人。当然，你难免会有与客户洽谈生意的时候，而开启瓶盖的那一瞬间往往就是使客户敞开心扉的时候。不过对于现代社会的人而言，只有能力较差的销售员才会选择这种摆酒宴的方法。许多人都会把公事和酒宴扯在一起，结果使自己在生意场上输得一败涂地。

通常情况下，当你渴望从员工身上得到更多回报的时候，员工同样有权期望从你那里获得更多的利益。如果你想让他们把公司的利益当做自己的利益，你必须让他们看到你把员工的利益当做自己的利益来看待。许多人之所以会努力工作就是希望得到一份荣誉，不过这类人应该是诗人，你不要指望在身边找出这类人。老板的赞扬的确可以使一些优秀员工长时间内干劲十足，而另外一些员工则会因为你的赞许之词而从此停滞不前。

当然，这个世上有许多马儿是不用鞭子抽就不肯向前走的，不过我们没有理由不去选择那些不必用鞭子抽就愿意前行的马儿！

许多人认为逆境和不公正的待遇不过是对一个人的考验而已——当你想要将员工身上的潜能激发出来的时候，事实的确如此。可是，相较于不公正的待遇而言，良好且公正的态度更容易促使员工克服自身缺点。不仅如此，员工为了表达对你的感激之情，必定会加倍努力工作。当然。对于那些不懂得感恩的员工你直接开除就对了——你身边的人应该都是精英。

那些坐在办公室里为你出谋划策的人是公司的"大脑"，那些销售员则是公司的"手"，而那跑业务的人员则是公司的"腿"。如果公司的"腿"能够做到"箭步如飞"，那么公司的"大脑"就不会思虑过度，"手"也不会忙乱无章了。

实战提升
Practising & Exercise

🍃导读

乔治·H·洛里默，美国著名作家兼报社主编。在任《星期六晚邮报》主编期间，洛里默以格雷厄姆公司老板约翰的名义，给他就读于哈佛大学的儿子皮埃尔庞特写信。他的家书在报上连载后立即产生了轰动效应，赢得了许多忠实读者，并很快编纂为《社会是一所大学》加以出版，这本书问世后曾连续两年荣获美国年度十大畅销图书的榜单，并因其独到的处事原则而被世人奉为年轻人的必读经典。

🍃单词注解🍃

inheritance [in'heritəns] *n.* 继承

remnant ['remnənt] *n.* 残余，剩余；遗迹

mostly ['məustli] *adv.* 大部分地；主要地

adversity [əd'və:siti] *n.* 逆境；厄运

deliver [di'livə] *v.* 投递；传送；运送

🍃诵读名句🍃

Health is like any inheritance—you can spend the interest in work and play，but you mustn't break into the principal.

Naturally，when you expect so much from your men，they have a right to expect a good deal from you.

Praise goes a long way with a good man，and some employers stop there.